STUDIES IN ETHICS

Edited by

Robert Nozick
Pellegrino University Professor
at Harvard University

A ROUTLEDGE SERIES

LEARNING AND COORDINATION

Inductive Deliberation, Equilibrium, and Convention

Peter Vanderschraaf

Routledge
New York & London

Published in 2001 by
Routledge
29 West 35th Street
New York, NY 10001

Routledge is an imprint of the Taylor & Francis Group

10 9 8 7 6 5 4 3 2 1

Library of Congress Cataloging-in-Publication Data
Vanderschraaf, Peter, 1962–
    Learning and coordination : inductive deliberation, equilibrium, and conven-
tion / Peter Vanderschraaf.
        p. cm. — (Studies in ethics)
    Includes bibliographical references and index.
    ISBN 0-8153-4039-7 (alk. paper)
    1. Social interaction—Mathematical models. 2. Socialization—Mathematical
models. 3. Game theory. I. Title. II. Studies in ethics (New York, N.Y.)
HM1111.V36 2001
302—dc21   00-045615

Printed on acid-free, 250-year-life paper.
Manufactured in the United States of America

For my parents,
Cornelia and John Vanderschraaf

Preface

I am singularly honored to have this book included in Routledge's Studies in Ethics series. This work is the product of my fascination with two closely intertwined problems. The first is that of giving a sufficiently precise and general analysis of *convention*, one that can aid us in understanding the proper role of convention in moral and political philosophy. The second is that of explaining how agents in a formal interaction problem or *game* can arrive at a mutually advantageous outcome or *equilibrium*.

The contributions of this book are best seen in light of the history of these two problems. In a sense, convention is a relative late-bloomer in philosophy. Already in the pre-Socratic era, philosophers considered claims that certain institutions are conventions. Yet a serious analysis of convention did not appear until 1740, when David Hume published the third book of *A Treatise of Human Nature*. Hume correctly observed that a convention is characterized not by any apparent arbitrariness in a given social practice, as many of his predecessors seem to have thought, but rather by the system of mutual expectations that lead the members of a society to follow this practice. In the 20th century, David Lewis developed this idea in his monograph *Convention* (1969). Lewis proposed a definition of convention in terms of the mathematical vocabulary of game theory. In 1944, John von Neumann and Oskar Morgenstern published their monumental *Theory of Games and Economic Behavior*, in which they presented a mathematical theory of interactive decisions. Lewis used von Neumann and Morgenstern's game theory as scaffolding for his own account of convention. John Nash proved that every game in which the agents each chose between finitely many alternative acts has a *Nash equilibrium*, which specifies for each agent a strategy which is best for this agent when the others follow their specified strategies (1950, 1951). Lewis identified the actions of individuals who follow a convention with the strategies in a game that define a *coordination equilibrium*, that is, a Nash equilibrium from which no one wishes anyone to deviate. Coordination equilibrium captures the intuition that a convention is a mutually beneficial social arrangement. To incorporate Hume's insight that mutual expectations underwrite convention, Lewis formulated a precise account of *common knowledge* and defined convention as a coordination equilibrium which individuals follow because it is common knowledge that all follow this equilibrium, and no other. Of course, both Hume's and Lewis' treatments of convention raise a critical question: How do individuals come to have the mutual expectations that make a given practice a convention?

Given a game-theoretic analysis of convention, the problem of explaining the origins of convention becomes a special case of the equilibrium selection problem in game theory. Nash's fundamental result did not provide a general method of identifying the "solution" of a game, for a game can have multiple Nash equilibria. At first blush, there is no *a priori* reason to suppose that agents in a game will choose one equilibrium over any of the others. Indeed, the classical game theory of von Neumann, Morgenstern and Nash cannot predict that agents will follow an equilibrium at all. For many years, game theorists tried to solve the equilibrium selection problem by augmenting the classical theory with *refinements* of the Nash equilibrium concept that would rule out certain equilibria as being somehow "unreasonable," ideally leaving only one Nash equilibrium as the solution of a game. The equilibrium refinements program has achieved important successes, and continues to this day. Nevertheless, this program ultimately fails to provide a fully satisfactory theory of equilibrium selection, and the coordination games that model alternative conventions illustrate this failure. In many elementary coordination games, a refinement that would rule out any one of the coordination equilibria would rule out all of them, resulting in the absurd conclusion that the agents would be irrational to follow any convention. In the end, no set of *a priori* arguments solves the equilibrium selection problem.

On the other hand, there is an alternative *a posteriori* justification of equilibrium selection. Agents who learn *inductively* through repeated trial-and-error plays of a game can converge to an equilibrium. I explored this approach to the equilibrium selection problem at Brian Skyrms' suggestion, and the outgrowth of this work resulted in my dissertation. Suppose that agents in a game are not initially at an equilibrium, and they note the strategies that each follows in a sequence of plays of the game, adjusting their beliefs about each other according to rules of Carnapian (1980) inductive logic. In its simplest form, this method of recursive belief updating is the *fictitious play* rule that George W. Brown introduced in a 1951 essay. Brown interpreted the belief updating process in an *a priori* way, with agents mentally simulating a sequence of plays they would play given strong common knowledge assumptions. But one can also interpret this process as learning through actual plays, which requires no initial common knowledge assumptions at all. This is my preferred interpretation of the fictitious play process, and all of the variants of fictitious play developed in this book have natural interpretations as actual play sequences, although for the sake of completeness I discuss the mental simulations interpretation for those variants in which I think this interpretation makes sense.

The crucial step I have taken away from the existing literature in inductive learning is to introduce the possibility of correlated strategies. Nash defined his equilibrium concept so that the agents' strategies at equilibrium are probabilistically uncorrelated. The fictitious play literature in game theory generally assumes uncorrelated strategies. This assumption is mathematically convenient, and ensures that a limit of the fictitious play process is a Nash equilibrium. Yet mathematical convenience is hardly a conceptual justification for this assumption. I contend there is no good reason to suppose that the strategies agents follow in a game are uncorrelated. Indeed, in a pair of landmark essays Robert Aumann (1974, 1987) generalized Nash's equilibrium concept by allowing agents to follow correlated strategies. In graduate school I analyzed a generalized fictitious play process which does not assume uncorrelated strategies. The results were striking and surprising. I discovered that in games with three or more agents who initially believe their strategies are uncorrelated, the generalized fictitious play process can converge to an equilibrium in which they believe their strategies are correlated. Correlation in beliefs can emerge "spontaneously" in the belief updating process, leading the agents to a kind of correlated equilibrium. But this limit was a correlated equilibrium different from Aumann's *correlated equilibrium*. By generalizing the dynamics that can explain the emergence of Nash equilibrium, I was led to formulate a new *endogenous correlated equilibrium* concept in game theory.

My interest in correlated inductive learning is also motivated by my desire to explain the origins of convention. Martin Shubik (1981) and Brian Skyrms (1990) suggest that convention might be best understood as a kind of correlated equilibrium, and Lewis himself gives an example of a convention which has a natural interpretation as a correlated equilibrium. I have pursued this idea in detail, and give a new definition of convention as a special kind of Aumann correlated equilibrium. To complement this definition of convention, I introduce a dynamical adjustment model that can be applied to explain the emergence of Aumann correlated equilibrium, and consequently, the emergence of Lewis-conventions as a special case. This models extends correlated fictitious play with the addition of random *signals* that the agents can observe and condition on as they update their beliefs about each other. Once again, correlation in beliefs can emerge "spontaneously" in the belief updating process. Agents who update their beliefs by conditioning on signals or "states of the world" can learn to follow an Aumann correlated equilibrium, even if their beliefs are initially uncorrelated with these states. And this simple model illustrates how agents who learn inductively can learn to follow a convention.

The present work is a revised version of my doctoral thesis. I have corrected all of the known errors in the original thesis, rearranged the material in places, and made significant changes in both the prose text and especially the mathematical notation that I hope have made the work far more clear. In the end I elected not to incorporate all I have learned about convention and equilibrium selection since leaving graduate school, because I still accept the main ideas I presented in my thesis, and hope to one day write a sequel to this book. I have made every effort to make this book self-contained. Readers should need no specific prior knowledge of either philosophy or game theory. Most of the analytical results and all of the computer simulation results presented in this book are original. I give detailed proofs of all original analytical results. For completeness, I occasionally include a result previously known to game theorists, and in most of these cases, I provide a different proof of the original theorem that appeared in scholarly journals that I hope readers will find easier to study than the originally published proof. Chapters 2 and 3 could be used as a first text in a graduate course in game theory. Philosophers and social scientists with a background in game theory may wish to proceed directly to Chapter 4 if they are most interested in convention, to Chapter 2 if they are most interested in generalizations of the Nash equilibrium concept, or to Chapter 3 if they are most interested in equilibrium selection.

The opening chapter sets the stage by discussing the general problem of social coordination, instances of which are solved by conventions. To better motivate the general problem, I review a series of more specific coordination problems, some relatively new and some taken from classics of political philosophy. I then introduce informally some of the basics of classical game theory, and recast the motivating examples in game-theoretic vocabulary to illustrate how the social coordination problem might be formulated more precisely as an equilibrium selection problem. Readers with a background in either social philosophy or game theory will find themselves occasionally treading on familiar ground. What may be less familiar even to many social scientists and philosophers is the fascinating interplay between concepts from game theory and the insights of moral and political philosophers. I hope I have captured something of the flavor of this interplay in this chapter.

Chapter 2 reviews solution concepts in game theory, and correlated equilibrium concepts in particular. I follow a number of authors who interpret the probabilities in the formal definition of the Nash equilibrium concept as an agent's *degrees of belief* regarding the strategies the other agents might follow. Here I argue that this *equilibrium-in-beliefs* interpretation produces spectacular generalizations of the Nash equilibrium concept when the simplifying assumption of uncorrelated strategies is dropped. Simply relaxing this assumption produces the endogenous correlated equilibrium concept. Adding "states of the world" on which agents can correlate their acts results in the Aumann correlated equilibrium concept. I also explore the relationship between common knowledge and equilibrium concepts and how the various solution concepts discussed here are interrelated. Finally, I discuss the relationship between correlated equilibrium and Richard Jeffrey's (1983) notion of *ratifiability* from decision theory.

Chapter 3 discusses inductive learning. I first review the traditional fictitious play process and how this process is a special case of Carnap's inductive logic applied to repeated play in games. In the bulk of the remainder of the chapter, I present a number of variants of fictitious play which relax the uncorrelated strategies assumption built into traditional fictitious play and explore the properties of these inductive learning models, which one might think of as "inductive learning with correlation." Simply dropping the uncorrelated strategies assumption of traditional fictitious play enables inductive deliberators to converge to an endogenous correlated equilibrium from initially uncorrelated beliefs. Introducing information from "states of the world" into the agents' belief updating enables inductive deliberators to converge to an Aumann correlated equilibrium from initially uncorrelated beliefs. This "spontaneous" appearance of correlation in beliefs and convergence to correlated equilibrium gives what I believe to be an especially powerful argument that correlated equilibrium concepts are the properly general solution concepts in game theory.

The concluding chapter returns to the social coordination problem and takes up the analysis of convention. I review Lewis' analysis of convention, and present a formal definition of convention as a special kind of Aumann correlated equilibrium which agents follow on account of their having common knowledge that their acts are appropriately correlated with publicly known "states of the world." I argue that this definition of convention as correlated equilibrium formulates Lewis' account more precisely and in its proper generality. A correlated equilibrium definition of convention gives a precise analytical framework for describing conventions and explaining why conventions remain stable over time. Yet the problem of explaining the origins of convention remains. Previous discussions of this problem in the literature, including Lewis', argue that conventions emerge either as a result of explicit agreement or because individuals recognize one arrangement as somehow focal or *salient*. To be sure, agreement and salience are the immediate explanations of many conventions. Nevertheless, I contend that this cannot be the end of the story. For agreements and salience themselves presuppose that the agents have solved certain higher-order coordination problems that enable them to form agreements or to regard an option as the salient option. That is, agreements and salience are parasitic on conventions. So a noncircular explanation of the origins of convention is needed. I argue that inductive learning can provide just such a noncircular explanation, since the results of Chapter 3 show that inductive belief updaters can converge to a correlated equilibrium convention even if their beliefs about each other are not initially correlated on any particular pattern of actions. In effect, individuals who do not happen to have any prior common conventions can establish a convention amongst themselves by trial and error learning. I also include convergence results that show that for certain classes of games, agents who update their beliefs about each other according to the inductive dynamics developed in Chapter 3 will converge almost surely to a correlated equilibrium convention. The results of this concluding chapter fall far short of providing a complete account of "spontaneous" convention, but I think they do constitute the beginnings of such an account and point to a rich new territory for philosophers and social scientists to explore.

Acknowledgments

Several institutions and many individuals have contributed either directly or indirectly to my doctoral dissertation and to the completion of this work as a volume in Routledge's series Studies in Ethics. It is a privilege as well as a pleasure to acknowledge them here.

First, I would like to thank the two philosophers who have most influenced my career thus far. In my undergraduate years at Loyola Marymount University, James Hanink gave me my first formal instruction in philosophy. Jim's exemplary teaching and the many hours he spent studying papers I wrote and arguing with me in his office sparked in me a lifelong passion for philosophy. Brian Skyrms worked closely with me from the moment I entered the doctoral program at the University of California at Irvine. Brian guided me through many false starts in my early research, directed my dissertation, and has given me far more support in my early career than anyone could expect from mere professional duty. I cannot thank Jim or Brian adequately for what they have done for me, but I do look forward to a continuing relationship with them as colleague and friend.

Many other professors, colleagues, and friends helped in various ways to prepare me to enter the philosophical profession as a graduate student. In particular, I would like to express special gratitude to Rob Allan, Bob Koerner, Patty Koerner, Michael Grady, Don White, Betsy White, Kari Regan, Joel Palmer, Roberta Sherbarth, Rosana Thrasher, and Linda Zagzebski.

Few graduate students are blessed with a supervising committee as supportive as was mine. I thank Vince Crawford and Joe Lambert for their wonderful patience, guidance, and encouragement over the years.

Cristina Bicchieri, Dean Foster, Drew Fudenberg, and Jim Joyce each read substantial portions of my doctoral thesis and gave me innumerable suggestions for its improvement, for which I now offer my thanks.

To my sorrow, I must acknowledge Gregory Kavka's contributions to my academic career and to this work posthumously. In my early days of graduate study, Greg's impact on my intellectual development through his teaching, writing and informal conversation was second only to Brian's. Greg also gave me much encouragement during some of the rougher periods of my early graduate education, again second only to Brian's in its importance to me. Before his early death, Greg served on my supervising committee, and gave me much help on early versions of the thesis. I am grateful for the all too brief time I was able to profit from his intellect and wisdom.

Paul Green, Peter Lewis, Kay Mathiesen, Ron Morales, and Amie Thomasson were my respected colleagues and much beloved friends during my graduate school years. I have had the good fortune to remain close to them professionally and personally, if not in physical distance, in the years that have followed. Their names appear often in the examples in this book, an insufficient tribute to the richness they have brought to my life.

The research for the doctoral thesis *A Study in Inductive Deliberation* which is the predecessor to this book was financially supported in part by the University of California at Irvine Humanities Associates, the Irvine Focused Research Program in Scientific Explanation and the Sarah Scaife Foundation.

Portions of this book were first published in alternate form in the following:

(with Brian Skyrms) "Deliberational Correlated Equilibria." *Philosophical Topics* 21, no. 1 (1994): 191–226.

"Inductive Learning, Knowledge Asymmetries and Convention." In *Theoretical Aspects of Reasoning About Knowledge V,* edited by Ronald Fagin, 284–304. Los Altos, California: Morgan Kaufman, 1994.

"Endogenous Correlated Equilibria in Noncooperative Games." *Theory and Decision* 38 (1995): 61–84.

"Convention as Correlated Equilibrium." *Erkenntnis* 42 (1995): 65–87.

Lanette Cornwell, Dawn McLaughlin, and Joanna Peters completed the formidable task of editing the entire manuscript and turning it into book form. I thank them for a magnificent job. Damon Zucca, my editor at Routledge, has been a joy to work with. I thank him for his guidance, his patience, and his unflappable good will.

My parents, Cornelia and John, and my brothers, Frits and Bob, have given me the support only a loving family could during the interminable years I spent in my formal education and in my philosophical career since leaving graduate school. I give my greatest thanks to Frits, Bob, Mom, and Dad. This work is dedicated to my parents.

Finally, I would like to express special thanks to Sharon Minichiello, formerly professor of history at Loyola Marymount University and now professor of history and Director of the Center for Japanese Studies at the University of Hawaii. During my undergraduate years at Loyola Marymount University Sharon helped me in more ways than she will ever realize, and it was she who gave me the encouragement that convinced me to pursue an academic career. Sharon, I hope this book is fruit worthy of your faith in me.

Contents

1 Social Interaction and Principles of Rational Decision   3
  §1.0 Introduction   3
  §1.1 Examples of Social Coordination Problems   6
  §1.2 Noncooperative Games 14
  §1.3 Nash Equilibrium 28
  §1.4 Examples Revisited 36
  §1.5 Equilibrium-in-Beliefs 47
  §1.6 Conclusion 50

2 Rationalizability and Correlated Equilibrium Concepts   53
  §2.0 Introduction 53
  §2.1 Rationalizability 55
  §2.2 Correlated Equilibrium Concepts 65
  §2.3 Correlated Equilibrium, Rationalizability, and Ratifiability . . . 82

3 Equilibrium Selection via Inductive Dynamic Deliberation   99
  §3.0 Introduction 99
  §3.1 The Dirichlet Rule 100
  §3.2 Inductive Deliberation with Endogenous Correlation 111
  §3.3 Correlating with "States of the World" 131
  §3.4 Dirichlet Dynamics with Imperfect Memory 149
  §3.5 Random Sampling Dirichlet Deliberation 163
  §3.6 Deliberators with Variable States 176

4 The Emergence of Social Convention   185
  §4.0 Introduction 185
  §4.1 Lewis' Characterization of Conventions 187
  §4.2 Convention as Correlated Equilibrium 194
  §4.3 Dynamical Explanations of Conventions 201

References   213

Index   219

List of Figures

Figure 1.2.1. Overlord 16
Figure 1.2.2. Overlord (ordinal utilities) 19
Figure 1.2.3. Overlord (cardinal utilities) 19
Figure 1.3.1. Prisoners' Dilemma (plea bargain interpretation) 30
Figure 1.3.2. Prisoners' Dilemma (ordinal utilities) 30
Figure 1.3.3. Hobbesian State of Nature as Prisoners' Dilemma 31
Figure 1.3.4. Chicken 32
Figure 1.4.1. The Encounter Problem 37
Figure 1.4.2. Hume's Rowboat 39
Figure 1.4.3. Battle of the Sexes 41
Figure 1.4.4. Telephone Tag 42
Figure 1.4.5. 2-Player Stag Hunt 42
Figure 1.4.6. 3-Player Stag Hunt, Division of Labor Interpretation . . 44
Figure 1.4.7. Public Good Provision of a "Lumpy" Good 46

Figure 2.1.1. Stag Hunt 56
Figure 2.1.2. A 3 × 3 Game with 4 Rationalizable Strategy Profiles . . 58
Figure 2.1.3. Game Reduced By Deleting a Dominated Pure Strategy . 58
Figure 2.1.4. The Same Game Reduced Again 59
Figure 2.1.5. Prisoner's Dilemma 59
Figure 2.2.1. Battle of the Sexes 67
Figure 2.2.2. Chicken 72
Figure 2.2.3. 3-Player Battle of the Sexes 75
Figure 2.2.4. 3-Player Prisoner's Dilemma 80
Figure 2.3.1. Brandenburger-Dekel Example 84
Figure 2.3.2. 3-Player Chicken 92

Figure 3.1.1. Battle of the Sexes 100
Figure 3.1.2. Convergence to Mixed Equilibrium-in-Beliefs in
        Battle of the Sexes 106
Figure 3.1.3. Two Populations Matched in Battle of the Sexes 108
Figure 3.2.1. 3-Player Chicken 111
Figure 3.2.2. Orbit of Independence-Deliberation in 3-Player Chicken 114
Figure 3.2.3. Orbit of Correlation-Deliberation in 3-Player Chicken . . 118
Figure 3.2.4. Public Good Provision 120

Figure 3.2.5. Battle of the Sexes *II* 126
Figure 3.3.1. Skyrms' 3-Player Example 135
Figure 3.5.1. Chicken 163
Figure 3.5.2. Young's Counterexample 171

Figure 4.1.1. Hume's Rowboat 187
Figure 4.1.2. Chicken 188
Figure 4.1.3. Battle of the Sexes 192
Figure 4.1.4. Telephone Tag 192
Figure 4.1.5. The Encounter Problem 194
Figure 4.2.1. Aumann's 3-Player Example 200
Figure 4.3.1. Battle of the Sexes *II* 206
Figure 4.3.2. A Non-Weakly Acyclic Game 210

List of Tables

Table 1.2.1. Overlord 18

Table 3.4.1. Battle of the Sexes
    Played by RRC-Dirichlet Deliberators 151
Table 3.6.1. Battle of the Sexes
    Played by VSC-Dirichlet Deliberators 178

LEARNING AND COORDINATION

Inductive Deliberation, Equilibrium, and Convention

Social Interaction and
Principles of Rational Decision

> Money has become by convention a sort of representative of demand; and this is why it has the name 'money'—because it exists not by nature but by law and it is in our power to change it and make it useless.
>
> Aristotle, *Nicomachean Ethics*

> Sometimes the interests of society may require a rule of justice in a particular case; but may not determine any particular rule, among several, which are all equally beneficial. . . .
>
> It is highly requisite, that prescription or long possession should convey property; but what number of days or months or years should be sufficient for that purpose, it is impossible for reason alone to determine. . . .
>
> *What is a man's property?* Anything which it is lawful for him, and for him alone, to use. *But what rule have we, by which we can distinguish these objects?* Here we must have recourse to statutes, customs, precedents, analogies, and a hundred other circumstances; some of which are constant and inflexible, some variable and arbitrary.
>
> David Hume, *Enquiry Concerning the Principles of Morals*

§1.0   Introduction

As Aristotle had already noted in his discussion of currency in the *Nicomachean Ethics*, one can explain the existence of seemingly arbitrary social arrangements in terms of mutual benefit. According to this kind of explanation, people coordinate their actions in certain ways, as when all use a common unit of currency, because each recognizes that doing so serves his self-interest. At the same time, mutual benefit does not generally determine the *details* of social coordination. This was Hume's point when he argued that the specific rules governing property rights in a society are not governed "by reason alone." The members of a particular community may regard a good as someone's property if she has possessed this good unchallenged for a year. Such a rule benefits the community members by forestalling many violent conflicts, so long as they generally abide by this rule. But a different community might require only one month's unchallenged possession as sufficient to convey ownership, and presumably this rule if generally followed would serve all as well as a one year rule. In most cases, people coordinate their activity in a certain way when they could have coordinated in a different way. Hence, an account of social coordination requires more than the premise that individuals will coordinate out of self-interest.

A central question I wish to address is this: *How do particular patterns of social coordination emerge?* The informal answer that motivates the work in this book is that *self-interested individuals can achieve mutually beneficial coordination by learning through experience.* This work falls in the long tradition that accounts for social coordination as the result of individual self-interest coinciding with mutual benefit. However, in the 20th century the development of the complementary theories of *expected utility* and *noncooperative games* have enabled philosophers, economists, and other social theorists to treat the question of social coordination much more precisely than ever before. In this work, I will develop a formal theory of inductive learning through experience which generalizes previous theories in the literature (Fudenberg and Kreps 1988; Skyrms 1991), and apply this theory to help account for the emergence of coordination patterns, modeled as equilibrium points of noncooperative games. Social interactions can be modeled as noncooperative games, which have *equilibrium outcomes* corresponding to coordination practices that each individual in the game is rational to follow, in the sense that following the equilibrium maximizes her expected utility. However, just as social situations can have many different coordination outcomes, a noncooperative game can have many different equilibrium points. The outstanding unresolved question of game theory is how to account for players selecting one equilibrium over others.

This book makes a contribution to a growing literature that accounts for players selecting an equilibrium of a game as the result of a *dynamical adjustment process.* I model players engaged in a game as *inductive deliberators,* who update their beliefs about one another recursively, using rules of Carnapian (1980) inductive logic, until they reach an *equilibrium* of the game. The theory of inductive deliberation I develop generalizes previous theories by allowing for the possibility of *correlation* in the beliefs of the deliberators. Most of the results of noncooperative game theory presuppose that the players' strategies are probabilistically independent. In particular, the *Nash equilibrium* concept, which has been the dominant solution concept in game theory, assumes probabilistic independence. Nearly every dynamic model in the game-theoretic literature also presupposes probabilistic independence at every stage of the dynamical process.

Assuming independence guarantees that the limit of such dynamics will be a Nash equilibrium. I will argue that such probabilistic independence assumptions are unfounded, and that agents should take into account the possibility that their opponents' actions are correlated. Relaxing the probabilistic independence assumption in noncooperative game theory leads to various *correlated equilibrium* concepts, which I argue are more appropriate solution concepts than the more restrictive Nash equilibrium concept. Relaxing the independence assumption in the inductive dynamics enables correlation in the deliberators' beliefs to emerge spontaneously, resulting in the deliberators converging to correlated equilibrium.

I devote the majority of the book to a formal theory of inductive deliberation, and its relationship to various correlated equilibrium concepts. In particular, I show the following: (1) Under suitable conditions, correlated equilibria correspond to fixed points of the dynamics, (2) The dynamics can "amplify" initially weak correlations in deliberators' beliefs, and (3) The dynamics can create correlation in beliefs from an initial uncorrelated state. In the final chapter, I argue that the emergence of correlated equilibria as a result of inductive deliberation can help to explain the origins of social coordination.

To set the stage for what follows, in the remainder of this introductory chapter I will describe the problem of social interaction in more detail, and review the roles that game theory and decision theory can play in explaining social interaction. In §1, I will present a variety of examples of social interaction problems meant to motivate the formal treatment of the social interaction problem that follows. §2 reviews the early attempt by Von Neumann and Morgenstern (1944) to model interactive decision problems mathematically as noncooperative games. Von Neumann and Morgenstern's treatment of the theory of games raises certain fundamental questions, which I attempt to address in subsequent sections. Von Neumann and Morgenstern focused their attention on solving a particular class of games, namely *zero-sum games*, and their method of solution was not satisfactory for solving games in general. In §3, I review Nash's (1950, 1951) introduction of a solution concept for games defined in terms of joint expected utility maximization. Nash showed that the games of the Von Neumann-Morgenstern theory in general have *Nash equilibrium points* at which every player maximizes her individual expected utility. However, Nash's analysis did not provide a general method for solving games, since a game need not have a unique Nash equilibrium. In §4, I return to the examples of §1 and apply game theory to restate the coordination problems of the examples more precisely. Finally, in §5 I argue for a reinterpretation of equilibrium concepts in game theory. The classical game theory of Von Neumann and Morgenstern (1944) and Nash (1950, 1951) defines the Nash equilibrium in terms of *mixed strategies*. I follow a number of authors

(Aumann 1987; Brandenburger and Dekel 1988; Skyrms 1991) who maintain that it is preferable to define equilibrium concepts in terms of players' *subjective beliefs*. Such a "subjectivist" reinterpretation of classical game theory opens up possibilities for spectacular generalizations of the Nash equilibrium concept, which will be considered in subsequent chapters.

§1.1   Examples of Social Coordination Problems

In this section, I give nine examples of situations in which individuals must coordinate their actions in order to interact "successfully." These examples are meant to illustrate some of the main problems faced by decision makers in social settings. One characteristic common to the interaction problems described in these examples is that not one has a unique resolution. In each example, the agents come to "solve" their interaction problem by settling upon one outcome they find mutually beneficial, when they could have settled upon a different mutually beneficial outcome. In later sections, I will use these examples to illustrate how the underlying logic behind the individuals' reasoning in social interaction problems can be formalized by employing the mathematical theory of games.

Example 1. The Encounter Problem

Two sales people, Amie and Kay, wish to meet in a two-story office building to plan for a forthcoming sales call. They do not care where they have their meeting, though they will both be very put out if they fail to meet. So long as Kay and Amie find each other, they will settle into the nearest vacant office and discuss their sales strategy. They will find one another if, and only if, each searches for the other on the same floor of the building. Clearly, Amie chooses which floor she will search for Kay on according to what floor she expects Kay to choose, and *vice versa*. This is a problem of *pure coordination* (Schelling 1960; Lewis 1969), since the interests of the agents making the choices coincide exactly. In this *Encounter Problem*, each individual arrives at her most desired outcome precisely when she coordinates her choice with the choice of the other individual, so that both arrive at their most desired outcome. Note that even though their interests coincide perfectly, this coordination problem is nontrivial because Kay and Amie can coordinate on two equally good outcomes. Which should they choose?

Example 2. Hume's Rowboat

David Hume was perhaps the first philosopher to fully appreciate the importance of coordination problems. In a famous passage in *A Treatise on Human Nature*, Hume considers the case of two rowers who must row in unison in order to move their boat forward. Hume notes that the rowers are able to synchronize their rowing, even though they do not explicitly promise one another to row in a certain way, so long as each expects the other to row as he rows.[1] This is a problem of pure coordination, since each rower gets what she most wants, which is to move the boat forward, precisely by choosing the same pattern of rowing as the other rower, so that the other rower gets what she most wants as well. Hume's Rowboat is evidently a more complicated problem than the Encounter Problem. Each rower can pull her oar at any one of many different rates, so that there are more than two ways for the rowers to coordinate their rowing, and many more than two ways for them to miscoordinate.

Example 3. Conventions of Language

In "On Sense and Reference," Frege asserts without argument that "one can hardly deny that mankind has a common store of thoughts which is transmitted from one generation to another."[2] While not all philosophers accept Frege's account of senses and thoughts as actual ideal entities, Frege's claim seems undeniably right.[3] Humans evidently do share and pass down a vast store of knowledge. The media for this knowledge transmission are human languages. In everyday human discourse, individual words convey meanings, and complete sentences convey what Frege called "thoughts" and Russell "propositions." People can ordinarily understand one another because they associate particular words with specific meanings. But how does this association take place? The actual verbal signs that people associate with particular meanings are at bottom arbitrary. As Shakespeare observed, "That which we call a rose, by any other name would smell as sweet."[4] Indeed, in Greece "$\tau\rho\iota\alpha\nu\tau\dot{\alpha}\varphi\upsilon\lambda\lambda o$" and in Russia "роза" have the same meaning to those who use Greek and Russian, respectively, as "rose" has for English users when they refer to the flower with thorns on its

---

[1] Hume (1740), p. 490.

[2] Frege (1892), p. 59.

[3] Note that Frege is not asserting that each member of the human race knows each thought in the "common store" of thoughts.

[4] *Romeo and Juliet*, Act II, scene 2.

stem.[5] Given the great variety of verbal signs that can serve the same purpose, how do conventions of language arise?

Conventions of language use are problems of pure coordination, like the Encounter Problem and Hume's Rowboat, in that all of the agents' interests coincide with their using the same word to refer to a particular entity. The language convention problem is far more complicated than either the Encounter Problem or Hume's Rowboat, since successful communication involves many individuals in a society coordinating on one of many possible verbal signals in order for this signal to become a word in the society's language.

Example 4. Dining Out

This is a variation of the Encounter Problem discussed above in the first example. Amie and Kay again wish to meet, this time to have dinner, but they have failed to prearrange the restaurant. Fortunately for them, they know that the options for restaurants each might choose to go to are limited. Amie knows that Kay will always go to her favorite restaurant, Mimi's European Cafe, unless Kay decides to go to Amie's preferred restaurant. Kay knows that Amie's favorite restaurant is the Cracker Barrel Southern Restaurant, and that Amie will always go to the Cracker Barrel unless she decides to defer to Kay's choice. Amie would definitely most prefer to meet Kay at the Cracker Barrel, and Kay would definitely most prefer to meet Amie at Mimi's. Nevertheless, each prefers meeting at her less favored restaurant over going to the restaurant the other does not choose and not meeting at all. This is a case of what might be termed *impure coordination*, since each individual wants to coordinate her choice with the other's choice, but their relative interests at each possible outcome of their joint choice do not perfectly coincide.[6]

Amie and Kay are likely to have much more difficulty resolving this problem than they have in the Encounter Problem, even if they are able to communicate before they choose their respective restaurants. If Amie is able to call Kay before dinner time, she might tell Kay that she will go to the Cracker Barrel no matter

---

[5] Of course, this discussion is not meant to give a full sketch of the Fregean theory of sense and reference. The only element of the Fregean theory relevant to the discussion here is the doctrine that linguistic entities, including words, have unique *senses* or *meanings* that map uniquely to the referents of the linguistic entities. Also, by using Fregean terminology, I do not mean to imply that an analysis of linguistic conventions commits one to accepting Frege's account of senses. I simply find the Fregean vocabulary particularly helpful in describing the problem of justifying linguistic conventions.

[6] To my knowledge, Gregory Kavka was the first to explicitly use the term 'impure coordination'. See Kavka (1986), p. 184. Nevertheless, the terminology is implicit in Lewis (1969).

what, in an attempt to intimidate Kay into giving in and going to the Cracker Barrel. For her part, Kay might reply that she will go to Mimi's no matter what, in hopes that Amie will give in. The two can meet only if exactly one of them gives in. If they both carry out threats to go to their preferred restaurants, or if they both give in, they will miscoordinate.

Example 5. Telephone Tag

Kay and Amie live in different cities and want to have a phone conversation. They coordinate and have their conversation if one calls and the other receives. However, each prefers to be the receiver, to avoid the charges of calling. Like the Dining Out problem of Example 4, this is an impure coordination problem, since each of the coordination points is more favorable to one of the two agents involved. The Telephone Tag problem shows that individuals do not always arrive at mutually beneficial outcomes by performing the same action. In Telephone Tag, the agents coordinate when each chooses the alternative opposite that which her counterpart chooses.

Example 6. Rousseau's Stag Hunt

In the *Discourse on the Origin and Foundations of Inequality Among Men*, Rousseau gives an example meant to explain the origin of cooperation among self-interested individuals so as to achieve mutual benefit:

> Taught by experience that love of well-being is the sole motive of human actions, he found himself in a position to distinguish the rare occasions when common interest should make him count on the assistance of his fellowmen, and those even rarer occasions when competition ought to make him distrust them. In the first case, he united with them in a herd, or at most in some sort of free association, that obligated no one and that lasted only as long as the passing need that had formed it. In the second case, everyone sought to obtain his own advantage, either by overt force, if he believed he could, or by cleverness and cunning, if he felt himself to be the weaker.

> This is how men imperceptibly acquire some crude idea of mutual commitments and the advantages to be had in fulfilling them, but only insofar as present and perceptible interest could require it, since foresight meant nothing to them, and far from concerning themselves about a distant future, they did not even give a thought to the next day. Were it a matter of catching a deer, everyone was quite aware that he must faithfully keep his post in order to achieve this purpose; but

if a hare happened to pass within reach of one of them, no doubt he would have pursued it without giving it a second thought, and that, having obtained his prey, he cared very little about causing his companions to miss theirs.[7]

As Rousseau frames the Stag Hunt problem, each hunter wants as much meat as he can get from the hunt. Assuming that enough deer and rabbits live in the woods, each individual hunter can guarantee himself a rabbit if he hunts for a rabbit. If they can agree to all hunt for a stag and all follow their agreement, then together they will capture a stag, and then each will have much more meat than the meat from a rabbit. However, if any hunter believes that any of the other hunters will fail to live up to the agreement, then he had better hunt for rabbit, since otherwise he will catch nothing. There are evidently two outcomes that the hunters can settle upon that are compatible with their individual interests, namely, all hunt for rabbit and all hunt for stag. All fare better if all hunt for stag, but each will be tempted to play it safe and hunt for a rabbit if he doubts any or all of the others' commitment to hunting for a stag. How can the hunters settle upon the better outcome in which they capture the stag?

Example 7. The Division of Labor

As it is by treaty, by barter, and by purchase, that we obtain from one another the greater part of those mutual good offices which we stand in need of, so it is this same trucking disposition which originally gives occasion to the division of labour. In a tribe of hunters or shepherds a particular person makes bows and arrows, for example, with more readiness and dexterity than any other. He frequently exchanges them for cattle or for venison with his companions; and he finds at last that he can in this manner get more cattle and venison, than if he himself went to the field to catch them. From a regard to his own interest, therefore, the making of bows and arrows grows to be his chief business, and he becomes a sort of armourer. Another excels in making the frames and covers of their little huts or moveable houses. He is accustomed to be of use in this way to his neighbors, who reward him in the same manner with cattle and with venison, till at last he finds it in his interest to dedicate himself entirely to his employment, and to become a sort of house-carpenter. In the same manner a third becomes a smith or a brazier, a fourth a tanner or dresser of hides or skins, the principal part of the clothing of savages. And thus the certainty of being able to exchange all that surplus part of the produce of his own labour, which is over and above his own consumption, for such parts of the produce of other men's

---

[7]Rousseau (1755), pp. 61–62.

labour as he may have occasion for, encourages every man to apply himself to a particular occupation, and to cultivate and bring to perfection whatever talent or genius he may possess for that particular species of business.[8]

Adam Smith argues in the quoted passage from *The Wealth of Nations* that the individual advantage persons derive from economic exchange leads to a mutually advantageous division of labor. Individuals' expectations that economic exchange will be possible underpin their willingness to specialize in their labor. Then they produce a greater aggregate of economic goods, which they can exchange, than they could produce if each fends for himself without specializing his labor.

Smith's account of the origin of the division of labor resembles Rousseau's Stag Hunt problem in that individuals in an economic community reason like the Stag Hunters to justify specializing their work. Each member of an economic community could act cautiously, and guarantee himself a modest level of economic well-being by farming for himself, hunting by himself, and otherwise working in isolation so as to provide for his own needs. If a community member "goes his own way," economically speaking, then he will have to consume all of the products of his labor, and will have no surplus of goods with which to trade with others. On the other hand, the members of the community all work far more efficiently if each specializes at a particular occupation in which he excels. In this case of divided labor, each can produce a substantial surplus that he can exchange with others for some of the fruits of their divided labor. In this manner, each individual enjoys a far greater level of economic prosperity than any can achieve under a system of undivided labor. However, specializing does involve a certain risk, since if one specializes his labor and then finds that the others have elected to go their own ways and not specialize, then he will not be able to exchange his surplus for the goods he needs but did not produce, and will thereby be worse off than if he had gone his own way. Again like in Stag Hunt, there appear to be two possible outcomes that are compatible with the self-interest of the members of the economy, namely, everyone specializes, or everyone "goes his own way." However, the coordination problem of the division of labor described by Smith may be more complicated than the Stag Hunt, in that there may be more than two such stable outcomes possible. A mutually beneficial division of labor may be possible even if only *most* of the members of the economic community specialize their labor, while in Rousseau's Stag Hunt all must run the risk in order to provide for the better overall outcome of the hunt.

---

[8] Smith (1776), pp. 27–28.

Example 8. Crisis Bargaining

In diplomatic crises, each negotiating party may threaten to act aggressively in order to intimidate the others into acquiescing to the party's demands. For instance, during the 1938 European crisis that ended with the Munich treaty, Hitler threatened to go to war against France and Great Britain unless these nations recognized Nazi Germany's immediate annexation of the Sudetenland. After they capitulated to Hitler's demands, Chamberlain and Daladier believed that they had averted an immediate war against Nazi Germany. Great Britain and France jointly suffered terrible losses in international prestige and in relative military strength as a result of their ministers' choice to appease Hitler. Nevertheless, the citizens of both nations rejoiced at the time, thinking that they had avoided the even worse consequence of war. On the other hand, Hitler and the Germans also wanted to avoid war. Had Chamberlain and Daladier informed Hitler that the British and French would fight rather than allow the Nazis to annex the Sudetenland, and had Hitler believed them, then in all likelihood Hitler would have backed down and Nazi Germany would have suffered a loss of international prestige.[9]

The Munich crisis exemplifies certain features common to crisis bargaining problems in which two sides must resolve a conflict of interest. First, each side has two options: "back down" and cooperate or at least act peacefully with the other side, or "strike" and act aggressively against the other side. Second, both sides fare better when they both back down than when both strike. Third, one side wins the conflict if it strikes and the other side backs down. Finally, if both sides strike, then the result is conflict, which is the worst possible outcome for each side.

Crisis bargaining problems present special difficulties for the sides trying to make their choices. Perhaps the outcome where each side backs down is intuitively the best overall outcome. This outcome preserves the "status quo" and allows each side to avoid conflict and not suffer the losses incurred if the other side strikes unilaterally. However, the standoff outcome is not a stable coordination point of a two-sided crisis bargaining problem. Each side is tempted to strike if it expects the other side to back down. The stable outcomes of a two-sided crisis bargaining problem are evidently the outcomes where one side strikes and the other backs down. If one side expects the other to strike, then it is best for this side to acquiesce and back down. If the other side knows that its opponent will back down, then it will strike, and neither side will deviate from this outcome. As a result, each side is prone to threaten to strike, and one side wins the crisis if it convinces the other side that its threats are genuine. In the Munich

---

[9]For a fascinating discussion of the Munich crisis, see Shirer (1960), Chapter 12.

Crisis, Nazi Germany emerged the clear victor because Chamberlain and Daladier believed Hitler's threat, enabling the Germans to strike unopposed. On the other hand, the diplomatic crisis over the 1990 Iraqi invasion of Kuwait resulted in the Persian Gulf War, which neither side wanted, because neither side was willing to back down in the face of the threats from the other side. Note that in such a crisis bargaining problem, both sides will be tempted to *threaten* to strike, even if one or the other side does not actually intend to strike. If one side intends to back down, then it may still threaten to strike in hopes of convincing the other side not to strike. Hence this kind of social coordination problem differs in kind from the other coordination problems considered so far. In a crisis bargaining problem, each side may want to try to keep the other side uncertain to some extent as to what it will do.

Example 9. Public Good Provision

Loosely speaking, a *public good* is a good that must be provided for by a relatively high percentage of the population if it is to be available at all, and that once available is available to every member of the population, whether or not this member contributes to the provision of the good. A paradigmatic example of a public good is an environment with low levels of pollution, so that among other things the air and the water are safe for all to use. If most members of the population take moderately expensive measures to curtail their pollution, then it can be to one's own advantage to limit one's own pollution in the same manner, and thus help keep the overall pollution level acceptably low. However, if few or none of the other members of society curtail their pollution, then one only loses by taking measures that curtail one's individual pollution, since these measures are somewhat costly and one cannot significantly lower the overall level of pollution by curtailing one's own pollution. There is clearly mutual advantage to having an environment with low pollution levels. But how can the members of a population come to curtail their overall pollution, when each member knows that she must rely upon the others curtailing their pollution in order to make curtailing her own pollution the rational thing for her to do?

§1.2   Noncooperative Games

> It is only a general sense of common interest; which sense all the members of the
> society express to one another, and which induces them to regulate their conduct
> by certain rules. I observe, that it will be for my interest to leave another in the
> possession of his goods, *provided* he will act in the same manner with regard
> to me. He is sensible of a like interest in the regulation of his conduct. When
> this common sense of interest is mutually express'd, and is known to both, it
> produces a suitable resolution and behavior.
>
> David Hume, *A Treatise of Human Nature*

Hume was perhaps the first to recognize that rational agents can achieve
mutually beneficial social arrangements as a consequence of their having appropriate reciprocal expectations. For instance, Hume notes all parties derive some
advantage if each individual refrains from stealing the material goods of others. The advantage thus gained accounts for the existence of property rights in
a society, according to Hume. Respecting property rights is only conditionally
advantageous for each member of society. If the other members in society do
not generally refrain from stealing, then one might as well steal also, and thus at
least avoid being exploited. Since respecting property rights benefits oneself only
conditionally, Hume wished to account for how respecting property rights does
not violate individual self-interested rationality. The answer, according to Hume,
lies in the beliefs or expectations that agents have regarding one another. Respecting property rights is the rational thing for an agent to do when she expects
everyone to conditionally respect property rights, and knows that everyone else
has the same expectation regarding her. Hume concludes that respecting property rights is a *jointly* rational policy when the members of a society have mutual
expectations that all will follow this policy.

More generally, Hume's contention is that a set of agents can each act so as to
achieve mutual benefit, and that each agent is rational to follow the arrangement
if the mutual benefit and the disposition of all to follow the arrangement is known
to all. These fundamental insights into the explanation of social cooperation have
been formulated more precisely in the 20th century as the mathematical theory
of *noncooperative games*. Modern noncooperative game theory, or *game theory*
for short,[10] was foreshadowed in papers by Zermelo (1913), Borel (1921, 1924),

---

[10]Beginning with Von Neumann and Morgenstern (1944), game theorists have distinguished two
branches of the theory: *cooperative* and *noncooperative*. Cooperative game theory is characterized
by players being able to establish binding agreements that restrict their actions. Noncooperative
game theory does not make this presupposition, and is generally regarded as the more fundamental

and Von Neumann (1928), though game theorists generally consider the theory to have been founded by Von Neumann and Morgenstern with the publication of their monumental treatise, *Theory of Games and Economic Behavior* (1944). In game theory, the notions of individual rationality, expectations, social interaction, and mutually beneficial arrangements are defined mathematically. An agent's decision is *rational in the Bayesian sense* when such a decision maximizes the agent's *expected utility*. To be able to choose according to the principle of Bayesian rationality in a social interaction problem, or *game*, an agent must rely upon his expectations regarding his situation, which are precisely defined as a probability distribution over the relevant states of the world, including his opponents' choices. A mutually beneficial social arrangement is modeled as an *equilibrium* of the game, that is, a combination of choices, each of which is Bayesian rational for each agent, given that she expects the other agents to follow this combination.

Before proceeding, I would like to comment briefly on the attribution of game-theoretic ideas to Hume, and more generally on the use of game theory as a means of addressing issues in social and moral philosophy. Certainly, Hume's insights into the individual rationality of social coordination are informal, while game theory is a mathematical theory. However, I see no reason not to credit these insights of Hume, and of like-minded philosophers and economists such as Hobbes and Smith, as game-theoretic insights. In a number of cases, a theory a philosopher has proposed informally has later been developed formally as part of a mathematical or scientific theory. To cite only one example, Glymour (1992, 229) credits Carnap with presenting the first theory of the mind as a computational program in *The Logical Structure of the World*, and as extending Hobbes' informal mechanistic theory of the mind in *De Copore*. One can concur with Glymour that Hobbes' and Carnap's informal theories laid the foundation of the formal theory of artificial intelligence. Similarly, one can regard game theory as a formal logic of interactive decision making, which builds upon the insights of Hume, and before Hume, Hobbes.[11] As a formal theory, game theory bears some interesting similarities with formal deductive logic. Formal logic enables us to better understand the core structure of arguments, whereas game theory enables us to better understand the reasoning of self-interested agents who make

---

branch of game theory. In this dissertation, I will use "game theory" to refer to noncooperative game theory when no confusion is likely to arise. This abuse of terminology has actually become a popular convention among many game theorists.

[11] For game-theoretic interpretations of Hobbes' arguments in *Leviathan*, see Gauthier (1969), Hampton (1986), and especially Kavka (1986).

Kavka (1989, 29–32) gives a similar argument in defense of the attribution of game-theoretic insights to Hobbes.

decisions in interactive contexts. Admittedly, people do not usually mentally construct formal models when they are trying to reason out how to decide upon a course of action. Still, these models are valuable in part because they make precise certain intuitive notions such as self-interested or other-interested behavior and beliefs regarding one's situation. Similarly, people do not typically think in terms of a predicate calculus, but we can use such a calculus to better understand the logical structure of an informal argument. Moreover, like formal logic, game theory is not a completely descriptive theory, but a normative theory. People can and do make mistakes when they choose, just as they make occasional logical mistakes in their arguments. Game theory helps to explain not what people do all of the time, but what people would do if they consistently followed certain principles of rational decision making. Finally, like formal logic, game theory has become a study unto itself, with many positive results and some interesting negative results.

Historically, formal game theory emerged as the result of the analysis of conflict rather than coordination. Consider the following caricature of the strategic dilemma faced by each side prior to the 1944 Allied invasion of Nazi-occupied France. The German and Allied high commands know that there are only two areas suitable for an Allied amphibious assault on occupied France: Calais and Normandy. The Allies have sufficient landing craft to assault only one of these areas. The Germans have sufficient forces to repel the invasion, provided that these forces are concentrated in the vicinity of the area the Allies will assault just prior to D-day. If the Germans disperse their forces more evenly between the two potential invasion areas, or concentrate their forces in the area not chosen by the Allies, then the Allied invasion will surely succeed. The Allies will win the war if the invasion is a success, while the Germans will win if their forces repel the invasion. Each side reasons that it has two viable strategic options. The Allies can invade either at Calais (C) or at Normandy (N). The Germans can concentrate their forces either at Calais (C) or at Normandy (N). This problem can be summarized in matrix form, as in Figure 1.2.1:

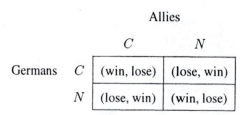

Figure 1.2.1. Overlord

In the matrix of this strategic problem, the Germans choose the row, and the Allies choose the column. Their options, C and N, are their *pure strategies*. As row chooser, the outcome for the Germans given both sides' selections of strategies is given by the first coordinate of each ordered pair in the corresponding cell of the matrix. Likewise, as column chooser, the outcome for the Allies given both sides' choices of strategies is given by the second coordinate of each ordered pair in the corresponding matrix cell. The strategy combinations that the two players settle upon can also be stated as ordered pairs, with the first coordinate containing the row chooser's strategy and the second coordinate containing the column chooser's strategy. For instance, the case in which the Germans concentrate at Calais and the Allies assault Normandy can be formally stated as the ordered pair (C, N), and the associated joint outcome, in which the Allied invasion is successful, is represented in the matrix as (lose,win). The formal model of the strategic dilemma in this section is known as a *noncooperative game*, which is called "Overlord" in reference to the historical Allied operation. The decision makers engaged in the game, namely the German and French high commands, are referred to as the *players*. The Germans will be referred to as the *row player* or *Player 1*, and the Allies will be referred to as the *column player* or *Player 2*. I will follow similar conventions for two-player games throughout this book. This kind of matrix representation is known as a *normal* or *strategic form game*. In a strategic form game, the players are modeled as choosing their strategies independently and in no particular temporal order. The situation of players engaged in a strategic form game is assumed to be such that each selects a strategy without being able to observe the strategies the opposing players select beforehand, so the players select their strategies as if they were choosing simultaneously. There are four possible strategy combinations for this game. In this case, the four combinations can produce one of two different results for the two sides as given in Table 1.2.1.

Given that each side prefers to win the war, the relative desirability of each strategy combination for the two sides can be represented by a second matrix representation of the game, given as Figure 1.2.2. The rankings for each player over the various strategy combinations are known as *ordinal utilities*. Note that the ordinal utilities in the matrix show that the desirability of each strategy option for each player depends crucially upon the strategy selected by the opposing player. The Germans' best option is C exactly in the case in which the Allies choose C as well, and N exactly in the case in which the Allies choose N. On the other hand, the Allies do best by choosing the *opposite* strategy of the Germans. Given that each side will want to choose the strategy that is best for its side, the Germans will choose C when they think it likely that the Allies will choose C,

Table 1.2.1. Overlord

Strategy Combination	Result
(C, C) Germans concentrate at Calais, Allies land at Calais	(win, lose) Germans win, Allies lose
(C, N) Germans concentrate at Calais, Allies land at Normandy	(lose, win) Germans lose, Allies win
(N, C) Germans concentrate at Normandy, Allies land at Calais	(lose, win) Germans lose, Allies win
(N, N) Germans concentrate at Normandy, Allies land at Normandy	(win, lose) Germans win, Allies lose

Allies

		C	N
Germans	C	(1st, 2nd)	(2nd, 1st)
	N	(2nd, 1st)	(1st, 2nd)

Figure 1.2.2. Overlord (ordinal utilities)

and N when they think it likely that the Allies will choose N. Similarly, the Allies will choose C when they think it likely that the Germans will choose N, and N when they think it likely that the Germans will choose C. Introducing the ordinal preferences of the players into the analysis of the game illustrates the fundamental distinguishing feature of strategic decision making in an interactive context: The best strategy for a player to select depends upon the strategies that this player expects the other players to select.

The analysis of the Overlord game in terms of ordinal utilities leaves important questions unanswered. Just what counts as a "best" strategy, given one's expectations? How likely must the Allies think it that the Germans choose C in order for the "best" Allied response to be N? In order to answer such questions and thereby come to some understanding of how this game might come to be "solved," it is necessary to know not only the *ordering* of the players' preferences for the various outcomes, but the *relative intensities* of these preferences. The relative intensities of preferences for various outcomes are quantified by *cardinal* or *numerical utilities*. In Overlord, if each player has a numerical utility of 1 for winning the war and -1 for losing the war, then the strategic problem each sides faces can be represented as in Figure 1.2.3:

Allies

		C	N
Germans	C	$(1, -1)$	$(-1, 1)$
	N	$(-1, 1)$	$(1, -1)$

Figure 1.2.3. Overlord (cardinal utilities)

The preferred strategy for each player depends upon that player's expectations regarding the opposing player. These expectations can be quantified as *probabilities* over the opponent's actions. Let $\mu_1(\cdot)$ and $\mu_2(\cdot)$ denote probability measures for the Germans and the Allies, respectively.[12]

These probability distributions, coupled with the numerical utilities for the outcomes of the game, enable us to give a more clear formulation of each player's best strategy. To satisfy requirements of individual rationality, each side will choose the strategy that maximizes *expected utility*, that is, the weighted average of the cardinal utilities of the alternative outcomes, the weighting factor being the player's probability distribution over the opponent's strategies. The expected utility of playing a strategy s for Player i, $i = 1, 2$, is denoted by $E_i(u_i(s))$. For instance, the expected utilities for the Germans' pure strategy options are

$$E_1(u_1(C)) = 1 \cdot \mu_1(\text{Allies choose } C) + (-1) \cdot \mu_1(\text{Allies choose } N)$$

and

$$E_1(u_1(N)) = (-1) \cdot \mu_1(\text{Allies choose } C) + 1 \cdot \mu_1(\text{Allies choose } N).$$

Since C and N are mutually exclusive and exhaust the Allies' alternative pure strategies,

$$\mu_1(\text{Allies choose } N) = 1 - \mu_1(\text{Allies choose } C)$$

so, setting $\alpha = \mu_1(\text{Allies choose } N)$, the Germans' expected utilities for the pure strategy alternatives can be rewritten as

$$
\begin{aligned}
E_1(u_1(C)) &= 1 \cdot \alpha + (-1)(1 - \alpha) = 2\alpha - 1 \\
E_1(u_1(N)) &= (-1) \cdot \alpha + 1(1 - \alpha) = 1 - 2\alpha.
\end{aligned}
$$

Similarly, setting $\beta = \mu_2(\text{Germans choose } C)$, the Allies' expected utilities for their alternative pure strategies are

(1.i)
$$
\begin{aligned}
E_2(u_2(C)) &= (-1) \cdot \beta + 1(1 - \beta) = 1 - 2\beta \\
E_2(u_2(N)) &= 1 \cdot \beta + (-1) \cdot (1 - \beta) = 2\beta - 1.
\end{aligned}
$$

The rational decision for each side is to select a strategy that maximizes expected utility. For instance, if $E_2(u_2(C)) > E_2(u_2(N))$, then the rational decision for

---

[12] A probability measure over a finite set Ω of events is a function $\mu(\cdot)$ that satisfies the following axioms:

A1. $\mu(\Omega) = 1$
A2. For each event $A \subseteq \Omega, \mu(A) \geq 0$
A3. For any pair of events $A, B \subseteq \Omega$, if $A \cap B = \emptyset$, then $\mu(A \cup B) = \mu(A) + \mu(B)$.

the Allies is to select C. By (1.i), if $\beta < \frac{1}{2}$, then choosing C is the rational decision for the Allies.

Ascribing numerical utilities and probabilities to the players engaged in Overlord permits a mathematically rigorous analysis of the game. However, is it legitimate to assume that players engaged in games do indeed have numerical probabilities and utilities? Before the publication of *Theory of Games and Economic Behavior*, a tradition in economics and moral philosophy culminating with the work of Pareto (1927) maintained that only ordinal utilities could sensibly be attributed to agents, and that consequently the Bayesian principle of expected utility maximization could never be practically applied. Von Neumann and Morgenstern (1944) gave a partial response to Paretian skepticism. They proved a representation theorem that showed that one can derive cardinal utilities for agents who have preferences over goods or prospects, and who follow certain axioms of decision making. Part of what Von Neumann and Morgenstern assumed was that agents have preferences over *gambles* on goods or prospects, and have a probability measure over the various outcomes of their decisions. Such *Von Neumann-Morgenstern utilities* are unique up to a choice of scale. Von Neumann and Morgenstern's work in *Theory of Games and Economic Behavior* secured the respectability of cardinal utility in economic theory. Interestingly, Von Neumann and Morgenstern had partly rediscovered some of the results in a paper by Frank Ramsey (1926) entitled "Truth and Probability." Ramsey showed that if an agent has a sufficiently rich ordering of preferences over gambles and follows certain axioms of coherent decision making, then the agent can derive both a cardinal utility function and a *subjective probability measure* over the various outcomes of his decisions. Ramsey argued that an agent who violated any of his axioms would be incoherent in that the agent would willingly accept a combination of gambles that would guarantee the agent a loss.[13] In short, Ramsey's achievement was to show that expected utility theory presupposes only coherent preferences. L.J. Savage (1954) revived Ramsey's program, and proved a representation theorem that most economists now refer to when they ascribe subjective probabilities and cardinal utilities to rational agents.[14]

---

[13] Ramsey (1926), p. 182. Ramsey's argument, which he presented only briefly, has sparked a literature on how having incoherent beliefs leaves one open to a *Dutch Book*, that is, a set of gambles that guarantees one a loss. See DeFinetti (1937) and Skyrms (1984) for detailed discussions of these Dutch Book arguments.

[14] See Savage (1954), chapter 5. Surprisingly, Ramsey's deep analysis of cardinal utility theory and subjective utility was little known among economists until the publication of Savage's seminal work. Savage's axiomatization of coherent decision making is different from Ramsey's, and Savage states his representation theorem in terms of modern (Kolmogorov 1933) probability calculus. Hence, most contemporary readers find Savage's presentation easier to follow than Ramsey's, and most

The Overlord game has the special property of being a *zero-sum game*, that is, a game in which the utilities of each outcome sum to zero. In this game, and in every such 2-player zero-sum game, each pure strategy combination results in one player receiving a positive quantity of utility and the other receiving a negative quantity of utility. Intuitively, in a 2-player zero-sum game, at every pure strategy outcome one player will be the "winner" and the other must be the "loser." Moreover, the amount of utility that the loser gives up equals the amount that the winner acquires, that is, one player's gain is the other player's loss. There can be no *net* gain in a zero-sum game. Since the interests of the players in this game are diametrically opposed, zero-sum games are sometimes called games of *pure conflict.*[15]

Given that there is no outcome in a game of pure conflict where all agents come out "ahead" in terms of utility, how can such games ultimately come to be resolved? Von Neumann and Morgenstern proposed a solution in *Theory of Games and Economic Behavior* (1944). They argued that the interdependence of the players' decisions in a zero-sum game implies that a "solution" of such a game must be the result of some procedure for selecting strategies such that each player would willingly follow the procedure knowing that the others follow the same procedure.

> Let us now imagine that there exists a complete theory of the zero-sum two-person game which tells a player what to do, and which is absolutely convincing. If the players knew such a theory then each player would have to assume that his strategy has been "found out" by his opponent. The opponent knows the theory, and he knows that a player would be unwise not to follow it. Thus the hypothesis of the existence of a satisfactory theory legitimizes our investigation of the situation when a player's strategy is "found out" by his opponent. And a satisfactory theory can exist only if we are able to harmonize the two extremes Γ_1 and Γ_2,— strategies of player 1 "found out" or of player 2 "found out."[16]

As Skyrms (1990, 13–16) points out, this argument evidently presupposes more than that the players use some general algorithmic procedure for selecting strategies and know that the other uses this procedure. If, for instance, in the Overlord game the players know the game's payoff structure and that they both follow the rule, consistent with Bayesian rationality,

---

textbook expositions of the derivation of subjective probabilities and cardinal utilities from preference orderings use Savage-like axioms.

[15] Schelling, (1960).

[16] Von Neumann and Morgenstern (1944), p. 148.

(1.*ii*)   Write a list of one's pure strategies, calculate their expected utilities, and choose the first pure strategy on the list that maximizes expected utility.

then their pure strategies are uniquely specified, but each player can still fail to know which strategy the opponent plays. If the players' beliefs regarding the opposing player are determined by

$$\alpha = \mu_1(\text{Allies choose } C) = \frac{6}{10} \text{, and}$$

$$\beta = \mu_2(\text{Germans choose } C) = \frac{3}{10}$$

and each player keeps its belief secret, then

$$E_1(u_1(C)) = 1 \cdot \frac{6}{10} + (-1) \cdot \frac{4}{10} = \frac{2}{10}$$

$$> -\frac{2}{10} = (-1) \cdot \frac{6}{10} + 1 \cdot \frac{4}{10} = E_1(u_1(N))$$

and

$$E_2(u_2(C)) = (-1) \cdot \frac{3}{10} + 1 \cdot \frac{7}{10} = \frac{4}{10}$$

$$> -\frac{4}{10} = 1 \cdot \frac{3}{10} + (-1) \cdot \frac{7}{10} = E_2(u_2(N))$$

and so the players will settle upon the strategy combination (C, C), but neither player will know before the fact that the opponent will choose C. This is because neither player knows one of the opponents' key *inputs* into the algorithm (1.*ii*), namely, the probability distribution $\mu_k(\cdot)$. Von Neumann and Morgenstern require that their "complete theory" of strategy selection is such that the players' strategies are mutually known. As the example just given implies, such a "complete theory" would have to include not only the common algorithm the players use, but all of the inputs to this algorithm, so that players would be able to reconstruct their opponents' reasoning and thereby know their chosen strategies. Von Neumann and Morgenstern are arguing, albeit in a rudimentary way, that a justification of a "solution" of a game is intimately connected with the assumptions made regarding the players' knowledge of their situation. The epistemic conditions which underpin solution concepts for games has become an area of research in its own right, and will be discussed in more detail in the second chapter.

Von Neumann and Morgenstern also require that the choices each player selects according to the theory are *optimal* in light of the choices of all of the players. In other words, they require that a "solution" to a zero-sum game must be such that no player will have reason to deviate from the solution given that every player follows the solution. Assuming that each player is rational in the Bayesian sense, a player *will* have reason to deviate from a particular strategy combination if, and only if, deviating unilaterally would yield the player a greater expected utility than following the combination would. Hence, the "solution" to a zero-sum game must be a strategy combination σ such that each player maximizes expected utility if all follow σ. A strategy profile that meets this condition is known as an *equilibrium* of the game.

The notion of an equilibrium in a zero-sum game was not completely new in *Theory of Games and Economic Behavior*. As hinted at in the beginning of this section, Hume had arrived at an informal understanding of equilibrium in *A Treatise on Human Nature*. In two papers written in the 1920s, Borel (1921, 1924) derived equilibrium solutions for a number of specific cases of zero-sum games. What is original in Von Neumann's work, published first in a 1928 essay and later in *Theory of Games and Economic Behavior*, is a general method for determining the equilibrium solutions of 2-player zero-sum games. In general, no combination of pure strategies is an equilibrium of a zero-sum game. In Overlord, at any of the four pure strategy combinations, one of the players will be the loser and want to switch strategies, if possible. This apparently implies that if each side knows the strategic reasoning of its opponent, then they can never resolve the game. If the Allies know that the Germans have decided on C, then the Allies will opt for N. But if they also know that the Germans can reconstruct their reasoning, the Allies will surmise that the Germans will switch to N, and so the Allies should switch to C. Since the Allies know that the Germans can reconstruct *this* line of reasoning, they know that Germans will anticipate the switch and switch themselves back to C. Hence, the Allies should switch again to N, which they know will lead the Germans to switch again to N, and so on. If the players are restricted to pure strategies, then there is no procedure of the kind envisioned by Von Neumann and Morgenstern such that both sides will be rational to follow the strategy the procedure recommends with full knowledge of the strategy the opponent plays.

Von Neumann's solution to this problem employs an idea, due primarily to Borel, for expanding the set of strategies available to the players engaged in a zero-sum game. In general, the players in a 2-player zero-sum game cannot be at equilibrium if both know in advance which pure strategy the opponent chooses. However, if each player selects a pure strategy according to the outcome of a random event, then he can prevent his opponent from anticipating his pure strategy with certainty. In Overlord, the Germans can prevent the Allies from guessing which pure strategy the Germans will follow by announcing over the radio that they will toss a fair coin, and opt for C if the coin lands heads up, and N

otherwise. The Allies can keep the Germans guessing as well by pegging their pure strategy on a random event that is probabilistically independent of the Germans' coin toss. These probabilistic strategies are known as *mixed strategies* because each player's strategy is a weighted average or probabilistic mixture of the player's pure strategies. A player can determine which mixed strategies are rational to follow by computing the expected utilities associated with the various mixed strategies. Using mixed strategies, the players engaged in a zero-sum game can in fact achieve equilibrium. Denoting the players' respective mixed strategies in Overlord by σ_1 and σ_2, where

$$\sigma_1 = (\mu_1(\text{choose } C), \mu_1(\text{choose } N)) = (\alpha, 1 - \alpha)$$
$$\sigma_2 = (\mu_2(\text{choose } C), \mu_2(\text{choose } N)) = (\beta, 1 - \beta),$$

their expected utilities are

$$E_1(u_1(\sigma_1)) = 1 \cdot \alpha\beta + (-1)\alpha(1 - \beta) + (-1)(1 - \alpha)\beta + 1 \cdot (1 - \alpha)(1 - \beta)$$
$$= (2\alpha - 1)(2\beta - 1)$$

and

$$E_2(u_2(\sigma_2)) = (-1) \cdot \alpha\beta + 1 \cdot \alpha(1 - \beta) + 1 \cdot (1 - \alpha)\beta + (-1)(1 - \alpha)(1 - \beta)$$
$$= (1 - 2\alpha)(2\beta - 1)$$

A strategy is *completely mixed* when each pure strategy has a positive probability of being the one selected by the mixing device. At the other extreme, choosing a pure strategy can be regarded as playing a mixed strategy in which the mixing device selects the pure strategy with probability one. Note that the notation for each player's probability distribution over the pure strategies agrees with the opponent's probability distribution regarding what the player chooses. This is no accident, since in order to be at equilibrium, each player's probability distribution regarding the opponent's play must agree with the distribution defining the player's mixed strategy. Indeed, when one plays a mixed strategy one should make this mixed strategy known to the opponent so that the opponent's beliefs over one's pure strategies conform with the probabilities determined by the mixing device. I will return to this point below. For now, note that since the Overlord game is a zero sum game, for any mixed strategies the players might choose,

$$E_1(u_1(\sigma_1)) = -E_2(u_2(\sigma_2))$$

that is, any *expected* gain Player 1 might make is Player 2's *expected* loss, and *vice versa*. If a set of mixed strategies $\sigma^* = (\sigma_1^*, \sigma_2^*)$ is an equilibrium of a

2-player zero-sum game, then neither player can increase expected utility by uni-laterally deviating from σ^*. Since one player's gain is the other's loss, at equi-librium neither player's expected utility can decrease if the other deviates. In other words, in the 2-player zero-sum case, at equilibrium each player plays a *security strategy*, that is, a strategy that yields the player the highest *guaranteed* expected utility given any strategy the opponent might employ. One can deter-mine one's security strategies by employing a decision-making criterion known as the *maximin rule*. Roughly speaking, the maximin rule recommends that one determine the minimum expected utility of each alternative strategy given any strategies the other agents can follow, and then select the strategy that yields the greatest of these minimum expected utilities. For instance, in the Overlord game, the Germans' minimum expected utility for either pure strategy is -1, since if they choose C the Allies might choose N, and if they choose N the Allies might choose C. If the Germans play a mixed strategy of choosing C with probability $\frac{1}{3}$ and choosing N with probability $\frac{2}{3}$, then their worst outcome occurs if the Allies follow the pure strategy C, in which case their expected utility is

$$E_1(u_1(\alpha = \frac{1}{3})) = 1 \cdot \frac{1}{3} + (-1) \cdot \frac{2}{3} = -\frac{1}{3}.$$

In this game, the Germans' security strategy turns out to be the mixed strategy

$$\sigma_1^* = (\mu_1(\text{choose } C), \mu_1(\text{choose } N)) = (\frac{1}{2}, \frac{1}{2}).$$

To see this, note that for any strategy

$$\sigma_2 = (\mu_2(\text{choose } C), \mu_2(\text{choose } N)) = (\beta, 1 - \beta)$$

that the Allies might play,

$$E_1(u_1(\sigma_1^*)) = 1 \cdot \frac{1}{2}\beta + (-1) \cdot \frac{1}{2}(1 - \beta) + (-1) \cdot \frac{1}{2}\beta + 1 \cdot \frac{1}{2}(1 - \beta) = 0$$

while for any other strategy $\sigma_1 = (\alpha, 1 - \alpha)$ where $\alpha < \frac{1}{2}$, the Germans will have a negative expected utility if the Allies play the pure strategy C, and for any other strategy $\sigma_1 = (\alpha, 1 - \alpha)$ where $\alpha > \frac{1}{2}$, the Germans will have a negative expected utility if the Allies play the pure strategy N.[17]

---

[17]To see this, note that if $\alpha < \frac{1}{2}$, then if the Allies play C, then

$$E_1(u_1(\sigma_1)) = 1 \cdot \alpha + (-1) \cdot (1 - \alpha) = 2\alpha - 1 < 0$$

and if $\alpha > \frac{1}{2}$, then if the Allies play N, then

$$E_1(u_1(\sigma_1)) = -1 \cdot \alpha + 1 \cdot (1 - \alpha) = 1 - 2\alpha < 0.$$

By a similar argument, the security strategy of the Allies is

$$\sigma_2^* = (\mu_2(\text{choose } C), \mu_2(\text{choose } N)) = (\frac{1}{2}, \frac{1}{2}).$$

As argued above, a necessary condition for an equilibrium σ^* of a 2-player zero-sum game it that the players choose a security strategy. Von Neumann (1928) proved that in general, this is also a sufficient condition. This fundamental result, known as the *Minimax Theorem*, can be stated as follows:

Theorem 1.2.1 (Minimax Theorem, Von Neumann, 1928). In a 2-player zero-sum game, the players are at equilibrium if, and only if, they each play a maximin strategy. □

To illustrate this result, consider that if the two players in the Overlord game follow the mixed strategy combination $\sigma^* = (\sigma_1^*, \sigma_2^*)$, then for any strategy $\sigma_1 = (\alpha, 1 - \alpha)$,

$$\begin{aligned}
E_1(u_1(\sigma_1^*)) &= 1 \cdot \frac{1}{2} \cdot \frac{1}{2} + (-1) \cdot \frac{1}{2} \cdot \frac{1}{2} + (-1) \cdot \frac{1}{2} \cdot \frac{1}{2} + 1 \cdot \frac{1}{2} \cdot \frac{1}{2} = 0 \\
&= 1 \cdot \alpha \cdot \frac{1}{2} + (-1) \cdot \alpha \cdot \frac{1}{2} + (-1) \cdot (1 - \alpha) \cdot \frac{1}{2} + 1 \cdot (1 - \alpha) \cdot \frac{1}{2} \\
&= E_1(u_1(\sigma_1))
\end{aligned}$$

so if the Germans believe that the Allies will follow their end of σ^* and play C with probability $\frac{1}{2}$, then the Germans can do no better than to follow σ^* and play C with probability $\frac{1}{2}$. Similarly, if the Allies believe that the Germans will follow σ^* and play C with probability $\frac{1}{2}$, then for any strategy $\sigma_2 = (\beta, 1 - \beta)$,

$$E_2(u_2(\sigma_2^*)) = 0 = E_2(u_2(\sigma_2))$$

so the Allies cannot do better by deviating from σ^*. Hence, σ^* is indeed an equilibrium, and has the property of being a *completely mixed equilibrium* since at this equilibrium both players follow completely mixed strategies.

The Overlord example shows how a strategic problem of pure conflict can be modeled mathematically as a zero-sum game. With the Minimax Theorem, Von Neumann and Morgenstern showed how such a problem in the 2-player case might be resolved in a way consistent with the individual rationality of the players. At the same time, the theory of zero-sum games raises a number of fundamental questions:

1. Is the applicability of the mathematical theory of games limited to cases of pure conflict? Put another way, does game theory provide a general logic of rational decision in an interactive context?

2. Does the Minimax Theorem of Von Neumann and Morgenstern provide a general method for "solving" games?

3. What must players know about their situation in order to come to a resolution of the game?

4. Since important real-world strategic decisions in the face of uncertainty like the Normandy invasion problem are not typically made by using random devices, do we have reason to suppose that rational decision makers would mix their strategies? Are mixed strategies legitimate?

I will consider each of these questions in the following sections.

§1.3   Nash Equilibrium

In one of the most famous passages of *Leviathan*, Hobbes describes the fate of individuals in a "State of Nature" that would exist in the absence of any government:

> during the time men live without a common Power to keep them all in awe, they are in that condition which is called Warre; and such a warre, as is of every man, against every man. . . . In such condition, there is no place for Industry; because the fruit thereof is uncertain: and consequently no Culture of the Earth; no Navigation, nor use of the commodities that may be imported by Sea; no commodious Building; no Instruments of moving, and removing such things as require much force; no Knowledge of the face of the Earth; no account of Time; no Arts; no Letters; no Society; and which is worst of all, continuall feare, and brutal danger of violent death; And the life of man, solitary, poore, nasty, brutish, and short.[18]

Why would persons in the Hobbesian State of Nature fall into such a sorry state? Hobbes' argument for this bleak conclusion can be summarized as follows: Each individual in the State of Nature can either cooperate with those he encounters or treat them as enemies. Treating another as an enemy implies that one will not trust another in anything and that one will attack the other if he thinks she lowers her guard. In the State of Nature, every person one encounters is strong enough and intelligent enough to pose a potential threat to one's own safety, particularly when one lowers one's guard. People desire security above

---

[18] Hobbes (1651), pp. 88–89.

all else, and in the State of Nature, the only way to make oneself more secure is to eliminate threats to oneself and acquire more goods, which one can do by attacking others successfully and taking their goods. Hence, every individual fears that any other person he meets will attack him in hope of gaining his goods and making her own position more secure, and also is tempted to attack preemptively in order to try and gain her goods and make his position more secure. If one acts cooperatively with another, then he lowers his guard and opens himself to attack. Hobbes concludes that in the State of Nature, the only rational choice for each individual is to treat others as enemies. Since all in the State of Nature reason in this manner, everyone treats everyone else as an enemy, so that life in the State of Nature becomes a cold, and at times hot, "war of all against all."

Several philosophers (Gauthier 1969; Hampton 1986; Kavka 1986) interpret Hobbes as giving an informal game-theoretical argument in Chapter 13 of *Leviathan* that foreshadows the reasoning of the players engaged in a game called *Prisoners' Dilemma*. The Prisoners' Dilemma is motivated by the following story:[19] Two men, Jules and Vincent, are filmed selling cocaine to a man they later discover is a police informant. The next day, police find the informant's bullet-ridden corpse. The district attorney suspects that Jules and Vincent are the killers. Soon afterward, the police apprehend Jules and Vincent and charge them with drug dealing and first-degree murder. The district attorney surmises that he already has the evidence to convict both suspects for drug dealing, but needs a confession from at least one of them in order to convict them for killing the informant. At the police station, the district attorney visits Jules in his cell and admits that if neither Jules nor Vincent confesses to the killing, then he can convict them for drug dealing only. The district attorney then offers Jules a plea bargain. If Jules confesses to shooting the informant, the district attorney promises to reduce the charges to drug dealing and manslaughter if Vincent also confesses, and to drop both charges if Vincent refuses to confess to the killing, in which case Vincent will be tried for both drug dealing and first-degree murder. Just before he leaves to let Jules think over the deal, the district attorney adds that he has already offered Vincent the same deal, and that Vincent is now deciding whether or not to plea bargain. Jules knows that the district attorney always wins his cases, and also knows that drug dealing and manslaughter each carry a sentence of two years in prison, while first-degree murder carries a life sentence. Jules considers his options in light of what Vincent might do. Jules reasons that if Vincent rejects the plea bargain, that he had better confess, since he will then go free, while if

---

[19]Game theorists credit A.W. Tucker with naming this game "Prisoners' Dilemma" and with first interpreting the game as two prisoners facing a plea-bargaining problem similar to the problem described here. See Luce and Raiffa (1957), pp. 94–95.

he does not confess, then he will be convicted for drug dealing and be sentenced to two years in prison. Jules also reasons that if Vincent plea bargains, he had better do likewise, since then he will be sentenced to only four years, while if he remains silent he will suffer a life sentence. Either way, Jules is better off if he confesses, so he accepts the plea bargain, and is not surprised later when he learns that Vincent has also accepted the plea bargain.

The Prisoners' Dilemma can be modeled as a 2-player game, summarized by the matrix in Figure 1.3.1:

Vincent

		S	P
Jules	S	(2 years, 2 years)	(life, freedom)
	P	(freedom, life)	(4 years, 4 years)

Figure 1.3.1. Prisoners' Dilemma (plea bargain interpretation)

Jules and Vincent each have the options of standing firm (S) and keeping silent, or accepting the plea bargain (P). The resolution of the Prisoners' Dilemma is apparently paradoxical, since each individual Prisoners' best strategy is to select P whatever the other prisoner does, so that they end up at (P, P), although both would fare better if both would select S and arrive at (S, S). This "paradox" becomes more evident upon examining the players' ordinal utilities, given in Figure 1.3.2:

Vincent

		S	P
Jules	S	(2nd, 2nd)	(4th, 1st)
	P	(1st, 4th)	(3rd, 3rd)

Figure 1.3.2. Prisoners' Dilemma (ordinal utilities)

Any 2-player game with this arrangement of ordinal utilities is a Prisoners' Dilemma game. In a Prisoners' Dilemma game, the strategy labeled P in the matrix is *strictly dominant* for both players, that is, P is the uniquely utility maximizing strategy for each player, regardless of which strategy the opponent selects. (P, P)

is the unique equilibrium of a Prisoners' Dilemma game. On the other hand, (P, P) is *suboptimal*, since both players prefer the results of outcome (S, S) over those of (P, P).[20]

The Prisoners' Dilemma game has a variety of other interpretations, but possibly the earliest informal description of a Prisoners' Dilemma is Hobbes' description of individual reasoning in the State of Nature. In the Hobbesian State of Nature, each individual can either *cooperate* with another individual he encounters (C) or *defect* against her, that is, treat her as an enemy (D). Mutual cooperation will result in a mutual benefit, but unilateral cooperation in the face of defection results in one being exploited. Defecting at least protects one against exploitation from a defector, and can result in a gain over that of mutual cooperation if one happens to have encountered a cooperator. The alternative payoffs for a pair of individuals in the Hobbesian State of Nature might be those given in the matrix of Figure 1.3.3:

Player 2

		C	D
Player 1	C	$(6, 6)$	$(2, 7)$
	D	$(7, 2)$	$(4, 4)$

Figure 1.3.3. Hobbesian State of Nature as Prisoners' Dilemma

This matrix summarizes a Prisoners' Dilemma. In any single pairwise encounter in the Hobbesian State of Nature under this interpretation, D is the dominant choice for each individual, even though both would fare better if both chose C. Hence such a State of Nature encounter would inevitably result in the cold, and occasionally hot, "war against all."

While the equilibrium of the Prisoners' Dilemma is suboptimal, it is not a game of *pure* conflict. By following the equilibrium, both players are *strictly* better off, and neither player gains at the expense of the other. Moreover, the equilibrium of the Prisoners' Dilemma does not require the players to mix their strategies, and the dominance argument that justifies equilibrium play in the Prisoners' Dilemma is a stronger justification than maximin reasoning.[21] In *Theory*

---

[20] An outcome *A* of a game is *(Pareto) optimal* if there is no other outcome *B* of the game such that every player's utility is at least as great as it is at *A* and is greater at *B* for at least one player than it is at *A*.

[21] This is because the *D* strategy in the Prisoners' Dilemma is not only the player's security strategy, but the unique strategy that maximizes the player's expected utility whatever the opponent does.

of Games and Economic Behavior, Von Neumann and Morgenstern emphasized the theory of zero-sum games and placed the Minimax Theorem in the limelight. Their presentation led many to conclude that game theory was applicable primarily to social interactions of pure conflict between two parties, and that maximin reasoning supports all equilibrium resolutions of noncooperative games. Both of these conclusions are mistaken. The Prisoners' Dilemma, possibly the most studied example in game theory, can be used to model situations in which people's interests *coincide* to some extent, and yet are such that they fail the achieve the outcome that would provide them with the greatest mutual benefit. Indeed, Hobbes may have been the first to use Prisoners' Dilemma reasoning to explain why people would be so wretched without any government that they would prefer to live under a sovereign's rule, however unjust the sovereign might be.[22]

Moreover, maximin reasoning does not always coincide with equilibrium. Consider a different example of a non-zero-sum game, which is summarized by the matrix in Figure 1.3.4:

Player 2

		C	D
Player 1	C	$(6, 6)$	$(2, 7)$
	D	$(7, 2)$	$(0, 0)$

Figure 1.3.4. Chicken

This game is known as *Chicken*, the name inspired by one of its best known interpretations, motivated by a famous scene in the film *Rebel Without A Cause*. Two individuals drive toward each other in their automobiles. Each driver can either "defy death" and stay the course (D) or "chicken out" and swerve away from the other at the last moment (C). If one driver defies death and the other chickens out, then the former gains in prestige and the latter loses face. If they both chicken out, then neither loses face. If both defy death, then they crash into each other, which is the worst possible outcome for them both. Chicken resembles the Prisoners' Dilemma in its Hobbesian interpretation in that both sides fare better if both adopt the more benign strategy C than they do if both adopt the more aggressive strategy D. However, unlike the Prisoners' Dilemma, (D, D) is not an equilibrium, since either player would be strictly better off by unilaterally deviating from (D, D). If the players in Chicken both follow their

---

[22] See Hobbes (1651), Chapters 17–19.

maximin strategies, then each will play C, so that they will arrive at (C, C). However, (C, C) is not an equilibrium, for each player would deviate to D if he thought the opponent would stick with his maximin strategy and play C.

Earlier I cited Von Neumann and Morgenstern's argument that any adequate theory for solving a zero-sum game must be such that every player will be able to determine the strategy the theory recommends to each of his opponents, and still be willing to follow the strategy the theory recommends. This argument in no way depends upon the game's being zero-sum. Hence, by Von Neumann and Morgenstern's own criterion, the Chicken example shows that the maximin criterion is an inadequate theory for solving games in general. General adherence to the maximin rule as a principle for individual decision making can contradict the players' Bayesian rationality. I should hasten to add that Von Neumann and Morgenstern did not claim that their theory for solving zero-sum games gives a general procedure for solving non-zero-sum games.

Any adequate solution concept for a game must be such that the players find it to their mutual advantage to follow an instance of this concept. Otherwise, players would be tempted to deviate from the so-called "solution," making nonsense of the claim that it was a solution in the first place. Hume recognized this informally in his account of social convention, and Von Neumann and Morgenstern had concluded much the same when they argued that a solution for a zero-sum game must be stable with respect to mutual knowledge of strategies. However, their method of solving 2-player zero-sum games cannot be extended to even the simplest of non-zero-sum games. In retrospect, this is perhaps not so surprising, since they made the maximin principle, and not the principle of expected utility maximization, the fundamental decision principle underlying their theory. In the 2-player zero-sum case, maximin reasoning agrees with expected utility maximization, so that Von Neumann and Morgenstern's theory successfully accounts for equilibrium play in this class of games. However, if expected utility maximization is the correct formal account of individual rational decision, then a more natural approach to defining an adequate solution concept for games would be to root such a concept in the Bayesian rationality principle.

This was the idea John Nash (1950, 1951) developed in a pair of seminal papers. Nash was the first to formally define an equilibrium concept for games defined in terms of individual expected utility maximization, and to show this *Nash equilibrium* can be applied as a solution concept to a very general class of games. In Nash's framework, each player in a game plays a mixed strategy σ_k which is probabilistically independent of the mixed strategies of his opponents.[23]

---

[23] Intuitively, the players' mixed strategies are *probabilistically independent* if the pure strategy a player's randomizing device recommends gives no evidence of which pure strategies the other

Players are at a Nash equilibrium if no player can improve upon his expected utility, given the strategies the opponents play, by unilaterally changing his strategy. More precisely,

Definition 1.3.1. In an n-player game, a strategy combination

$$\sigma^* = (\sigma_1^*, \ldots, \sigma_n^*)$$

is a *Nash equilibrium* if, and only if, for each player k and for any mixed strategy σ_k open to player k,

$$E_k(u_k(\sigma^*)) \geq E_k(u_k((\sigma_1^*, \ldots, \sigma_{k-1}^*, \sigma_k, \sigma_{k+1}^*, \ldots, \sigma_n^*))) \quad \square$$

Nash (1950) noted that in the 2-player zero-sum case, the Nash equilibrium concept predicated on expected utility maximization coincides with the equilibrium players achieve by applying the maximin rule. However, Nash was able to show that players who are expected utility maximizers can achieve equilibrium in a much more general class of games than can maximin players. Nash proved that every game with finitely many players, each of whom has finitely many pure strategies, has a Nash equilibrium in mixed strategies.[24] Moreover, by definition every player follows the Bayesian principle of utility maximization if the players follow a Nash equilibrium, so a Nash equilibrium is mutually beneficial in terms of expected utility. Another way of phrasing Nash's result is that for every game with finitely many possible outcomes, there is an outcome such that individual Bayesian rationality coincides with mutual benefit. Nash's fundamental theorem, perhaps the single most important development in the history of game theory, led to the Nash equilibrium becoming the central solution concept for noncooperative games. In recent years, alternate interpretations of mixed strategies have led to generalizations of the Nash equilibrium concept (Aumann 1974, 1987; Bernheim 1984; Pearce 1984; Vanderschraaf 1992), which I will discuss in the following chapter.

Nash proved the existence of an equilibrium for a wide class of games, but did not give a general method for solving games, since a game need not

---

players' randomizing devices recommend to them. Formally, the players mixed strategies are probabilistically independent if the joint probability distribution over the pure strategy combinations defined by their strategies is a product measure of each player's individual mixed strategy, that is, if $\sigma = (\sigma_1, \sigma_2, \ldots, \sigma_n)$ is the joint probability distribution over the pure strategies, then the players' strategies are probabilistically independent if $\sigma = \sigma_1 \cdot \sigma_2 \cdots \sigma_n$.

[24] Note that this does not imply that every such game has a *completely mixed* Nash equilibrium. For instance, the unique Nash equilibrium in the Prisoners' Dilemma (Hobbesian interpretation) is the strategy profile (D, D), which the players can achieve by playing the degenerately mixed strategy profile $\sigma^* = (\sigma_1^*, \sigma_2^*)$ where $\sigma_1^*(D) = \sigma_2^*(D) = 1$.

have a unique Nash equilibrium. Chicken provides a dramatic example of this phenomenon. Chicken has two distinct equilibria in pure strategies: (C, D) and (D, C). Chicken also has a completely mixed equilibrium, in which each player plays C with probability $\frac{2}{3}$, and which yields each player an expected utility of $4\frac{2}{3}$. By following any of these equilibria, the players all satisfy the principle of Bayesian rationality conditional on their mutual expectations. If each player expects the opponent to follow a certain equilibrium, then she maximizes her expected utility by following this equilibrium as well. In Chicken, the (C, D) equilibrium is more favorable for Player 2, while the (D, C) equilibrium is more favorable for Player 1. The mixed Nash equilibrium σ^* characterized by $\sigma_1^*(C) = \sigma_2^*(C) = \frac{2}{3}$ yields each player the same expected utility, but there is no apparent reason why this property should lead the players to follow σ^*. Indeed, before play one would expect that each player would if possible threaten to play D no matter what, in an attempt to intimidate the opponent into acquiescing and playing C. In cases like Chicken in which there are multiple equilibria, how would players pick one equilibrium over the others? For that matter, would one expect that players engaged in a game would settle upon an equilibrium at all?

Any justification of equilibrium play depends upon what one assumes the players know about their situation and what they believe about each other. More precisely, one can account for equilibrium play if one supposes the following:

(i) Each player is an expected utility maximizer,

(ii) Each player knows the payoff structure of the game,

(iii) Each player believes that the opponents will play their ends of the equilibrium, and

(iv) (i)–(iii) are *common knowledge* among the players (Lewis 1969), that is, each player knows that every opponent knows (i)–(iii), and she knows that her opponents know that she knows (i)–(iii), and so on.

This sort of justification of equilibrium play is already present informally in Hume, who argues that two people are rational to follow a mutually beneficial convention "When this common sense of interest is mutually express'd, and is known to both."[25] In Chicken, there is no *a priori* reason to suppose that players would settle upon any of the three Nash equilibria. What if we suppose that the players have common knowledge that they are Bayesian rational and know that they are engaged in a game of Chicken? These assumptions alone do not justify equilibrium play, for if each player believes that the opponent will certainly

---

[25] Hume (1740), p. 490.

chicken out and play C, then Bayesian rationality will recommend that each defy death and play D, so that they arrive at (D, D) and crash. However, if the players also have common knowledge of the strategies they expect one another to play, then one can explain equilibrium play if their expectations happen to be aligned on one of the game's equilibria. If, say, Player 1 is certain that Player 2 will chicken out, and if Player 2 is certain that Player 1 will defy death, and these beliefs are common knowledge, then each player maximizes expected utility precisely when he follows his end of the equilibrium (D, C) and knows that the opponent does likewise, so they will follow the equilibrium (D, C). Of course, this common knowledge account of equilibrium play raises certain fundamental questions, including: (1) Where do the players' expectations regarding each other come from? (2) Why would players' expectations regarding each other settle upon one equilibrium over other equilibria? (3) For that matter, must the players' expectations settle upon an equilibrium at all? and (4) What happens if these common knowledge assumptions are relaxed?

I will address these and other related questions in much greater detail in the subsequent chapters. For the present, I would like to return to the nine motivating examples of §1, and show how game theory can help to clarify the reasoning of the agents in these various coordination problems.

§1.4   Examples Revisited

Example 1. The Encounter Problem

Amie's and Kay's attempt to meet in the office building can be modeled as a game in which each player has two pure strategies, namely, search for the other on the first floor (A_1) or search on the second floor (A_2). The payoff matrix of this game is given in Figure 1.4.1. Since Kay's and Amie's interests agree completely at each possible outcome of their search for one another, at each of the four possible outcomes their payoffs are identical. This property of the payoff structure characterizes the Encounter Problem as a game of *pure coordination*.[26]

Note that one player achieves her best outcome precisely when the other player achieves her best outcome. The Encounter Problem contrasts sharply with the Overlord game, in which one player does best precisely when the other does worst. Indeed, one can think of the payoff structures of Overlord and the Encounter Problem as modeling two extreme cases of social interactions between two individuals, the first being one in which their interests are diametrically

---

[26]Schelling (1960), p. 84, Lewis (1969), p. 14.

Kay

		A_1	A_2
Amie	A_1	$(1,1)$	$(0,0)$
	A_2	$(0,0)$	$(1,1)$

A_1 = search on first floor, A_2 = search on second floor

Figure 1.4.1. The Encounter Problem

opposed and the second in which their interests coincide perfectly. Thomas Schelling developed this idea in *The Strategy of Conflict* (1960). Schelling argued that most social interaction problems are best modeled by games that contain elements of *both* cooperation and conflict. Schelling also argued that pure conflict and pure coordination games represent extreme cases of what players desire their opponents to know regarding the pure strategies they select. In a pure coordination game, a player will want all of the other players to know which pure strategy she will play. Conversely, in a zero-sum game, each player will want to keep his selection of pure strategy a secret.

> the intellectual processes of choosing a strategy in pure conflict and choosing a strategy of coordination are of wholly different sorts.... In the pure-coordination game, the player's objective is to make contact with the other player through some imaginative process of introspection, of searching for shared clues; in the minimax strategy of a zero-sum game—most strikingly so with randomized choice—one's whole objective is to avoid any meeting of minds, even an inadvertent one.[27]

Schelling proposed a reorientation of game theory, in which all noncooperative games should be regarded as falling along a continuum of which the games of pure conflict and pure coordination are the endpoints. The payoff structure of a game-theoretic model of an interaction should reflect the extent to which the players' interests agree, and correspondingly, to what extent each player will want his opponents to be able to guess his choice of pure strategy. The more the agents' interests disagree, the closer the corresponding game's payoffs will be to those of a zero-sum game, while the more their interests agree, the closer the game's payoffs will be to those of a pure coordination game. Perhaps more than any other single work, Schelling's now-classic text helped to expand the

---

[27] Schelling (1960), p. 96.

application of game theory beyond pure conflict resolution problems to problems of social interaction in general.

The Encounter Problem has three Nash equilibria, namely, the pure strategy equilibria (A_1, A_1) and (A_2, A_2), and a mixed equilibrium $\sigma^* = (\sigma_1^*, \sigma_2^*)$ characterized by $\sigma_1^*(A_1) = \sigma_2^*(A_1) = \frac{1}{2}$. At either of the pure strategy Nash equilibria, the player's expected payoff vector is $(1, 1)$. At the mixed equilibrium, the expected payoff vector is $(\frac{1}{2}, \frac{1}{2})$. Under this game-theoretic interpretation, we can now rephrase the problem that Kay and Amie face. Finding each other corresponds to reaching one of the game's equilibrium points. If they play the mixed equilibrium, then they find each other with probability $\frac{1}{2}$.[28] If they play one of the pure strategy equilibria, they find each other for certain. Still, from the players' individual perspectives, either pure strategy equilibrium is as good as the other. Which equilibrium should Kay and Amie select?

Example 2. Hume's Rowboat

The coordination problem Hume's rowers face can also be modeled as a pure coordination game, since both rowers achieve what they most want, which is to move their boat forward, by synchronizing their rowing. Hence, each rower will want the other rower to know which way she intends to row. The Rowboat game is somewhat more complicated than the Encounter Problem, since each rower can pull her oar at one of more than two different rates. Suppose that Amie and Kay are Hume's rowers. Suppose further that they have brought a metronome with them and run it on a low speed so that each times her stroke according to the metronome in one of three ways: stroke on every click (A_1), stroke on every third click (A_2), or stroke on every other click (A_3). If both know that each patterns her rowing according to one of these tempos, then each can easily synchronize her rowing with the other's rowing if she knows which tempo her companion has chosen. Figure 1.4.2. summarizes the corresponding pure coordination game.

The Rowboat game has three Nash equilibria in pure strategies: (A_1, A_1), (A_2, A_2), and (A_3, A_3). There is also a mixed Nash equilibrium at which each

---

[28] At the mixed equilibrium each player plays A_1 and A_2 with probability $\frac{1}{2}$, and their probability distributions are independent, so

$$
\begin{aligned}
\sigma^*(\text{Kay and Amie meet}) \;=\;& \sigma^*(\text{Kay plays } A_1, \text{Amie plays } A_1) \\
& + \sigma^*(\text{Kay plays } A_2, \text{Amie plays } A_2) \\
=\;& \sigma_1^*(\text{Kay plays } A_1) \cdot \sigma_2^*(\text{Amie plays } A_1) \\
& + \sigma_1^*(\text{Kay plays } A_1) \cdot \sigma_2^*(\text{Amie plays } A_1) \\
=\;& \frac{1}{2} \cdot \frac{1}{2} + \frac{1}{2} \cdot \frac{1}{2} = \frac{1}{2}.
\end{aligned}
$$

Kay

		A_1	A_2	A_3
	A_1	$(3,3)$	$(0,0)$	$(0,0)$
Amie	A_2	$(0,0)$	$(1,1)$	$(0,0)$
	A_3	$(0,0)$	$(0,0)$	$(2,2)$

Figure 1.4.2. Hume's Rowboat

rower follows the A_1 pattern with probability $\frac{2}{11}$, the A_2 pattern with probability $\frac{6}{11}$, and the A_3 pattern with probability $\frac{3}{11}$, and which yields each rower an expected payoff of $\frac{6}{11}$. Note that the four Nash equilibria are not equally good from the rowers' point of view. This reflects the intuition that some patterns of rowing may move the boat forward faster than others. The choice of equilibrium in the Rowboat game may seem easy at first glance. Since (A_1, A_1) is the Pareto optimal equilibrium, one might suppose that the players would naturally settle upon rowing at the rate of one stroke per click. However, this need not be the case. A variety of other factors might drive the rowers to settle upon a different equilibrium, or even miscoordinate altogether. If, for instance, Amie and Kay have rowed together in the past, and they have followed the (A_3, A_3) equilibrium before, then each might expect the other to stroke on every other click on this occasion, so that they would again follow (A_3, A_3) even though they both know they would move the boat faster by following (A_1, A_1). Indeed, if Amie were to row in the A_1 pattern in hopes of moving the boat as fast as possible while Kay were to follow precedent and row according to the A_3 pattern, then they would miscoordinate and move their boat in circles.

One might argue that Kay and Amie can try to solve their problem by crying "Pull!" at certain clicks of the metronome, so that each can indicate to the other how she rows. This way they can *correlate* their rowing to the metronome. The role of signaling devices and correlated strategies in games will play a central role in what is to follow. However, I should note that simply introducing signaling in this manner does not immediately resolve the coordination problem the rowers face. One would expect Amie and Kay to successfully coordinate their rowing to their signals only if they signal each other at the same rate, which means that each will have to anticipate when the other will cry "Pull!" Allowing each rower to signal her intentions to the other evidently turns the rowboat problem into a second-order coordination problem. How do the rowers settle upon one signalling pattern rather than another in order to coordinate their rowing?

Example 3. Conventions of Language

One can regard the establishment of a meaning convention in a particular language as a pure coordination game, in which an equilibrium corresponds to the state at which all the agents using the language associate the same meaning to a particular signal. In such a model, English users would be at equilibrium with respect to their usage of the verbal signal "rose" precisely when all English users associate the same meaning with this signal. Note that coordination could occur if the English users all associate with "rose" a meaning corresponding to some entity other than the flower with thorns on its stem. Also, as hinted in the Shakespeare quotation, coordination could occur if all of the English users were to settle upon a different signal as having the meaning that English users have in fact come to associate with "rose." The structure of such a pure coordination game would be immensely complicated, since the number of players and the number of alternative strategies would be very large. Lewis took the first steps toward the formal analysis of this problem by introducing a class of coordination games called *signaling games*.[29] Game theorists have applied Lewis' theory to formally model conventions of meaning among small groups of individuals having a limited number of alternative signals available to them. The game-theoretic analysis of human language conventions is still very much in its infancy, due to the complexity of the problem. Still, conventions of language are similar in kind to the much simpler Encounter and Rowboat pure coordination problems. The problem in all these cases is that of selecting one from among many equilibria of a pure coordination game.

Example 4. Dining Out

Amie's and Kay's dining problem is summarized as a game in Figure 1.4.3. Both players would like to coordinate their choices, but each prefers the outcome of one of the coordinated act pairs over the other. The game is one of impure coordination, since the players' payoffs do not coincide exactly at the outcomes at which they coordinate.

This game is known in the literature as "Battle of the Sexes" because in one of its earliest interpretations, the players were a woman and a man who had to resolve an impure coordination problem.[30] Battle of the Sexes has three Nash

---

[29] See Lewis (1969), Chapter 4.

[30] In this older interpretation, a woman (Player 1) and a man (Player 2) are trying to decide upon an activity for the evening. They have two options: attend a ballet (A_1) or attend a prize fight (A_2). Following certain stereotypes, the woman is assumed to prefer the ballet over the prize fight and the man to prefer the prize fight over the ballet. However, both prefer attending either the prize fight or

Kay

		A_1	A_2
Amie	A_1	$(2, 1)$	$(0, 0)$
	A_2	$(0, 0)$	$(1, 2)$

A_1 = Cracker Barrel, A_2 = Mimi's

Figure 1.4.3. Battle of the Sexes

equilibria, namely the two pure strategy equilibria (A_1, A_1) and (A_2, A_2), and a third mixed equilibrium in which Amie plays A_1 with probability $\frac{2}{3}$, and Kay plays A_1 with probability $\frac{1}{3}$. The payoff vectors associated with the pure strategy equilibria are $(2, 1)$ and $(1, 2)$, and the payoff vector of the mixed strategy equilibrium is $(\frac{2}{3}, \frac{2}{3})$. As noted in §1, even though the players want to coordinate their strategies, in this game of impure coordination each player might be tempted to threaten the other player by insisting that she will play her end of the equilibrium best for her no matter what. But if both make and carry out such threats, they will miscoordinate on (A_1, A_2). On the other hand, if each believes the other's threat and both give in, they will miscoordinate on (A_2, A_1). To be certain of coordinating at one of the two pure strategy Nash equilibria, exactly one player will have to give in. Who shall it be?

Example 5. Telephone Tag

Bicchieri (1993, 234–235) models Telephone Tag as an impure coordination game, which can be described by Figure 1.4.4. One might think of Telephone Tag as Battle of the Sexes in reverse. Like Battle of the Sexes, in Telephone Tag each player prefers one of the coordination points over the other. However, in this game, Amie and Kay coordinate on a pure strategy equilibrium by playing opposite strategies.

Telephone Tag has three Nash equilibria, namely, the pure strategy equilibria (A_1, A_2) and (A_2, A_1), and a mixed equilibrium at which Amie plays A_1 with

---

the ballet together over going to different events. The earliest presentation of the Battle of the Sexes game and of this interpretation I have found is in Luce and Raiffa (1957), pp. 90–91, although they do not claim originality.

There are a variety of interpretations of Battle of the Sexes in the literature. To give just one other example here, Hampton (1986), pp. 161–162, and Kavka (1986), pp. 184–185, interpret this game as a simple example of selecting a political leader. In this case, there are two candidates and an electorate of just two voters, who must both vote for the same candidate or else be deadlocked. Each party favors one candidate over the other, but both prefer to elect somebody rather than be deadlocked.

Kay

		A_1	A_2
Amie	A_1	$(0,0)$	$(1,2)$
	A_2	$(2,1)$	$(0,0)$

$A_1 = $ Call, $A_2 = $ Receive

Figure 1.4.4. Telephone Tag

probability $\frac{2}{3}$, and Kay plays A_1 with probability $\frac{1}{3}$. The equilibrium selection problem for Amie and Kay is essentially the same as the problem they face in Battle of the Sexes, except that they coordinate by choosing different pure strategy options. To be certain of reaching a pure strategy equilibrium, exactly one player must give in and call. Who calls?

Example 6. Rousseau's Stag Hunt

In Rousseau's description of the Stag Hunt, defecting from the hunting party by hunting rabbit is a security strategy for each hunter. However, if they all cooperate by hunting stag, all will end up with a much better overall payoff. A 2-player version of the Stag Hunt game is given in Figure 1.4.5.[31]

Kay

		A_1	A_2
Amie	A_1	$(2,2)$	$(0,1)$
	A_2	$(1,0)$	$(1,1)$

$A_1 = $ cooperate by hunting stag, $A_2 = $ defect by hunting rabbit

Figure 1.4.5. 2-Player Stag Hunt

Stag Hunt has the pure strategy Nash equilibria (A_1, A_1), corresponding to both hunters cooperating and catching a stag, and (A_2, A_2), the equilibrium at which both defect by hunting rabbit. There is also a mixed equilibrium at which

---

[31] The game of Figure 1.4.5 is the most widely accepted game-theoretic interpretation of Rousseau's description of the Stag Hunt. However, Binmore (1994, 120–125) argues that Rousseau's passage is actually best interpreted as a version of Prisoners' Dilemma.

each hunter plays A_1 with probability $\frac{1}{2}$. The (A_1, A_1) equilibrium is clearly the Pareto optimal equilibrium. However, the players will not reach this equilibrium unless each has a high enough expectation that the other will cooperate. If Kay has little or no confidence that Amie will cooperate, then Kay must defect in order to avoid her worst payoff. If the players mistrust one another and each decides to play it safe and take the payoff guaranteed by defecting, then they will settle upon the Pareto inferior equilibrium (A_2, A_2). Even though the (A_1, A_1) equilibrium is the best equilibrium of this game, it cannot be sustained without a high degree of mutual trust. In Stag Hunt, the equilibrium selection problem becomes one of explaining how and to what extent players come to trust or mistrust one another.

Example 7. The Division of Labor

Smith's explanation of the origins of labor specialization is a Stag Hunt explanation. Each member of the economy can follow a security strategy of "going it alone" and providing for one's own needs very inefficiently in isolation from the rest of the community, or follow a strategy of specializing one's labor and generating a large surplus for exchange. Exchange is possible only if all or at least most people specialize their labor, but when exchange takes place all fare much better than when all go it alone. As Smith puts it in one of his most famous passages,

> It is not from the benevolence of the butcher, the brewer, or the baker that we expect our dinner, but from their regard to their own interest. We address ourselves, not to their humanity but to their self-love, and never talk to them of our own necessities but of their advantages.[32]

A 3-player Stag Hunt game is summarized by the matrices in Figure 1.4.6. Under a Division of Labor Interpretation, the butcher chooses the row, the baker chooses the column, and the brewer chooses the matrix. Each can either cooperate by specializing his labor (A_1) or defect by going it alone (A_2).

As in the 2-player version of Stag Hunt, there are only two Nash equilibria in pure strategies, namely, (A_1, A_1, A_1) and (A_2, A_2, A_2). Once more, the (A_1, A_1, A_1) equilibrium at which all cooperate is the unique Pareto optimal equilibrium, and the (A_2, A_2, A_2) equilibrium results if all play their security strategies. As in the 2-player version, in this 3-player Stag Hunt game if the butcher, the baker, and the brewer are able to achieve the optimal equilibrium, they will have to trust one another to a certain degree. However, the optimal

---

[32] Smith (1776), pp. 26–27.

	A_1	A_2
A_1	(2, 2, 2)	(0, 1, 0)
A_2	(1, 0, 0)	(1, 1, 0)

	A_1	A_2
A_1	(0, 0, 1)	(0, 1, 1)
A_2	(1, 0, 1)	(1, 1, 1)

A_1 = cooperate by specializing, A_2 = defect by "going it alone"

Figure 1.4.6. 3-Player Stag Hunt, Division of Labor Interpretation

equilibrium at which all three players specialize their labor is intuitively harder to achieve than the optimal equilibrium of the 2-player Stag Hunt, since now each player has two opponents, either of whom can make specialization useless by defecting. Indeed, as the number of players engaged in Stag Hunt increases, the likelihood that they achieve the optimal equilibrium generally decreases.[33]

Example 8. Crisis Bargaining

One can model a diplomatic crisis like the crisis leading to the 1938 Munich agreement as Chicken. Referring back to the game summarized in Figure 1.3.4, under a crisis bargaining interpretation, each side can either back down (C) or strike (D). Suppose that Hitler assumes the role of Player 1 and Chamberlain and Daladier assume the role of Player 2. If both players first intend to back down, then each side would be tempted to strike if it were to discover the opponent's strategy. However, if both strike, the outcome corresponding to (D, D) is war, which is the worst possible outcome for each side. Chicken has two pure strategy Nash equilibria, namely (A_1, A_2), at which Chamberlain and Daladier win the crisis, and (A_2, A_1), at which Hitler wins. Chicken also has a third mixed equilibrium at which each player plays A_1 with probability $\frac{2}{3}$, and which yields each player an expected payoff of $4\frac{2}{3}$.

Chicken resembles the impure coordination games Battle of the Sexes and Telephone Tag in that exactly one player must yield and accept a less preferred equilibrium in order for the players to be certain of reaching a pure strategy Nash equilibrium solution. Each player is tempted to threaten the opponent, in hopes of convincing the opponent to back down. However, in Chicken, each player prefers that the opponent plays A_1, no matter which strategy he adopts himself. If Hitler intends to be aggressive and play A_2, then he wants Chamberlain and Daladier to back down so that they reach the equilibrium at which Hitler wins.

---

[33] See van Huyck, Battalio, and Beil (1990).

However, if Hitler actually intends to play it safe and play A_1, he still prefers that Chamberlain and Daladier play A_1, since the standoff point (A_1, A_1) is better for Hitler than the equilibrium (A_1, A_2) at which Hitler loses the crisis. Hence, unlike the previous examples, in Chicken it can be to a player's advantage to keep the opponent somewhat uncertain as to which pure strategy he will actually play. In Schelling's continuum of games, Chicken is closer to a game of pure conflict than any of the previous examples. Still, in Chicken the players again face the problem of equilibrium selection. Even though each player wants its opponent to back down *no matter what*, the only stable resolutions of Chicken are the equilibria. How do the players settle upon one equilibrium rather than any of the other equilibria?[34]

Example 9. Public Good Provision

The problem of public good provision is frequently a *threshold* problem. Each individual has the option of either cooperating by contributing toward the provision of the good or defecting by free-riding. The public good may be a step or "lumpy" good, in the sense that no amount of the public good is provided unless a certain threshold of the population cooperates. For example, in attempting to curtail the pollution of a lake, a minimum number of the businesses that use lake water must implement costly pollution control measures in order for there to be any ecological benefit. If this minimal level is not achieved, then there is a loss of joint gains, because the lake will be so polluted that the water is unsafe for any use. However, if more than enough of the businesses implement pollution control measures so that the lake water is safe for use, then any single manufacturer would be tempted to free-ride. Negotiating an agreement to limit pollution into the lake is a coordination problem with conflictual elements, since each company would prefer to fall in the group that does not cooperate, while enjoying the benefits of improved water quality paid for by the cooperating companies. Other environmental agreements that share this theoretical structure include the over-exploitation of resources such as fishing stocks and whaling, the

---

[34] One might object that in many real-life crisis situations, the parties do sometimes sustain a standoff or fall into conflict. This is not necessarily irrational from a game-theoretic standpoint, if the parties are thinking ahead to *future* interactions with the same (or even similar) opposing parties. A sequence of repeated crisis interactions can be modeled as a *repeated* Chicken game. In repeated game theory, a variety of strategy combinations emerge as equilibria which involve strategies that are not equilibrium strategies in the single round case. For instance, a strategy of responding to a strike in the current round by striking back can be part of an equilibrium in repeated Chicken, if such retaliation convinces the opponent that future strikes will be punished, and thereby leads the opponent to follow more cooperative behavior in the future.

use of ecosystems such as tropical rain forests, and restrictions on global commons use such as the radio spectrum and orbital arcs. A simple game-theoretic model that captures the intuitive problem each participant faces in a threshold public goods problem is given in Figure 1.4.7:

	A_1	A_2
A_1	$(6,6,6)$	$(2,7,2)$
A_2	$(7,2,2)$	$(0,0,0)$

	A_1	A_2
A_1	$(2,2,7)$	$(0,0,0)$
A_2	$(0,0,0)$	$(0,0,0)$

A_1 = cooperate and contribute, A_2 = defect and free-ride

Figure 1.4.7. Public Good Provision of a "Lumpy" Good

In this 3-player game, each player is tempted to defect (A_2) and leave the cost of providing the public good to the other two players. However, if all players or any two of the three players fail to cooperate (A_1), then no public good is provided and the outcome is detrimental to all players. There are four pure strategy Nash equilibria: the three cases in which exactly one player defects and the case where all players defect. The game also has a mixed Nash equilibrium σ^* characterized by the mixed strategies

$$\sigma_k^*(A_1) = \frac{4}{5}, \ \sigma_k^*(A_2) = \frac{1}{5}, \ k = 1, 2, 3$$

that yields each player an expected payoff of 4.48. As in all of the other examples, the problem these players face is one of selecting an equilibrium. This game resembles Chicken in that each player is tempted to appear to be a noncooperator, in hopes of driving the other players to cooperate. If one can convince the others that one will defect, if neither of the others can do likewise, and this is common knowledge among the players, then they will settle upon the equilibrium most favorable to oneself. However, unlike in Chicken, cooperation is not a "play it safe" strategy. If any two players succeed in convincing their opponents that they will not cooperate, and their success is common knowledge, then each player will reason that there is no benefit to be had from cooperating, so they will settle upon the equilibrium at which all defect, which is in fact the worst pure strategy Nash equilibrium.

§1.5   Equilibrium-in-Beliefs

The primary solution concept in noncooperative game theory has been the Nash equilibrium concept. Under the traditional interpretation introduced by Von Neumann and Morgenstern (1944) and Nash (1950, 1951), players are at a Nash equilibrium if each player employs a mixed strategy that maximizes her expected utility given the other players' mixed strategies. However, this traditional interpretation of Nash equilibrium has come under challenge on several counts. First, some authors question the rationality of explicitly mixing strategies in certain circumstances. Second, it turns out that it is never necessary for a player to explicitly mix her strategy in order to conform with the principle of Bayesian rationality. Finally, the very reason that mixed strategies were introduced as a means of resolving games of pure conflict makes it possible to define the Nash equilibrium concept without reference to mixing devices. One can reinterpret the probabilities defined by a mixing device as the *beliefs* of the other players, quantified as their subjective probability distributions, regarding the strategies one plays. Under this "subjectivist" interpretation of mixed strategies, players are at a Nash *equilibrium-in-beliefs* when each player plays a pure strategy that is optimal given all of the players' beliefs regarding what their opponents will do, and assuming that these beliefs satisfy probabilistic *consistency* and *independence*. I concur with a number of authors (Aumann 1987; Brandenburger and Dekel 1988; Skyrms 1991) who argue that it is preferable to adopt the equilibrium-in-beliefs interpretation of Nash equilibrium. To do so is to accept a definition of Nash equilibrium that is mathematically equivalent to that of the traditional Nash equilibrium, but that has a different and (hopefully) more plausible intuitive justification. In the next chapter I will argue that the subjectivist interpretation of the probabilities has profound implications for what counts as a "solution" of a noncooperative game.

To illustrate the contrast between the traditional interpretation of Nash equilibrium as equilibrium in mixed strategies and Nash equilibrium-in-beliefs, let us reconsider the Battle of the Sexes coordination problem, which has the payoff structure shown in Figure 1.4.3. Under the traditional interpretation, at Nash equilibrium each player pegs her strategy on the outcome of a random experiment, such as a coin toss or a roulette wheel spin, and the players' experiments are probabilistically independent. However, in the absence of *correlation* in the players' mixed strategies, there is no decisive reason why a player would ever base her strategy on a random experiment. At either pure strategy equilibrium in Battle of the Sexes, each player has a unique pure strategy best response, so there is no need for either player to randomize. For instance, at the equilibrium

(A_1, A_1), each player chooses to play the pure strategy A_1 given that she believes with certainty that her opponent will also play A_1. Under the traditional interpretation of Nash equilibrium, each player's mixed strategy is defined by the degenerate probability distribution $\sigma_k^*(A_1) = 1, k = 1, 2$. Each player could mix her strategy by performing an experiment and playing A_1 whatever the outcome of the experiment turns out to be, but this is clearly unnecessary. At this equilibrium, each player simply selects the pure strategy that is her unique best response given her belief that her opponent will play her end of the equilibrium. As for the mixed equilibrium, each player can maximize expected utility by playing the corresponding mixed strategy under the traditional interpretation, but this mixed strategy is *not* her unique best reply to her opponent's strategy.

There is no decisive reason why either player in Battle of the Sexes should play the mixed strategy that is her end of the mixed equilibrium, as long as her beliefs about her opponent agree with the opponent's end of the mixed equilibrium under the traditional interpretation. For instance, if Kay believes that Amie will play A_1 with probability $\frac{2}{3}$, then *any* strategy that Kay might play, pure or mixed, is a best reply, so Kay has no decisive reason to peg her strategy to a mixing device and to play A_1 with probability $\frac{1}{3}$. This phenomenon holds for any mixed equilibrium of a noncooperative game. If a player's probability distribution over his opponents' strategies agrees with the distribution that would be defined by their playing the mixed strategies of the "traditional" Nash equilibrium, whether or not the opponents do in fact play mixed strategies, then *any* strategy the player might select is a best reply. The player expects to do just as well by selecting a pure strategy without the aid of a random experiment, so why should she bother explicitly mixing his strategy?

Luce and Raiffa (1957, 75) point out that the primary argument in favor of supposing that players would ever mix their strategies is that mixing can keep one's opponents uncertain as to which pure strategy one will ultimately play. For instance, defenders of mixed strategies argue that if Kay and Amie were to play a zero-sum game with the payoff structure of the Overlord game defined by the matrix in Figure 1.2.3, Amie would be justified in tying her strategy to the outcome of a random experiment in order to keep Kay in the dark as to which pure strategy Amie will play. If Kay knew in advance Amie's pure strategy, Kay would choose the pure strategy that would result in Amie's receiving her worst payoff. If Amie announces that she will play the mixed strategy of tossing a fair coin and playing A_1 if the coin lands heads-up and A_2 if the coin lands tails-up, then $\sigma_2(\text{Amie plays } A_1) = \frac{1}{2}$, and so Kay cannot be sure of anticipating which pure strategy Amie will ultimately play. Indeed, given Kay's probability distribution over Amie's actions, Kay cannot even play a strategy that would be strictly favorable to her, and hence strictly unfavorable to Amie, in terms of expected utility. Given Kay's beliefs, which correspond with Amie's end of the unique Nash equilibrium for this game, Kay can maximize her expected utility by playing any strategy, including the mixed strategy of playing A_1 with probability $\frac{1}{2}$. If Kay plays this mixed strategy, then she keeps Amie uncertain as to which pure strategy she will play, just as Amie keeps Kay uncertain as to which pure strategy she will play by mixing her strategies.

However, it is not necessary for a player to mix her own strategies in order to generate uncertainty in the minds of her opponents. An alternate way to interpret probabilities over pure strategies in game theory is as the probabilities *in the minds of the other players* as to what one will do, rather than as explicitly mixed strategies. This enables one to reinterpret the Nash equilibrium as an equilibrium-in-beliefs regarding the strategies one's opponents play.

Suppose that in Overlord the players do not announce their intended strategies, either pure or mixed. Each player still has a probability distribution reflecting uncertainty regarding her opponent's actions, which might be a function of a variety of conditions. In particular, I shall argue in a subsequent chapter that *players can form their probabilities for their opponents' strategies by learning inductively from what they have observed these opponents do in the past.* If Kay's probability that Amie chooses A_1 is $\frac{1}{2}$, then Kay's expected payoff for choosing A_1 equals her expected payoff for choosing A_2, so Kay is at her end of a mixed Nash equilibrium-in-beliefs. Similarly, if Amie's probability that Kay chooses A_2 is $\frac{1}{2}$, then she is at her end of a mixed Nash equilibrium-in-beliefs. Note that if Amie and Kay are at equilibrium-in-beliefs regarding what the other will do, then each may choose a pure strategy to play her end of the equilibrium strategy combination. Hence the equilibrium-in-beliefs interpretation of the Nash equilibrium concept sidesteps the objections raised by some authors (McLennen 1978; Rubinstein 1991) against the classical game theory of Von Neumann and Morgenstern which criticize the rationality of playing mixed strategies. Moreover, replacing randomized strategies in game theory with probability distributions over a player's opponents appears to reflect the actual predicament facing the players. Each player wants to maximize her expected utility, which she can always do by choosing a pure strategy *given what she believes her opponents will do*, and her beliefs may be quantified by a subjective probability distribution over the opponents' act combinations.

For these reasons, we will use the equilibrium-in-beliefs interpretation of Nash equilibria in the remainder of this book. These arguments favoring a "subjectivist" interpretation of mixed acts extend to cases in which the players are not at a Nash equilibrium. In particular, Aumann (1974, 1987) and Vanderschraaf

(1992) interpret generalizations of the Nash equilibrium concept known as *correlated equilibrium concepts* as equilibrium-in-beliefs concepts.

One possible objection to the subjectivist interpretation of Nash equilibrium is that in the case of a completely mixed equilibrium, the strategies the players choose are not uniquely specified. In other words, at a completely mixed equilibrium-in-beliefs, one cannot *predict* the exact pure strategy profile the players will select. However, as Bicchieri (1993, 65) points out, the traditional Nash equilibrium in terms of mixed strategies is equally unpredictive for the case of purely mixed equilibria. Under either interpretation, at a completely mixed equilibrium every strategy for every player maximizes expected utility, so neither interpretation uniquely determines the strategies the players should play. Indeed, under the traditional interpretation, at a completely mixed equilibrium each player could *ignore* the results of the randomizing device if she wanted to without violating Bayesian rationality, and choose some pure strategy other than the one the mixing device would dictate. Those who favor the equilibrium-in-beliefs interpretation of the Nash equilibrium concept simply accept this phenomenon. At a completely mixed Nash equilibrium, every pure strategy profile maximizes expected utility for every player, and so the subjectivists recognize that any pure strategy profile might be chosen. In the special case of completely mixed equilibrium, the pure strategy profile the players settle upon stems from their best guesses as to which strategy each should play, which is a psychological rather than a logical process.

§1.6   Conclusion

I began this chapter by raising the problem of explaining how rational agents might come to coordinate their activities so as to achieve a mutually beneficial outcome. The difficulty in coming up with a satisfying account is the multiplicity of possible solutions to a given social coordination problem. Why do people coordinate their activity in a certain way, when they might have coordinated in a different way? Game theory enables us to recast this problem as that of *equilibrium selection*. Modeling social interactions as games summarizes the strategic problem faced by individuals trying to coordinate, and gives a precise account of a pattern of coordination as an equilibrium of a certain game. However, the classical game theory of Von Neumann and Morgenstern (1944) and Nash (1950, 1951) falls short of providing a satisfactory account of coordination. Classical game theory gives no general method for choosing one Nash equilibrium in a game over the game's other equilibria. Moreover, reinterpreting mixed strategies as players' subjective beliefs may lead us to reevaluate the centrality of the Nash equilibrium concept. In the next chapters, I will consider alternative solution concepts for noncooperative games, and develop a theory of inductive deliberation that one can apply to the equilibrium selection problem.

CHAPTER 2

Rationalizability and Correlated Equilibrium Concepts

§2.0   Introduction

In this chapter, I discuss various solution concepts for noncooperative games that generalize the Nash equilibrium concept. Each of the solution concepts I will consider generalizes the Nash equilibrium concept by relaxing, in one way or another, various assumptions that justify the Nash equilibrium concept. A common approach to accounting for Nash equilibrium play in a game presupposes that the following are common knowledge among the players:

(1) the game's payoff structure,

(2) the *Bayesian rationality* of the players, and

(3) the players' beliefs about one another.

In addition, any Nash equilibrium must satisfy the following:

(4) Players regard their opponents' strategies as *probabilistically independent*, and

(5) Players' beliefs must be *consistent*, in a sense to be made precise below.

I argue in this chapter that some of these assumptions make sense, while others are unfounded. Consequently, the Nash equilibrium is the appropriate solution concept for noncooperative games only in limited contexts. I argue below that in general *correlated equilibrium* concepts are preferable to the Nash equilibrium concept.

In §2.1 I review a solution concept for noncooperative games known as *rationalizability*, introduced by Bernheim (1984) and Pearce (1984). Of the various solution concepts for noncooperative games in the literature, rationalizability requires the weakest common knowledge assumptions. Hence, I regard rationalizability as a suitable starting point for the present discussion. I contend that rationalizability makes sense in contexts where players will play a game only once, knowing nothing about their opponents other than the fact that they are

Bayesian rational. However, rationalizable strategy profiles become unstable in cases where players learn about each others' beliefs. Hence, rationalizability is not a suitable solution concept for games in which the players are modeled as *inductive deliberators*, as they are so modelled in this book,[1] since inductive deliberation gives an account of how players can learn about each others' beliefs over time.

The primary solution concepts for noncooperative games in this book are *correlated equilibrium* concepts, which I discuss in §2.2. Most of the results of noncooperative game theory presuppose that the choices rational agents make in noncooperative games are probabilistically independent. I contend that there is no *a priori* reason for rational agents to assume probabilistic independence, and that in fact there are good reasons to suppose that the choices of rational agents in a game are correlated. Relaxing the probabilistic independence assumption leads to spectacular changes in equilibrium concepts. In two seminal papers, Aumann (1974, 1987) introduced a solution concept for noncooperative games, the *Aumann correlated equilibrium*, in which players achieve equilibrium when their beliefs, quantified as probability distributions, are correlated with some external signal. The Aumann correlated equilibrium concept generalizes the Nash equilibrium concept, given the traditional mixed strategy interpretation, by relaxing the assumption that the players' mixed strategies are stochastically independent. Vanderschraaf (1992) introduces an alternate correlated equilibrium concept for noncooperative games called an *endogenous correlated equilibrium*, which generalizes the Nash equilibrium concept by dropping probabilistic independence in players' probability distributions without introducing signaling devices. In §2.2 I review the discussion in Vanderschraaf (1992) and contrast the endogenous correlated equilibrium with the correlated equilibrium defined by Aumann (1974, 1987). I conclude that in cases in which the players have no information over and above the payoff structure and the beliefs they have regarding each others' play, the endogenous correlated equilibrium concept is a more appropriate solution concept for noncooperative game theory than the less general Nash equilibrium concept. In contexts in which the players receive information from an external signaling device or recommended strategies from an arbiter, the Aumann correlated equilibrium concept is the appropriate solution concept. In Chapter 3, we shall see that the beliefs of players modeled as *inductive deliberators* can converge to either type of correlated equilibrium, depending on the information they have at their disposal.

Finally, in §2.3 I discuss the interrelationships between endogenous correlated equilibrium, Aumann correlated equilibrium, and rationalizability. If

---

[1] See Chapter 3 below.

the players' beliefs over their opponents are allowed to be completely arbitrary, then the resulting *subjective* Aumann correlated equilibrium concept contains the rationalizability concept, which in turn contains the endogenous correlated equilibrium concept. When players' beliefs are restricted so as to be consistent, then the resulting *objective* Aumann and endogenous correlated equilibrium concepts overlap, but neither objective correlated equilibrium concept contains the other.

§2.1   Rationalizability

In order to justify any solution concept for noncooperative games, one must specify what the players in the game know about their situation. A modest starting point is to assume that the players are sophisticated enough to know the full payoff structure of the game they are engaged in and that they are all expected utility maximizers. Suppose that in a game the payoff structure of the game and the *Bayesian rationality* of each of the players are both *common knowledge* in Lewis' (1969) sense:

(C1) Each player knows the payoff vector for every strategy combination of the game,

(C2) Each player knows that she is Bayesian rational, that is, she acts so as to maximize her expected utility, and

(C*) Each player knows that each of her opponents knows (C1) and (C2), and she knows that her opponents know that she knows (C1) and (C2), and so on.

Suppose further that no other information is common knowledge. In other words, each player knows that her opponents are expected utility maximizers, but does not in general know exactly which strategies they will choose or what their probabilities for her acts are. These common knowledge assumptions motivate the solution concept for noncooperative games known as *rationalizability*, introduced independently by Bernheim (1984) and Pearce (1984). Roughly speaking, a *rationalizable strategy* is any strategy a player may choose without violating Bayesian rationality given (C1), (C2), and (C*). Bernheim and Pearce argue that when only the structure of the game and the players' Bayesian rationality are common knowledge, the game should be considered "solved" if every player plays a rationalizable strategy. For instance, in the "Stag Hunt" game with payoff structure defined by Figure 2.1.1, if Kay and Amie have common knowledge of all of the payoffs at every strategy combination, and they have common knowledge that both are Bayesian rational, then any of the four pure strategy profiles is rationalizable.

Kay

		A_1	A_2
Amie	A_1	$(2, 2)$	$(0, 1)$
	A_2	$(1, 0)$	$(1, 1)$

Figure 2.1.1. Stag Hunt

If, say,

(2.*i*) $\mu_1(\text{Kay plays } A_1) = \mu_1(A_1) = .7$

and

(2.*ii*) $\mu_2(\text{Amie plays } A_1) = \mu_2(A_1) = .4$

then

$$E_1(u_1(A_1)) = .7 \cdot (2) + .3 \cdot (0) = 1.4 > 1.0 = .7 \cdot (1) + .3 \cdot (1) = E_1(u_1(A_1))$$

and

$$E_2(u_2(A_2)) = .4 \cdot (1) + .6 \cdot (1) = 1.0 > .8 = .4 \cdot (2) + .6 \cdot (0) = E_2(u_2(A_1))$$

so Amie and Kay maximize expected utility by playing A_1 and A_2, respectively. The players both conform with Bayesian rationality by playing their respective ends of the strategy combination (A_1, A_2) *given their beliefs*, even though (A_1, A_2) is not an equilibrium, since Amie would want to defect from this strategy combination if she knew for certain that Kay was going to play A_2. A key reason that the strategy combination (A_1, A_2) is rationalizable for Amie is that she knows that Kay is Bayesian rational, but she does not know Kay's probability distribution for her own (Amie's) alternative. Kay is similarly situated, that is, she knows that Amie will try to maximize expected utility but does not know the distribution by which Amie calculates her expected utility. If Amie did know Kay's beliefs for her own actions, she would conclude that Kay will play A_2, and consequently *Amie would have to revise her belief that Kay is more likely to* *play* A_1. Indeed, if Kay and Amie are to play the Stag Hunt game repeatedly, then after the first play they will presumably both want to revise their beliefs regarding what the other player will do in light of the fact that they have played (A_1, A_2). A systematic account of belief revision and its relationship to various solution concepts of noncooperative games is presented in Chapter 3. The point of the present example is that players can conform with Bayesian rationality by playing a nonequilibrium strategy combination if they have common knowledge of the game's payoff structure and of their Bayesian rationality *only*. As we shall see below in §2.2, the Nash equilibrium concept which has been the dominant solution concept in game theory, as well as the various correlated equilibrium concepts discussed in the literature (Aumann 1974, 1987; Vanderschraaf 1992) require stronger common knowledge assumptions than (C1), (C2), and (C*).

Continuing with the Stag Hunt example, to show that any pure strategy combination is rationalizable, note that in general

$$
\begin{aligned}
E_1(u_1(A_1)) &= 2\mu_1(\text{Kay plays } A_1) \\
E_1(u_1(A_2)) &= \mu_1(\text{Kay plays } A_1) + \mu_1(\text{Kay plays } A_2) \\
E_2(u_2(A_1)) &= 2\mu_2(\text{Amie plays } A_1) \\
E_2(u_2(A_2)) &= \mu_2(\text{Amie plays } A_1) + \mu_2(\text{Amie plays } A_2)
\end{aligned}
$$

so it is rational for Amie to play A_1 whenever

(2.*iii*) $\qquad 2\mu_1(A_1) \geq \mu_1(A_1) + \mu_1(A_2) \text{ or } \mu_1(A_1) \geq \mu_1(A_2)$

and it is rational for Amie to play A_2 whenever

(2.*iv*) $\qquad\qquad\qquad \mu_1(A_1) \leq \mu_1(A_2).$

Similarly, it is rational for Kay to play A_1 whenever

(2.*v*) $\qquad\qquad\qquad \mu_2(A_1) \geq \mu_2(A_2)$

and it is rational for Kay to play A_2 whenever

(2.*vi*) $\qquad\qquad\qquad \mu_2(A_1) \leq \mu_2(A_2)$

So, given appropriate values for $\mu_1(A_1)$ and $\mu_2(A_1)$, any pure strategy combination of this game can be rationalizable. If equality obtains in (2.*iii*) and (2.*iv*), then Amie can maximize expected utility by playing *either* pure strategy. Likewise, if equality obtains in (2.*v*) and (2.*vi*), then Kay can maximize expected utility by playing either one of her pure strategies. Note that the game's pure strategy Nash equilibria, (A_1, A_1) and (A_2, A_2), are rationalizable, since it is rational for Amie and Kay to conform with either equilibrium given appropriate distributions. In general, the set of a game's rationalizable strategy combinations contains the set of the game's pure strategy Nash equilibria, and this example shows that the containment can be proper.

Nevertheless, in certain games some strategy combinations are not rationalizable. Consider the 2-player game with payoff structure defined by Figure 2.1.2:

Kay

		A_1	A_2	A_3
	A_1	$(4, 3)$	$(1, 2)$	$(3, 4)$
Amie	A_2	$(1, 1)$	$(0, 5)$	$(1, 1)$
	A_3	$(3, 4)$	$(1, 3)$	$(4, 3)$

Figure 2.1.2. A 3 × 3 Game with 4 Rationalizable Strategy Profiles

In this game, A_1 and A_3 strictly dominate A_2 for Amie, so Amie cannot play A_2 on pain of violating Bayesian rationality. Kay knows this, so Kay knows that the only pure strategy profiles that are possible outcomes of the game will be among the six profiles in which Amie does not choose A_2. In effect, the 3 × 3 game is reduced to the 2 × 3 game defined by Figure 2.1.3:

Kay

		A_1	A_2	A_3
Amie	A_1	$(4, 3)$	$(1, 2)$	$(3, 4)$
	A_3	$(3, 4)$	$(1, 3)$	$(4, 3)$

Figure 2.1.3. Game Reduced By Deleting a Dominated Pure Strategy

In this reduced game, A_2 is strictly dominated for Kay by A_1, and so Kay will rule out playing A_2. Amie knows this, and so she rules out strategy combinations in which Kay plays A_2. The rationalizable strategy profiles are the four profiles that remain after deleting all of the strategy combinations in which either Amie or

Kay play A_2. In effect, common knowledge of Bayesian rationality reduces the 3×3 game of Figure 2.1.2 to the 2×2 game defined by Figure 2.1.4, since Amie and Kay both know that the only possible outcomes of the game are (A_1, A_1), (A_1, A_3), (A_3, A_1) and (A_3, A_3).

Kay

		A_1	A_3
Amie	A_1	$(4, 3)$	$(3, 4)$
	A_3	$(3, 4)$	$(4, 3)$

Figure 2.1.4. The Same Game Reduced Again

In certain games, the set of rationalizable strategies might be only a single strategy profile. A simple example of this phenomenon is the 2-player Prisoners' Dilemma game with payoff structure defined by Figure 2.1.5:

Kay

		C	D
Amie	C	$(3, 3)$	$(1, 4)$
	D	$(4, 1)$	$(2, 2)$

Figure 2.1.5. Prisoner's Dilemma

In the Prisoners' Dilemma, D is the strictly dominant strategy for each player, no matter what her distribution is over her opponent's actions. Since both players know this, they will both rule out C, so (D, D), which happens to be the game's only Nash equilibrium, is the only rationalizable strategy profile for the Prisoners' Dilemma. If the set of rationalizable profiles for a game is a singleton, as in Prisoners' Dilemma, then the game is said to be *dominance solvable*.

Rationalizability is an attractive solution concept for noncooperative games because its underlying common knowledge assumptions are in a sense "minimal." In order for the players to play a rationalizable strategy combination, and to know that all are conforming with Bayesian rationality when they do so, it suffices that the players have common knowledge of the game's payoff structure and of Bayesian rationality. Moreover, these common knowledge assumptions are intuitively quite plausible. (C1) simply says that each player knows what game he is in fact engaged in, and (C2) is just the statement that he is Bayesian rational. So if the players have common knowledge of (C1) and (C2), each player knows that he is playing a game with opponents *like himself* with respect to Bayesian rationality, and that everyone has the same knowledge of the game that he has.

Nevertheless, the drawback to rationalizability is that this solution concept becomes *unstable* when the players learn more about their situation than (C1), (C2), and (C*). As the Stag Hunt example shows, a rationalizable strategy combination can be unstable with respect to belief revelation, since in that example Amie will defect from (A_1, A_2) if she learns Kay's probability distribution. Moreover, if players play the same game repeatedly, then what the players *learn* by playing a rationalizable strategy combination can lead them to change beliefs and strategies. Again, in the Stag Hunt example, if Kay and Amie play (A_1, A_2) based upon their distributions (2.*i*) and (2.*ii*), and are then to continue playing Stag Hunt, it hardly seems reasonable to suppose that Amie will leave her probability $\mu_1(\text{Kay plays } A_1) = .7$ *unrevised* given that Kay has played A_2, which gives evidence that Kay is likely to play A_2 in future rounds. Given that Kay has played A_2, Amie will presumably want to modify her beliefs, and perhaps switch her strategy to A_2 as well. Indeed, it seems right to say that Amie would be *irrational* to stubbornly leave her beliefs unchanged and to continue playing A_1 if Kay consistently plays A_2. This of course raises the question: How are players to revise their beliefs in light of what they learn beyond the common knowledge assumptions (C1), (C2), and (C*)? I will address this question in detail in Chapter 3.

In summary, I think that rationalizability is a suitable solution concept for noncooperative games in a *static* setting, in which they will play the game once and in which their common knowledge is limited to (C1), (C2), and (C*). Given stronger common knowledge assumptions, or given a *dynamic* setting in which players can *learn* about one another, perhaps by playing the game repeatedly, then rationalizability becomes unstable, and I think we must then look to other solution concepts for games.

Rationalizability can be defined formally in two ways. Bernheim (1984) defines rationalizability in terms of each player maximizing his expected utility given a set of beliefs he has regarding his opponents' actions that is consistent with the common knowledge assumptions (C1), (C2), and (C*). Pearce (1984) defines rationalizability in terms of iterated deletion of strictly dominated strategies.[2] In both papers, the alternative definitions are shown to be logically

---

[2]Brandenburger and Dekel (1987) give a third definition of rationalizability in terms of *best reply sets*. I discuss this characterization of rationalizability in §2.3.

equivalent.[3] Bernheim and Pearce both assume, on rather weak grounds, that players' beliefs about their opponents must satisfy probabilistic independence. Following Brandenburger and Dekel (1988), I will state variations of Bernheim's and Pearce's definitions here, in which their assumption of probabilistic independence is relaxed. The resulting definitions of *correlated rationalizability* are logically equivalent, which I show below. I first give the usual definitions of a game in strategic form, expected utility, and players' distributions over their opponents' strategies to establish notation.

Definition 2.1.1. A *game* Γ is an ordered triple $(N, S, \boldsymbol{u})$ consisting of the following elements:

(*a*) A finite set $N = \{1, 2, \ldots, n\}$, called the *set of players*.

(*b*) For each player $k \in N$, there is a finite set $S_k = \{A_{k1}, A_{k2}, \ldots, A_{kn_k}\}$, called the *alternative pure strategies* for player k. The Cartesian product $S = S_1 \times \cdots \times S_n$ is called the *pure strategy set* for Γ.

(*c*) A map $\boldsymbol{u} : S \to \mathbb{R}^n$, called the *utility* or *payoff function* on the pure strategy set. At each strategy combination $\boldsymbol{A} = (A_{1j_1}, \ldots, A_{nj_n}) \in S$, player k's particular payoff or utility is given by the kth component of the value of $\boldsymbol{u}$, that is, player k's utility u_k at $\boldsymbol{A}$ is determined by

$$u_k(\boldsymbol{A}) = I_k \circ \boldsymbol{u}(A_{1j_1}, \ldots, A_{nj_n}),$$

where $I_k(\boldsymbol{x})$ projects $\boldsymbol{x} \in \mathbb{R}^n$ onto its kth component. $\qquad\square$

The subscript '$-k$' indicates the result of removing the kth component of an n-tuple or an n-fold Cartesian product. For instance,

$$S_{-k} = S_1 \times \cdots \times S_{k-1} \times S_{k+1} \times \cdots \times S_n$$

denotes the strategy combinations that player k's opponents may play.

Now let us formally introduce a system of the players' beliefs into this framework. $\mathcal{P}_k(S_{-k})$ denotes the set of probability distributions over the measurable space $(S_{-k}, \mathfrak{F}_k)$, where $\mathfrak{F}_k$ denotes the Boolean algebra generated by the strategy combinations S_{-k}. Each player k has a probability distribution $\mu_k \in \mathcal{P}_k(S_{-k})$, and this distribution determines the *expected utilities* for each of k's possible acts:

$$(2.vii) \quad E_k(u_k(A_{kj})) = \sum_{A_{-k} \in S_{-k}} u_k(A_{kj}, \boldsymbol{A}_{-k}) \cdot \mu_k(\boldsymbol{A}_{-k}), \quad j = 1, 2, \ldots, n_k.$$

---

[3] See Proposition 3.2 in Bernheim (1984) and Proposition 2 in Pearce (1984).

If i is an opponent of k, then i's individual strategy A_{ij} may be characterized as a union of strategy combinations $\bigcup \{A_{-k} | A_{ij} \in A_{-k}\} \in \mathfrak{F}_k$, and so k's marginal probability for i's strategy A_{ij} may be calculated as follows:

$$\mu_k(A_{ij}) = \sum_{\{A_{-k} | A_{ij} \in A_{-k}\}} \mu_k(A_{-k}).$$

Definition 2.1.2. Given that each player $k \in N$ has a probability distribution $\mu_k \in \mathcal{P}_k(S_{-k})$, the system of beliefs

$$\boldsymbol{\mu} = (\mu_1, \ldots, \mu_n) \in \mathcal{P}_1(S_{-1}) \times \cdots \times \mathcal{P}_n(S_{-n})$$

is *Bayes concordant* iff,

(2.*viii*)   For $i \neq k$, $\mu_i(A_{kj}) > 0 \Rightarrow A_{kj}$ maximizes k's expected utility
for some $\sigma_k \in \mathcal{P}_k(S_{-k})$,

and (2.*viii*) is common knowledge. A pure strategy combination

$$\boldsymbol{A} = (A_{1j_1}, \ldots, A_{nj_n}) \in S$$

is *rationalizable* iff the players have a Bayes concordant system $\boldsymbol{p}$ of beliefs and, for each player $k \in N$,

(2.*ix*) $E_k(u_k(A_{kj_k})) \geq E_k(u_k(A_{ki_k}))$ for $i_k \neq j_k$.

The set of *correlated rationalizable strategy combinations* is denoted by $S^\star$.[4] $\square$

The only substantive difference between this definition of rationalizability and Bernheim's original definition is that Bernheim requires the players' distributions over their opponents' strategies to satisfy probabilistic independence. Formally, Bernheim requires that for each player k and for each

$$\boldsymbol{A}_{-k} = (A_{1j_1}, \ldots, A_{k-1j_{k-1}}, A_{k+1} \ldots, A_{nj_n}) \in S_{-k}$$

k's joint probability must equal the product of k's marginal probabilities, that is,

(2.*x*) $\mu_k(\boldsymbol{A}_{-k}) = \mu_k(A_{1j_1}) \cdots \mu_k(A_{k-1j_{k-1}}) \cdot \mu_k(A_{k+1j_{k+1}}) \cdots \mu_k(A_{nj_n}).$

Bernheim argues that the probability distributions of the players must satisfy independence, because the rationalizability model presumes that the players choose

---

[4] In his original paper, Bernheim (1984) calls a Bayes concordant system of beliefs a "consistent" system of beliefs. Since the term "consistent beliefs" is used in this paper to describe probability distributions that agree with respect to a mutual opponent's strategies, I use the term "Bayes concordant system of beliefs" rather than Bernheim's "consistent system of beliefs."

their strategies independently, without being able to influence one another prior to play. However, as I shall argue in more detail below in §2.2, Bernheim's argument and arguments like it conflate the *causal independence* of the player's strategy choices with the notion of *evidential independence*. Even if one's opponents choose their strategies without being able to influence each other by communicating or some other means, the choice of one opponent might give *evidence* for how some of the other opponents will play if the opponents are alike (or different) in some way relevant to their decision-making processes. Such similarities or differences can be reflected in a probability distribution that has some of the opponents' acts correlated. Consequently, in Definition 2.1.2 the players' probability distributions over their opponents are not required to satisfy probabilistic independence. Since any Nash equilibrium-in-beliefs μ is clearly Bayes concordant, the set $S^{\star}$ is nonempty for any game Γ. The following result shows that the common knowledge restriction on the distributions in Definition 2.1.2 formalizes the assumption that the players have common knowledge of Bayesian rationality.

Proposition 2.1.3. In a game Γ, common knowledge of Bayesian rationality is satisfied iff (2.*viii*) is common knowledge.

Proof. Suppose first that common knowledge of Bayesian rationality is satisfied. Since it is common knowledge that player i knows that player k is Bayesian rational, it is also common knowledge that if $\mu_i(A_{kj}) > 0$, then A_{kj} must be optimal for k given some belief over S_{-k}, so (2.*viii*) is common knowledge.

Suppose now that (2.*viii*) is common knowledge. Then, by (2.*viii*), player i knows that player k is Bayesian rational. Since (2.*viii*) is common knowledge, all statements of the form 'For $i, j, \ldots, k \in N$, i knows that j knows that $\ldots k$ is Bayesian rational' follow by induction. $\qquad\square$

It is also easy to extend Pearce's definition of rationalizability to allow for correlation in the players' distributions. Given a distribution $\mu_k \in \mathcal{P}_k(S_{-k})$, by Bayesian rationality, player k must choose an action A_{kj} which solves

$$\max_{A_{ki} \in S_k} \left(\sum_{A_{-k} \in S_{-k}} u_k(A_{ki}, \boldsymbol{A}_{-k}) \cdot \mu_k(\boldsymbol{A}_{-k}) \right).$$

Following standard terminology, A_{kj} is called a best reply to μ_k. If any act A_{kl} is *strictly dominated*, that is, A_{kl} is not a best reply to any $\mu_k \in \mathcal{P}_k(S_{-k})$, then k cannot choose A_{kl}. Let $S_k^0 = S_k$ and

$$S_k^1 = \{A_{kj} \in S_k^0 | A_{kj} \text{ is a best reply to some } \mu_k \in \mathcal{P}_k(S_{-k})\}.$$

In other words, S_k^1 is the subset of k's pure strategies that are not strictly dominated. Since the Bayesian rationality of the players is common knowledge, player k knows that opponent j can choose only strategies that are in S_j^1. Hence, if player k is to have a distribution $\mu_k \in \mathcal{P}_k(S_{-k})$ consistent with this knowledge, μ_k can assign positive probabilities only to act combinations in $S_{-k}^1 = S_1^1 \times \cdots \times S_{k-1}^1 \times S_{k+1}^1 \times \cdots \times S_n^1$. Hence, k should choose an action only from the strategies in the set

$$S_k^2 = \{A_{kj} \in S_k^1 | A_{kj} \text{ is a best reply to some } \mu_k \in \mathcal{P}_k(S_{-k}^1)\}.$$

By the common knowledge assumption (C*), this reasoning can be extended indefinitely. Define inductively

$$S_k^m = \{A_{kj} \in S_k^{m-1} \mid A_{kj} \text{ is a best reply to some } \mu_k \in \mathcal{P}_k(S_{-k}^{m-1})\}.$$

Since there are only finitely many strategies, there must be a value M such that $S_k^m = S_k^M \neq \emptyset$ for all $m \geq M$. S_k^M is the set of strategies that player k can choose given the assumption of common knowledge of Bayesian rationality.

Definition 2.1.4. $S^M = S_1^M \times \cdots \times S_n^M$ is the set of the game's *Pearce-correlated rationalizable* strategy combinations. □

If the sets $\tilde{S}_k^m$ are defined inductively in the same way as S_k^m except that each distribution $\mu_k \in \mathcal{P}_k(\tilde{S}_{-k}^{m-1})$ meets the probabilistic independence condition (2.x), then $\tilde{S}_k^M$ is the set of player k's "uncorrelated" rationalizable strategies as defined originally in Pearce (1984). Clearly, $\tilde{S}_k^M \subseteq S_k^M$ for each $k \in N$.

The proof that the two definitions of correlated rationalizability are equivalent is similar to Bernheim's and Pearce's proofs for rationalizability with probabilistic independence. To show this, another preliminary result is needed.

Lemma 2.1.5. In a game Γ, if Bayesian rationality is common knowledge, then for each $k \in N$

$$\mu_k(\boldsymbol{B}_{-k}) > 0 \Rightarrow \boldsymbol{B}_{-k} \in S_{-k}^M.$$

Proof. The proof is by finite induction on m. If $\mu_k(\boldsymbol{B}_{-k}) > 0$, then $\mu_k(B_{ij}) > 0$ for each $B_{ij} \in \boldsymbol{B}_{-k}$. Since Bayesian rationality is common knowledge, by Proposition 2.1.3,

(1) $\mu_k(B_{ij}) > 0 \Rightarrow B_{ij}$ is a best reply to some $\sigma_i \in \mathcal{P}_i(S_{-i})$,

so $\boldsymbol{B}_{-k} \in S_{-k}^1$, so the lemma is proved for $m = 1$. Note further that (1) is common knowledge, since, by common knowledge of Bayesian rationality, each player k knows that each opponent $i \neq k$ will also reason as k reasons and assign positive probability only to act combinations in S^1_{-i}.

Now suppose that for $m = l$,

$$(2) \qquad \mu_k(\boldsymbol{B}_{-k}) > 0 \Rightarrow \boldsymbol{B}_{-k} \in S^l_{-k}.$$

and that (2) is common knowledge. In other words, it is common knowledge that all players assign zero probability to the act combinations in $S - S^l$. Since Bayesian rationality is common knowledge, if $\mu_k(\boldsymbol{B}_{-k}) > 0$, then for each $B_{ij} \in \boldsymbol{B}_{-k}$, B_{ij} is a best reply to some $\sigma_i \in \mathcal{P}_i(S^l_{-i})$. Hence, $\boldsymbol{B}_{-k} \in S^{l+1}_{-k}$, so the lemma is proved for $m = l$. $\qquad\square$

Proposition 2.1.6. The set of correlated rationalizable strategy combinations is equivalent to the set of Pearce-correlated rationalizable strategy combinations, that is, $S^\star = S^M$.

Proof. Suppose that $\boldsymbol{A} = (A_{1j_1}, \ldots, A_{nj_n}) \in S^\star$ given the Bayes concordant system of distributions $\boldsymbol{\mu} = (\mu_1, \ldots, \mu_n)$. By Lemma 2.1.5, for $k \in N$, μ_k is a probability measure that assigns zero probability to each strategy combination in $S_{-k} - S^M_{-k}$, so the restriction of μ_k to S^M_{-k} is a probability measure over S^M_{-k}. Hence, A_{kj_k} is a best reply to $\mu_k \in \mathcal{P}_k(S^M_{-k})$, so $A_{kj_k} \in S^M_k$, and so $\boldsymbol{A} \in S^M_1 \times \cdots \times S^M_n$.

Now suppose that $\boldsymbol{A} \in S^M$. Then for each player k, there is some distribution $\sigma_k \in \mathcal{P}_k(S^M_{-k})$ such that

$$\sum_{\boldsymbol{B}_{-k} \in S^M_{-k}} u_k(A_{kj_k}, \boldsymbol{B}_{-k})\sigma_k(\boldsymbol{B}_{-k}) \geq \sum_{\boldsymbol{B}_{-k} \in S^M_{-k}} u_k(A_{ki_k}, \boldsymbol{B}_{-k})\sigma_k(\boldsymbol{B}_{-k}).$$

Since $\boldsymbol{A}$ is Pearce-rationalizable, player k must assign zero probability to each act combination $\boldsymbol{B}_{-k} \in S_{-k} - S^M_{-k}$. But this implies that condition (2.*viii*) is satisfied, and, moreover,

$$\sum_{\boldsymbol{B}_{-k} \in S_{-k}} u_k(A_{kj_k}, \boldsymbol{B}_{-k})\sigma_k(\boldsymbol{B}_{-k}) \geq \sum_{\boldsymbol{B}_{-k} \in S_{-k}} u_k(A_{ki_k}, \boldsymbol{B}_{-k})\sigma_k(\boldsymbol{B}_{-k}),$$

that is, condition (2.*ix*) is satisfied. Hence $\boldsymbol{\sigma} = (\sigma_1, \ldots, \sigma_n)$ is a Bayes concordant system of distributions, and so $\boldsymbol{A} \in S^\star$. $\qquad\square$

§2.2 Correlated Equilibrium Concepts

In this section, I discuss *correlated equilibrium* concepts, which generalize the Nash equilibrium concept and which I shall argue are the appropriate solution concepts given that the players have common knowledge of the games' payoff structure, of Bayesian rationality, and each others' beliefs. These are some of the same common knowledge assumptions which justify the Nash equilibrium concept, but I shall argue that the additional assumption of *probabilistic independence* inherent in the Nash equilibrium is unfounded, and that correlated equilibrium concepts should be regarded as the primary solution concepts for noncooperative game theory.

Most of the results of noncooperative game theory assume that the players' strategies are probabilistically independent. In particular, the Nash equilibrium concept assumes probabilistic independence between the players' choices. However, the set of equilibrium solutions available to players engaged in a game may change profoundly if they are allowed to consider correlated strategies. In two landmark essays, Robert Aumann (1974, 1987) formalized a notion of *correlated equilibrium* for multi-player noncooperative games. Aumann showed that players in a game can achieve a correlated equilibrium by pegging their strategies on an external event, and gave examples where this correlated equilibrium resulted in payoffs for each player superior to those of any of the game's Nash equilibria. Vanderschraaf (1992) introduces an *endogenous correlated equilibrium* for noncooperative games involving three or more players, which generalizes the Nash equilibrium concept by relaxing the assumption that the strategies of a player's opponents are probabilistically independent. This endogenous correlated equilibrium does not require the players to tie their strategies to an external event, and consequently applies to situations in which Aumann's correlated equilibrium is inappropriate.

In the remainder of this section, I give examples which illustrate and contrast Aumann's correlated equilibrium concept and the endogenous correlated equilibrium concept. I argue that an agent participating in a noncooperative game has no *a priori* reason to assume that the others' choices are probabilistically independent. Consequently, I contend that game theorists should focus on correlated equilibrium concepts rather than the less general Nash equilibrium concept as the primary solution concepts in noncooperative game theory. I also give the formal definitions of the endogenous and Aumann correlated equilibrium concepts. In §2.3, I will discuss the interrelationships between correlated rationalizability, endogenous correlated equilibrium, and Aumann correlated equilibrium.

Below I present two examples to illustrate and contrast the correlated equilibrium concept first defined formally in Aumann (1974) and the alternative endogenous correlated equilibrium concept introduced in Vanderschraaf (1992). I begin by adopting a "subjectivist" interpretation of mixed strategies, in which randomized strategies are replaced by players' subjective probability distributions over their opponents' actions. When players have probability distributions over their opponents' strategies, it is natural for them to consider correlated strategies. Aumann (1974) showed that players can achieve a correlated equilibrium if they believe that their opponents' strategies are correlated with an external event space. Example 2.2.1 illustrates this kind of correlation. In games having three or more players, correlation in a player's subjective probability distribution is possible without an external event space. Example 2.2.2 shows that players can achieve an endogenous correlated equilibrium if they do not assume that their opponents' actions are probabilistically independent.

Example 2.2.1.

Consider first the familiar Battle of the Sexes coordination problem from Example 4 of Chapter 1, which has the payoff structure shown in Figure 2.2.1:

Kay

		A_1	A_2
Amie	A_1	(2, 1)	(0, 0)
	A_2	(0, 0)	(1, 2)

Figure 2.2.1. Battle of the Sexes

Both players would like to coordinate their choices, but each prefers the outcome of one of the coordinated act pairs over the other one. Battle of the Sexes has three Nash equilibria, namely the two pure strategy equilibria (A_1, A_1) and (A_2, A_2), and a third mixed equilibrium in which Amie plays A_1 with probability $\frac{2}{3}$ and Kay plays A_1 with probability $\frac{1}{3}$. The payoff vectors associated with the pure strategy equilibria are (2,1) and (1,2), and the payoff vector of the mixed strategy equilibrium is $(\frac{2}{3}, \frac{2}{3})$.

A Nash equilibrium may also be regarded as an *equilibrium-in-beliefs* regarding the strategies one's opponents play.[5] For instance, if Kay's probability that Amie chooses A_1 is $\frac{2}{3}$, then Kay's expected payoff for choosing A_1 equals her expected payoff for choosing A_2, so Kay is at her end of a mixed Nash equilibrium-in-beliefs. Similarly, if Amie's probability that Kay chooses A_2 is $\frac{2}{3}$, then she is at her end of a mixed Nash equilibrium-in-beliefs. Note that if Amie and Kay are at equilibrium-in-beliefs regarding what the other will

---

[5] John Harsanyi may have been the first to interpret Nash equilibria in this way. See Harsanyi (1977), p. 103.

do, then each may choose a pure act to play her end of the equilibrium strategy combination. Hence the equilibrium-in-beliefs interpretation of the Nash equilibrium concept sidesteps the objection some raise against game theory that rational agents should not base important decisions on mixed acts.[6] Moreover, replacing randomized strategies in game theory with probability distributions over a player's opponents appears to reflect the actual predicament of the players. Each player wants to maximize her expected utility, which she can always do by choosing a pure strategy *given what she believes her opponents will do*, and her beliefs may be quantified by a subjective probability distribution over the opponents' act combinations. For these reasons, I will use the equilibrium-in-beliefs interpretation of Nash equilibria throughout this book. Of course, these arguments favoring a "subjectivist" interpretation of mixed acts extend to cases in which the players are not at a Nash equilibrium. Aumann (1974, 1987) introduced his correlated equilibrium concept as an equilibrium-in-beliefs concept. The endogenous correlated equilibrium concept introduced in Vanderschraaf (1992) is also an equilibrium-in-beliefs concept.

If the two players are allowed to communicate prior to playing this game, they can agree to play a correlated strategy that will yield a payoff vector they both prefer to that of the mixed Nash equilibrium and that is itself an equilibrium. For example, Luce and Raiffa (1957) note that if the two individuals play repeated Battle of the Sexes over time, they can obtain an average payoff vector of $(\frac{3}{2},\frac{3}{2})$ by alternating between (A_1,A_1) and (A_2,A_2) on successive plays. In a single play of this game, no mixed strategy combination can achieve the payoff vector $(\frac{3}{2},\frac{3}{2})$. However, Luce and Raiffa also note that the players in Battle of the Sexes *can* achieve this *expected* payoff vector in a single play if they toss a fair coin and both play A_1 if the coin lands heads-up ("H"), and both play A_2 if the coin lands tails-up ("T").[7] Then the combinations (A_1,A_1) and (A_2, A_2) are each played with probability $\frac{1}{2}$, and the uncoordinated strategy combinations are played with probability zero. This strategy combination is *correlated* because the players peg their individual strategies on the outcome of the same event, namely the coin toss. By playing their ends of this correlated strategy combination, both players have an expected payoff of $\frac{1}{2} \cdot 2 + \frac{1}{2} \cdot 1 = \frac{3}{2}$. The payoff vector $(\frac{3}{2},\frac{3}{2})$ Pareto dominates the payoff vector $(\frac{2}{3},\frac{2}{3})$ of the mixed Nash equilibrium, and moreover this correlated strategy combination is an equilibrium. Neither player

---

[6]For instance, Martin Shubik gives an interesting argument that throws the rationality of playing mixed strategies into doubt on the grounds that a mixed strategy Nash equilibrium can be very unstable with respect to even minute changes in one of the player's probabilities. See Shubik (1982), pp. 249–251.

[7]See Luce and Raiffa (1957), pp. 115–120. This is the earliest discussion of a correlated equilibrium that I am aware of. Stergios Skaperdas first alerted me to this section of *Games and Decisions*.

would unilaterally deviate from this strategy combination. If Amie computes her conditional expected payoffs, she will note that

$$E_1(u_1(A_1)|H) = 2 \quad > \quad 0 = E_1(u_1(A_2)|H) \, , \text{ and}$$
$$E_1(u_1(A_2)|T) = 1 \quad > \quad 0 = E_1(u_1(A_1)|T)$$

so she will not want to defect from the correlated strategy of playing A_1 if H and A_2 if T. Similarly, Kay will want to adhere to her end of this correlated strategy combination. Pre-game communication permits the two players to achieve a mutually beneficial *Aumann correlated equilibrium*, as defined in Aumann (1974, 1987). $\qquad\qquad\qquad\qquad\qquad\qquad\qquad\qquad\qquad\qquad\qquad\qquad$ $\square$

Aumann's (1974, 1987) correlated equilibrium concept has players correlating their strategies with an event space external to the game. For instance, in Example 2.2.1 the external event space is the set of outcomes $\Omega = \{H, T\}$ resulting from the coin toss. As Aumann's correlated equilibrium requires the external event space, it can be called an *exogenous* equilibrium concept.[8] Since Aumann's correlated equilibrium concept imposes a somewhat artificial structure upon the game, it does not in general replace the Nash equilibrium concept in noncooperative game theory. To use Aumann's exogenous correlated equilibrium concept, one must rely upon a story that explains why players tie their strategies to an event that is not a part of the original game. For example, an exogenous correlated equilibrium might result from pre-game communication, but noncooperative game theory does not typically assume that the players communicate with one another prior to the game. In Chapter 3, I shall explore the possibility of players learning to correlate their strategies with an external event space without pre-play communication.

As Aumann (1987) shows, the players do not necessarily have to observe outcomes of the external event space themselves in order to correlate their strategies. If the only information each receives is a recommended strategy from a colleague or arbiter, then they can correlate on the external event space *indirectly*. For instance, in Example 2.2.1, the colleague could toss the fair coin in private and recommend that Amie and Kay play (A_1, A_1) if H and (A_2, A_2) if T. Kay and Amie can have nontrivial probability distributions over their own acts, even without actually mixing their strategies, if they decide to abide by what the colleague recommends. When a player decides to follow the recommendation of another, say a trusted arbiter, then her probability for her own action is her probability over what the arbiter will recommend. If Amie and Kay each believe that what the arbiter recommends to her is correlated with what the arbiter

---

[8] The term "exogenous correlated equilibrium" is mine, not Aumann's.

recommends to her opponent, then they can achieve the same Aumann correlated equilibrium described in Example 2.2.1 without ever seeing the arbiter flip the coin. Prior to the arbiter's recommendation, their distributions over the joint outcomes of the game are

$$\mu_k(A_1, A_1) = \mu_k(A_2, A_2) = \mu_k(H) = \mu_k(T) = \frac{1}{2}, \ k = 1, 2.$$

Again, the players are at a correlated equilibrium with expected payoff $\frac{3}{2}$ for each, because in this case neither player would unilaterally deviate from what the arbiter recommends. For instance, if Kay computes her conditional expected payoffs, where she conditions on her recommended strategy, she will note that

$$E_2(u_2(A_1)|A_1) = 1 \quad > \quad 0 = E_2(u_2(A_2)|A_1), \text{ and}$$
$$E_2(u_2(A_2)|A_2) = 2 \quad > \quad 0 = E_2(u_2(A_1)|A_2)$$

so she will not want to deviate from what the arbiter recommends, and similarly, Amie will want to adhere to her recommended strategy. In this example, the players each know what the arbiter recommends to the opponent as well as to herself. However, we shall presently see the players do not always have to know each others' recommended strategies in order to be at Aumann correlated equilibrium.

Aumann's (1974) fundamental insight is that an equilibrium solution of a noncooperative game can involve correlated strategies even in the absence of binding agreements. As noted above, Luce and Raiffa (1957) present an early example of correlated equilibrium. However, they mistakenly characterize correlated equilibrium as a solution concept for cooperative games. Prior to Aumann's 1974 essay, game theorists typically assumed that correlated strategies were only possible in cooperative game theory. In noncooperative games, it was supposed that the players' strategies had to be probabilistically independent because by definition the players are not cooperating. Aumann observes that correlated equilibrium does not in fact require a binding agreement, though players can decide to correlate their strategies as a result of pre-play *communication*. An Aumann correlated equilibrium is *self-enforcing*, despite the fact that players correlate their strategies without a binding commitment. In Example 2.2.1, since neither Amie nor Kay would want to deviate from the strategy (A_1, A_1) if H and (A_2, A_2) if T, they do not require a binding agreement to guarantee that each must follow the correlated equilibrium or to be assured that the opponent will follow her end of the correlated equilibrium. Aumann argues that it is the self-enforcing nature of the relevant solution concepts, and not the lack of correlation in strategies, that distinguishes noncooperative game theory from the cooperative theory.

In the correlated equilibrium described in Example 2.2.1, Amie and Kay both have $\mu_k(H) = \mu_k(T) = \frac{1}{2}$, that is, Amie's and Kay's probabilities for the events in Ω are *consistent*. However, it is not essential to the correlated equilibrium concept that the players' subjective probabilities for the same event always agree. Aumann (1974) presented a variety of examples of *subjective equilibria* (both correlated and "uncorrelated") in which players have *inconsistent probabilities*, that is, different subjective probabilities for the same event. Indeed, a different correlated equilibrium can be achieved in Battle of the Sexes if the players have inconsistent subjective probabilities. Suppose that Kay and Amie wish to play Battle of the Sexes once more, and that they have decided to correlate their strategies to the result of the confederate's penny toss as in Example 2.2.1. However, this time Amie believes that the colleague favors her by flipping a trick penny which lands heads-up with probability .55. Likewise, Kay believes that the colleague favors her by flipping a biased penny which lands tails-up with probability .60. Then Amie's expected payoff is $.55 \cdot 2 + .45 \cdot 1 = 1.55$ and Kay's expected payoff is $.40 \cdot 1 + .60 \cdot 2 = 1.60$. Neither Amie nor Kay will wish to deviate from this strategy, so they are at a subjective correlated equilibrium with payoff vector $(1.55, 1.60)$. Some authors object to subjective correlated equilibria on the grounds that the players would be irrational to have inconsistent probabilities. This objection has bite, I think, only if each player knows not only all of the probabilities that characterize the equilibrium-in-beliefs, but also how each of her opponents has derived his probabilities for his opponents' act combinations, *and* that they started with the same prior probability distribution over Ω. I think each of these assumptions is open to question, and that the latter *common prior assumption* is especially problematic. In any event, those who reject inconsistent probabilities prefer to focus on *objective correlated equilibria*, in which all the players' probabilities are consistent.

The Aumann correlated equilibrium concept does not require that the players receive *identical* information from the external event, as Aumann (1974, 1987) shows.[9] To see this, note that in the 2-player "Chicken" game with payoff matrix given in Figure 2.2.2, Kay and Amie can achieve an Aumann correlated equilibrium if they tie their strategies to the result of a fair coin toss, as in Example 2.2.1, and this time play (A_1, A_2) if H and (A_2, A_1) if T. In this case, the expected payoff for each player is $\frac{1}{2} \cdot 2 + \frac{1}{2} \cdot 7 = 3$.

However, the players can do even better by following the following correlated strategy: An arbiter will roll a fair six-sided die, with outcomes denoted by ω_k, where k is the number of spots on the upward face of the die after the roll. After noting the result of the die roll, the arbiter will tell Amie privately either

---

[9] The following example is due to Aumann. See Aumann (1974), p. 71 and Aumann (1987), p. 5.

Kay

$$
\begin{array}{ccc}
 & C & D \\
\end{array}
$$

Amie $\quad C \quad \boxed{(6,6)} \ \boxed{(2,7)}$

$\quad\quad\quad\ \ D \quad \boxed{(7,2)} \ \boxed{(0,0)}$

Figure 2.2.2. Chicken

that the event

$$H_{11} = \{\omega_1, \omega_2, \omega_3, \omega_4\}$$

or that the event

$$H_{12} = \{\omega_5, \omega_6\}$$

occurred. The arbiter will also tell Kay privately either that the event

$$H_{21} = \{\omega_1, \omega_2\}$$

or that the event

$$H_{22} = \{\omega_3, \omega_4, \omega_5, \omega_6\}$$

has occurred. In other words, Amie's and Kay's *private information partitions* are defined as $\mathcal{H}_1 = \{H_{11}, H_{12}\}$ and $\mathcal{H}_2 = \{H_{21}, H_{22}\}$, respectively. They will play the correlated strategy combination $f : \Omega \to S$ defined by

(2.*xi*) $\quad\quad f(\omega) = \begin{cases} (A_1, A_2) & \text{if } \omega_k \in \{\omega_1, \omega_2\}, \\ (A_1, A_1) & \text{if } \omega_k \in \{\omega_3, \omega_4\}, \\ (A_2, A_1) & \text{if } \omega_k \in \{\omega_5, \omega_6\}. \end{cases}$

At every point of the event space, neither player will want to deviate from the correlated strategy combination f. To see this, note that $\omega_k \in \{\omega_1, \omega_2\}$ implies that

$$
\begin{aligned}
E_1(u_1 \circ f | \mathcal{H}_1)(\omega_k) &= E_1(u_1(A_1) | H_{11}) \\
&= \frac{1}{2} \cdot 2 + \frac{1}{2} \cdot 6 \\
&= 4 \\
&> \frac{7}{2} \\
&= \frac{1}{2} \cdot 0 + \frac{1}{2} \cdot 7 \\
&= E_1(u_1(A_2) | H_{11}) = E_1(u_1(A_2) | \mathcal{H}_1)(\omega_k)
\end{aligned}
$$

and

$$E_2(u_2 \circ f | \mathcal{H}_2)(\omega_k) = E_2(u_2(A_1) | H_{21})$$
$$= 6 < 7$$
$$= E_2(u_2(A_2) | H_{21}) = E_2(u_2(A_2) | \mathcal{H}_2)(\omega_k),$$

$\omega_k \in \{\omega_3, \omega_4\}$ implies that

$$E_1(u_1 \circ f | \mathcal{H}_1)(\omega_k) = E_1(u_1(A_1) | H_{11})$$
$$= \frac{1}{2} \cdot 2 + \frac{1}{2} \cdot 6$$
$$= 4$$
$$> \frac{7}{2}$$
$$= \frac{1}{2} \cdot 0 + \frac{1}{2} \cdot 7$$
$$= E_1(u_1(A_2) | H_{11}) = E_1(u_1(A_2) | \mathcal{H}_1)(\omega_k)$$

and

$$E_2(u_2 \circ f | \mathcal{H}_2)(\omega_k) = E_2(u_2(A_1) | H_{22})$$
$$= \frac{1}{2} \cdot 6 + \frac{1}{2} \cdot 2$$
$$= 4$$
$$> \frac{7}{2}$$
$$= \frac{1}{2} \cdot 7 + \frac{1}{2} \cdot 0$$
$$= E_2(u_2(A_2) | H_{22}) = E_2(u_2(A_2) | \mathcal{H}_2)(\omega_k)$$

and $\omega_k \in \{\omega_3, \omega_4\}$ implies that

$$E_1(u_1 \circ f | \mathcal{H}_1)(\omega_k) = E_1(u_1(A_1) | H_{12})$$
$$= 6 < 7$$
$$= E_1(u_1(A_2) | H_{12}) = E_1(u_1(A_2) | \mathcal{H}_1)(\omega_k)$$

and

$$
\begin{aligned}
E_2(u_2 \circ f | \mathcal{H}_2)(\omega_k) &= E_2(u_2(A_1)|H_{22}) \\
&= \frac{1}{2} \cdot 6 + \frac{1}{2} \cdot 2 \\
&= 4 \\
&> \frac{7}{2} \\
&= \frac{1}{2} \cdot 7 + \frac{1}{2} \cdot 0 \\
&= E_2(u_2(A_2)|H_{22}) = E_2(u_2(A_2)|\mathcal{H}_2)(\omega_k)
\end{aligned}
$$

Hence, at every point in Ω, Amie and Kay will both want to follow the strategy combination defined by f, and so f is a correlated equilibrium. For each player the overall expected payoff is $\frac{1}{3} \cdot 2 + \frac{1}{3} \cdot 6 + \frac{1}{3} \cdot 7 = 5$. This correlated equilibrium is outside the convex hull of the game's Nash equilibria, and Pareto dominates the correlated equilibrium (A_1, A_2) if H and (A_2, A_1) if T described above, in which the players have the identical knowledge of the outcome of the event space. Indeed, the correlated equilibrium characterized by (2.xi) relies upon the players receiving *different* private information from the external event space. If, for instance, ω_3 occurs then both players follow the correlated equilibrium by playing A_1. If Kay and Amie were to learn each others' signals, each thinking she had done so in secret, then they each would conclude that $\{\omega_3, \omega_4\}$ has occurred, in which case each will expect the other to play A_1 for certain. Consequently, the equilibrium would break down and both will play A_2.   □

The next example illustrates an alternate correlated equilibrium concept, the *endogenous correlated equilibrium* (Vanderschraaf 1992).

Example 2.2.2.

If a game involves three or more players, then another form of correlation is possible, which can result in an alternate type of correlated equilibrium. For instance, consider now a 3-player Battle of the Sexes game, which has the payoff structure given in Figure 2.2.3, where Amie now chooses the row, Kay chooses the column, and Ron chooses the matrix. Like the 2-player version of Battle of the Sexes, in this game the players all want to coordinate their choices, but each player clearly prefers one coordinated act combination over the others. This game has four Nash equilibria: the pure strategy equilibria (A_1, A_1, A_1), (A_2, A_2, A_2), and (A_3, A_3, A_3), and a mixed equilibrium where each player k believes that each opponent j plays j's preferred alternative with probability $\frac{1}{2}$

	A_1	A_2	A_3
A_1	$(2,1,1)$	$(0,0,0)$	$(0,0,0)$
A_2	$(0,0,0)$	$(0,0,0)$	$(0,0,0)$
A_3	$(0,0,0)$	$(0,0,0)$	$(0,0,0)$

	A_1	A_2	A_3
A_1	$(0,0,0)$	$(0,0,0)$	$(0,0,0)$
A_2	$(0,0,0)$	$(1,2,1)$	$(0,0,0)$
A_3	$(0,0,0)$	$(0,0,0)$	$(0,0,0)$

	A_1	A_2	A_3
A_1	$(0,0,0)$	$0,0,0$	$(0,0,0)$
A_2	$(0,0,0)$	$(0,0,0)$	$(0,0,0)$
A_3	$(0,0,0)$	$(0,0,0)$	$(1,1,2)$

Figure 2.2.3. 3-Player Battle of the Sexes

and the other two alternatives with probability $\frac{1}{4}$. The payoff vectors for the pure strategy Nash equilibria are $(2,1,1)$, $(1,2,1)$, and $(1,1,2)$, and the payoff vector for the mixed Nash equilibrium is $(\frac{1}{8}, \frac{1}{8}, \frac{1}{8})$.

If the players allow for the possibility that their opponents' act combinations are correlated, then they have a number of new equilibria to consider. Set

$$x_{ij} = \mu_1(A_i \wedge A_j) = \mu_1(\text{Kay chooses } A_i, \text{Ron chooses } A_j), \; i,j = 1,2,3,$$
$$y_{ij} = \mu_2(A_i \wedge A_j) = \mu_2(\text{Amie chooses } A_i, \text{Ron chooses } A_j), \; i,j = 1,2,3,$$

and

$$z_{ij} = \mu_3(A_i \wedge A_j) = \mu_3(\text{Amie chooses } A_i, \text{Kay chooses } A_j), \; i,j = 1,2,3$$

At a mixed equilibrium-in-beliefs, each player is indifferent to her pure act choices, that is,

(1) $$E_k(u_k(A_1)) = E_k(u_k(A_2)) = E_k(u_k(A_3)), \; k = 1,2,3.$$

Suppose that Amie's expected payoffs satisfy (1). Then

(2) $$2x_{11} = x_{22} = x_{33}$$

and since $x_{11} + x_{22} + x_{33} \leq 1$, (2) implies that

(3) $$x_{22} \leq \frac{2}{5}.$$

If equality obtains in (3), then $x_{22} = x_{33} = \frac{2}{5}$, $x_{11} = \frac{1}{5}$, and $x_{ij} = 0$ if $i \neq j$, and in this case

$$E_1(u_1(A_1)) = E_1(u_1(A_2)) = E_1(u_1(A_3)) = \frac{2}{5}$$

so (1) is satisfied. Indeed, for any $\alpha_1 \in \left(0, \frac{2}{5}\right]$, Amie's expected payoffs satisfy (1) if

(4) $x_{22} = x_{33} = \alpha_1$ and $x_{11} = \dfrac{\alpha_1}{2}$.

Similarly, if $\alpha_2 \in \left(0, \frac{2}{5}\right]$, then Kay's expected payoffs satisfy (1) if

(5) $y_{11} = y_{33} = \alpha_2$ and $y_{22} = \dfrac{\alpha_2}{2}$

and if $\alpha_3 \in \left(0, \frac{2}{5}\right]$, then Ron's expected payoffs satisfy (1) if

(6) $z_{11} = z_{22} = \alpha_3$ and $z_{33} = \dfrac{\alpha_3}{2}$.

If (4), (5), and (6) all obtain, then the three players are at an *endogenous correlated equilibrium*. If $\alpha_1 = \alpha_2 = \alpha_3 = \frac{2}{5}$, then the payoff vector for this correlated equilibrium is $\left(\frac{2}{5}, \frac{2}{5}, \frac{2}{5}\right)$, which Pareto-dominates the payoff vector of the mixed Nash equilibrium. Since the set of endogenous correlated equilibria is determined by the parameters α_1, α_2, and α_3, this game has infinitely many endogenous correlated equilibria. Note that at the mixed Nash equilibrium, Amie's probabilities for her opponents' coordinated act combinations are $x_{11} = \frac{1}{4} \cdot \frac{1}{4} = \frac{1}{16}$, and $x_{22} = x_{33} = \frac{1}{2} \cdot \frac{1}{4} = \frac{1}{8}$, so (4) is satisfied. Similarly, at the mixed Nash equilibrium Kay's probabilities satisfy (5) and Ron's probabilities satisfy (6), so the mixed Nash equilibrium belongs to the set of the game's endogenous correlated equilibria.   □

The endogenous correlated equilibrium concept generalizes the Nash equilibrium concept simply by dropping the assumptions that the actions of each player's opponents are probabilistically independent and that the players' subjective probabilities are all consistent. The only structure the endogenous correlated equilibrium concept requires beyond the payoff structure of the game is the system of the players' beliefs regarding their opponents' actions, which is simply one of the structures one may import into game theory to justify mixed Nash equilibria. In particular, the endogenous correlated equilibrium concept does not assume that the players engage in pre-game communication. Players can achieve an Aumann correlated equilibrium when they have good reason to expect each other to tie their choices to some external event. In simpler contexts, in which the players choose their strategies apart from any externalities, the endogenous correlated equilibrium is the more appropriate correlated equilibrium concept.

As with Aumann's exogenous correlated equilibrium concept, it is possible to distinguish between *subjective* and *objective endogenous correlated equilibria*. If the players are at a subjective correlated equilibrium, then their probabilities could be inconsistent, that is, two players could have different probabilities for a mutual opponent's strategies. If all the players' probabilities are consistent, then they are at an objective endogenous correlated equilibrium. For instance, in Example 2.2.2 Amie, Kay and Ron are at an objective endogenous correlated equilibrium when $\alpha_1 = \alpha_2 = \alpha_3 = \frac{2}{5}$.[10] If one insists upon consistent subjective probabilities, then all of a game's endogenous correlated equilibria are objective endogenous correlated equilibria. However, as noted above I do not object to inconsistent subjective probabilities in general, and below I define the endogenous correlated equilibrium as a subjective correlated equilibrium concept.

One might ask whether in general the endogenous correlated equilibrium concept is a more appropriate solution concept for noncooperative games than the much better known Nash equilibrium concept. I suggest that, in general, the players engaged in a game should focus on the more general correlated equilibrium concept. The endogenous correlated equilibrium is conceptually simpler than the Nash equilibrium, since an endogenous correlated equilibrium does not require the independence assumption characteristic of Nash equilibria. So the question really reduces to whether or not players engaged in a noncooperative game should assume that their opponents' moves are probabilistically independent. Some claim that noncooperative game theory must assume probabilistic independence precisely because the players are not cooperating. In a noncooperative game, each player's only goal is maximizing his own expected utility, regardless of how this may affect the others' utilities, which would seem to rule out correlated strategies among players. As noted in §2.1, B.D. Bernheim (1984) argues for this position, stating:

---

[10]Note that if $\alpha_1 = \alpha_2 = \alpha_3 = \frac{2}{5}$, then

$$\mu_2(\text{Amie chooses } A_1) = y_{11} + y_{12} + y_{13} = \frac{2}{5} + 0 + 0 = \frac{2}{5},$$

and

$$\mu_3(\text{Amie chooses } A_1) = z_{11} + z_{12} + z_{13} = \frac{2}{5} + 0 + 0 = \frac{2}{5},$$

so Kay's and Ron's subjective probabilities for the event {Amie chooses A_1} agree. Similarly, each pair of player's subjective probabilities for a mutual opponent's act agree, so Kay's, Amie's and Ron's subjective probabilities are all consistent.

A question arises here as to whether an agent's probabilistic conjectures can allow for correlation between the choices of other players. In a purely non-cooperative framework, such correlation would be nonsensical: The choices of any two agents are by definition independent events; they cannot affect each other.[11]

However, even if the players choose their strategies independently, without trying to influence the others' choices, this causal independence between strategies does not imply probabilistic independence. After all, the opponents might be alike in certain ways relevant to the game, and their similarities can be reflected in a probability distribution that has some of the opponents' acts correlated. For instance, in Example 2.2.2 Kay might be aware that Amie and Ron have worked closely together for the same company in the past, and as a result Amie's choice is a fairly good indicator of what Ron will choose, and *vice versa*, even if in this particular instance Amie and Ron do not communicate with one another before they choose their strategies. Hence if the actions of one's opponents are causally independent, one has no *a priori* reason to suppose that they are also probabilistically independent. In a noncooperative game with no pre-play communication or other externalities, players should allow for the possibility of correlation among their opponents' actions, and consider the game resolved should they find themselves at an endogenous correlated equilibrium.[12]

In the remainder of this section, I give the formal definitions of the endogenous correlated equilibrium concept and Aumann's correlated equilibrium concept. The notations of §2.1 remain in force in this section.

Definition 2.2.1. Given that each player $k \in N$ has a probability distribution $\mu_k \in \mathcal{P}_k(S_{-k})$, the system of beliefs

$$\boldsymbol{\mu} = (\mu_1, \ldots, \mu_n) \in \mathcal{P}_1(S_{-1}) \times \cdots \times \mathcal{P}_n(S_{-n}),$$

---

[11] Bernheim (1984), p. 1014.

[12] One might object that if the players in a game know *nothing* about one another, then they should not be able to achieve an endogenous correlated equilibrium. However, this objection applies to the Nash equilibrium as well. Suppose that Kay knows nothing about Amie or Ron before they play the game. If one insists upon probabilistic independence in this case, then I think one should also insist that Kay have a uniform distribution over Amie's and Ron's acts, since any distribution other than the uniform would presumably reflect something Kay knows about her opponents. Of course, if Kay *does* have a uniform distribution over her opponents' strategies, then the players are not at equilibrium at all. This objection raises the issue of how players ought to form their beliefs regarding their opponents. This question is dealt with at length in Vanderschraaf and Skyrms (1993) and in Chapter 3 of this book.

is an endogenous correlated equilibrium iff

(2.*xii*)
  For $i \neq k$, $\mu_i(A_{kj}) > 0 \Rightarrow A_{kj}$ maximizes k's expected utility given μ_k.

If μ is an endogenous correlated equilibrium, a pure strategy combination $A = (A_{1j_1}, \ldots, A_{nj_n}) \in S$ is an *endogenous correlated equilibrium strategy combination given μ* iff, for each player $k \in N$,

(2.*xiii*) $E_k(u_k(A_{kj_k})) \geq E_k(u_k(A_{ki_k}))$ for $i_k \neq j_k$.

The ordered pair (A, μ) is called an *endogenous correlated equilibrium pair*. $\square$

Condition (2.*xiii*) is the statement that the players in a game are at equilibrium if and only if no player can gain by unilaterally defecting from the strategy combination. Condition (2.*xiii*) restricts the players' beliefs by formalizing the following assumptions:

(C1) Each player knows the entire payoff structure of the game,

(C2) Each player chooses a strategy that maximizes her expected utility,

(C3) Each player knows the beliefs of all of the players, including herself, and

(C*) Each player knows that each of her opponents knows (C1)–(C3), and she knows that her opponents know that she knows (C1)–(C3), and so on.

These common knowledge assumptions underlying the endogenous correlated equilibrium concept will be discussed in detail in §2.3. Note that this definition of an equilibrium says nothing about whether or not the players regard their opponents' strategy combinations as probabilistically independent. Also, this definition does not require that the players' probabilities are consistent, in the sense that players' probabilities for a mutual opponent's acts agree.

A simple refinement of the endogenous correlated equilibrium concept characterizes the Nash equilibrium concept.

Definition 2.2.2. A system of players' beliefs μ is a *Nash equilibrium* iff

(*a*) Condition (2.*xii*) is satisfied,

(*b*) For each $k \in N$ and each $A_{-k} \in S_{-k}$, condition (2.*x*) is satisfied, and

(*c*) For each $A_{kj} \in S_k$, if $i, l \neq k$ then $\mu_i(A_{kj}) = \mu_l(A_{kj})$. $\square$

In other words, an endogenous correlated equilibrium is a Nash equilibrium (in beliefs) when each player regards the moves of his opponents as probabilistically independent and the players' probabilities are consistent. Note that in the 2-player case, conditions (*b*) and (*c*) of the Definition 2.2.2 are always satisfied, so for 2-player games the endogenous correlated equilibrium concept reduces to the Nash equilibrium concept.

Since a Nash equilibrium is a special case of endogenous correlated equilibria, by Nash's Theorem (1951) every game has at least one endogenous correlated equilibrium. Example 2.2.2 shows that a game can have a continuum of distinct endogenous correlated equilibria, even though it has only finitely many Nash equilibria. On the other hand, the set of endogenous correlated equilibria is not larger than the set of Nash equilibria in all cases, even when there are three or more players. For instance, in the 3-player version of the Prisoners' Dilemma, which has the payoff structure given in Figure 2.2.4, D is the dominant strategy for all three players, no matter what probability distribution each player has over the others' act combinations.

	C			D	
	C	D		C	D
C	$(3,3,3)$	$(1,4,1)$	C	$(2,1,1)$	$(1,2,2)$
D	$(4,1,1)$	$(2,2,1)$	D	$(2,2,1)$	$(2,2,2)$

Figure 2.2.4. 3-Player Prisoner's Dilemma

Hence, in this game, the only endogenous correlated equilibrium is the game's one Nash equilibrium (D, D, D), characterized by the distributions

$$\mu_k(\text{opponent 1 plays } D, \text{ opponent 2 plays } D) = 1, \quad k = 1, 2, 3.$$

It may be instructive to compare the definition of endogenous correlated equilibrium with that of Aumann's (1974, 1987) correlated equilibrium concept.

Definition 2.2.3. Given a game $\Gamma = (N, S, u)$ and a finite probability space Ω, a function $f : \Omega \to S$ defines a set of *exogenously correlated strategy n-tuples*. Each player $k \in N$ has an *information partition* $\mathcal{H}_k$ of Ω, such that if $\omega \in \Omega$ occurs, then k is informed that a particular event $H_{ki}(\omega) \in \mathcal{H}_k$ has occurred. Then $f = (f_1, \ldots, f_n)$ is an *Aumann correlated equilibrium* iff, for each $k \in N$,

(*a*) f_k is an $\mathcal{H}_k$-measurable function, that is, for each $H_{kj} \in \mathcal{H}_k$, $f_k(\omega')$ is constant for each $\omega' \in H_{kj}$, and (*b*) For each $\omega \in \Omega$ such that $\mu_k(\omega) > 0$,

$$(2.xiv) \qquad E_k(u_k \circ f | \mathcal{H}_k)(\omega) \geq E_k(u_k(f_{-k}, g_k) | \mathcal{H}_k)(\omega)$$

for any $\mathcal{H}_k$-measurable function $g_k : \Omega \to S_k$.[13] □

The set Ω is known as the *states of the world*, and player k's information about which ω has occurred is represented by k's information partition $\mathcal{H}_k$. $f(\omega)$ gives each player a recommended strategy $f_k(\omega) \in f(\omega)$. Player k can either follow the recommendation by playing $f_k(\omega)$ or deviate by playing some other strategy. The players are at an exogenous correlated equilibrium if at each state of the world $\omega \in \Omega$, no player will want to deviate from the recommended strategy given his information $H_{ki}(\omega)$. The measurability restriction *(a)* on f_k formalizes the intuition that at each state of the world, Player k knows which pure strategy he will follow.

Certain common knowledge assumptions are implicit in the definition of Aumann *a posteriori equilibrium*. First, the players must have common knowledge that they are all Bayesian rational, in the sense that every player chooses a strategy that maximizes his expected payoff given his beliefs regarding his opponents at every cell of his information partition. The payoff structure of the game, the partitions of Ω, and the function $f : \Omega \to S$ all must be common knowledge in order for the players to be able to compute one another's expected payoffs and thereby know that they are at correlated equilibrium. Note that Aumann's correlated equilibrium concept generalizes the Nash equilibrium concept. Players are at a Nash equilibrium $f = (f_1, \ldots, f_n)$ if each player k pegs his strategy f_k on a randomizing device Ω_k that is probabilistically independent of the randomizing devices of his opponents and such that $f_k(\omega)$ is optimal for k given the strategies of k's opponents.[14] Hence f is formally a correlated equilibrium where $\Omega = \Omega_1 \times \cdots \times \Omega_n$.

---

[13]The restriction that $\mu_k(\omega) > 0$ is needed in order for the conditional expectation to be defined. If $\mu_k(\omega') = 0$, this reflects k's belief that the strategy profile $f(\omega)$ will never be played, unless there is some $\omega' \neq \omega$ such that $\mu_k(\omega') > 0$ and $f(\omega) = f(\omega')$. A refinement of the Aumann correlated equilibrium concept, the *a posteriori correlated equilibrium*, extends the definition of conditional probability to sets of measure zero and requires that (a) hold for all $\omega \in \Omega$, including cases where $\mu_k(\omega) = 0$. I shall discuss *a posteriori* correlated equilibrium below in §2.3.

[14]By the monotonicity of expectation, if (4.*i*) obtains, then

$$(1) \qquad E_k(u_k \circ f) = E_k(E_k(u_k \circ f | \mathcal{H}_k)(\omega))$$
$$\geq E_k(E_k(u_k \circ (f_{-k}, g_k) | \mathcal{H}_k)(\omega)) = E_k(u_k \circ (f_{-k}, g_k))$$

and, when f satisfies probabilistic independence, (1) is the condition on f that characterizes the Nash equilibrium concept.

As noted already, the primary difference between Aumann's correlated equilibrium and the endogenous correlated equilibrium is that in Aumann's correlated equilibrium, the players correlate their strategies to some event $\omega \in \Omega$ that is external to the game. This difference is reflected in the way that players who correlate their strategies exogenously calculate their expected utilities. In Aumann's model, each player has a prior probability distribution η_k over Ω, which k can use to calculate the probabilities that the various act combinations $A \in S$ are played. It can be shown that Aumann's correlated equilibrium condition is equivalent to the following: The players $k \in N$ are at Aumann correlated equilibrium iff for every k and for every A_{kj} such that $\eta_k(A_{kj}) > 0$,

$$(2.xv) \quad \sum_{A_{-k}} u_k(A_{kj}, A_{-k})\eta_k(A_{-k}|A_{kj}) \geq \sum_{A_{-k}} u_k(A_{ki}, A_{-k})\eta_k(A_{-k}|A_{kj})$$

for all $A_{ki} \in S_k$.[15] In other words, each player calculates expected utilities conditional on his obeying the recommended strategy. On the other hand, the players are at an endogenous correlated equilibrium if for every k,

$$(2.xvi) \quad \sum_{A_{-k}} u_k(A_{kj}, A_{-k})\mu_k(A_{-k}) \geq \sum_{A_{-k}} u_k(A_{ki}, A_{-k})\mu_k(A_{-k})$$

for all $A_{ki} \in S_k$. The utilities in (2.xvi) are computed according to the formula (2.vii), which is the definition of expected utility given in Savage (1954). In the endogenous correlated equilibrium framework, a player has no *recommended* strategy to play, and therefore calculates expected utility subject to an unconditional distribution over the opponents' act combinations.

§2.3 Correlated Equilibrium, Rationalizability, and Ratifiability

Rationalizability is closely related to correlated equilibrium concepts. In its most general formulation, the Aumann correlated equilibrium concept contains rationalizability. Brandenburger and Dekel (1987) show that when players correlate their strategies to an external event space Ω and calculate expected utilities conditional on information partitions over Ω, then the notion of correlated rationalizability is equivalent to a refinement of Aumann's subjective exogenous correlated equilibrium concept, namely the *a posteriori correlated equilibrium*.

---

[15]For a proof, see Fudenberg and Tirole (1992), pp. 57–58.

Subjective endogenous correlated equilibrium is a special case of correlated rationalizability, so subjective *a posteriori correlated equilibrium* contains the subjective endogenous correlated equilibrium concept. However, neither of the *objective* Aumann or correlated equilibrium concepts contains the other.

The definition of Aumann correlated equilibrium places no consistency restrictions upon the beliefs of the players. As a result, every rationalizable strategy profile $A^* = (A_1^*, \ldots, A_n^*)$ with a corresponding Bayes concordant system σ^* of distributions is formally a subjective Aumann correlated equilibrium, as Brandenburger and Dekel (1987) show. I repeat a variation or their argument here.

Lemma 2.3.1. Given a game Γ, if $A^* = (A_1^*, \ldots, A_n^*) \in S^\star$, then there is a subjective Aumann correlated equilibrium f of Γ such that $f_k = A_k^*$ for each player k.

Proof. Let σ^* be a Bayes concordant system of beliefs such that (2.*ix*) is satisfied for each player k. Note that one may consider each strategy A_k^* as the strategy an arbiter secretly recommends to player k, and k's *conditional* distribution given the recommendation to play A_k^* defined as $\sigma_k(B_{-k}|A_k^*) = \sigma_k^*(B_{-k})$ for each $B_{-k} \in S_{-k}$. Since k will play A_k^* as if he had received a recommendation to play A_k^*, $\sigma_k(A_k^*) = 1$, and, by rationalizability,

$$\sum_{B_{-k}} u_k(A_k^*, B_{-k})\sigma_k(B_{-k}|A_{kj}) \geq \sum_{B_{-k}} u_k(A_{ki}, B_{-k})\sigma_k(B_{-k}|A_{kj})$$

for each $A_{ki} \in S_k$, so (2.*xv*) is satisfied. $\square$

Since, as I will show below, the correlated rationalizability concept contains the subjective endogenous correlated equilibrium concept, subjective endogenous correlated equilibrium is a special case of subjective Aumann correlated equilibrium. Recall that in order for players to *know* that they are at a correlated equilibrium, they must have common knowledge of each others' beliefs. On the other hand, rationalizability does not require that players know each others' beliefs, and indeed, as we have seen above, players may wish to deviate from a rationalizable strategy combination if they learn each others' beliefs. However, it still makes sense to interpret a rationalizable strategy profile as an Aumann correlated equilibrium as in the above construction, if one assumes that the players have common knowledge of each others' conditional distributions, but *not* their recommendations. Since the arbiter in the construction recommends A_k^* to each player k and keeps the other recommendations secret, k can know his opponents' distributions *given what their recommendations are,* but still not know what his opponents' beliefs are after each receives his recommendation, since k only knows his own recommendation.

However, not every strategy profile determined by a subjective Aumann correlated equilibrium need be rationalizable. Brandenburger and Dekel (1987) give the following example of a game with payoff structure defined by Figure 2.3.1, together with an event space $\Omega = \{\omega_1, \omega_2\}$, where Amie observes which of $\omega_k \in \Omega$, $k = 1, 2$, occurs, but Kay receives no information from Ω, so that

$$\mathcal{H}_1 = \{\{\omega_1\}, \{\omega_2\}\}, \text{ and } \mathcal{H}_2 = \{\omega_1, \omega_2\}.$$

Amie's and Kay's subjective probability distributions over Ω are defined, respectively, by

$$\mu_1(\omega_1) = 1$$

and

$$\mu_2(\omega_1) = \mu_2(\omega_2) = \frac{1}{2}.$$

Kay

		C	D
Amie	C	$(3,0)$	$(1,2)$
	D	$(0,4)$	$(0,1)$

Figure 2.3.1. Brandenburger-Dekel Example

Given these distributions, the function $f : \Omega \to S$ defined by

(2.xvii) $$f(\omega) = \begin{cases} (A_1, A_1) & \text{if } \omega = \omega_1 \\ (A_2, A_1) & \text{if } \omega = \omega_2 \end{cases}$$

is a subjective Aumann correlated equilibrium, since

$$E_1(u_1 \circ f|\{\omega_1\}) = 3 > 0 = E_1(u_1(A_2, f_{-1})|\{\omega_1\})$$

and, for any value of $\omega \in \Omega$,

$$\begin{aligned} E_2(u_2 \circ f|\mathcal{H}_2)(\omega) &= E_2(u_2 \circ f) \\ &= 0 \cdot \frac{1}{2} + 4 \cdot \frac{1}{2} \\ &= 2 > \frac{3}{2} \\ &= 2 \cdot \frac{1}{2} + 1 \cdot \frac{1}{2} \\ &= E_2(u_2(f_{-2}, A_2)) = E_2(u_2(f_{-2}, A_2|\mathcal{H}_2)(\omega). \end{aligned}$$

However, this equilibrium relies upon Amie playing a strictly dominated strategy if ω_2 occurs, so $f(\omega_2) = (A_2, A_1)$ is not rationalizable.

Brandenburger and Dekel (1987) show that if an Aumann correlated equilibrium is such that each player's recommended strategy is optimal for her, including those she assigns zero probability, then every strategy profile defined by the correlated equilibrium is rationalizable. Consequently, there is an equivalence between the notion of correlated rationalizability and this refinement of subjective Aumann correlated equilibrium, called *a posteriori equilibrium* (Aumann 1974; Brandenburger and Dekel 1987). I will review Brandenburger and Dekel's equivalence result, after giving the formal definition of *a posteriori equilibrium*. As Brandenburger and Dekel (1987) point out, this definition of *a posteriori correlated equilibrium* requires the conditional expectations to be defined and condition (2.*xiv*) to be met even if some players assign zero probabilities to some of the cells of their information partitions. Following their lead, I require in the following definition that for every player $k \in N$,

(a) $\mu_k(\cdot|H_{ki})$ is a probability measure on Ω, and

(b) $\mu_k(H_{ki}|H_{ki}) = 1$

for each $H_{ki} \in \mathcal{H}_k$. Of course, these conditions follow immediately from the conventional definition of conditional probability if $\mu_k(H_{ki}) > 0$, but the point is that imposing (a) and (b) on every cell of every player's information partition extends the definition of conditional probability to events of zero probability.

Definition 2.3.2. Given a game $\Gamma = (N, S, u)$ and a finite probability space Ω together with information partitions $\mathcal{H}_k$, $k \in N$, of Ω, a function $f : \Omega \to S$ is an *a posteriori Aumann correlated equilibrium*, or simply *a posteriori equilibrium* iff, for each $k \in N$,

(a) f_k is $\mathcal{H}_k$-measurable, and

(b) For each $\omega \in \Omega$,

$$E_k(u_k \circ f|\mathcal{H}_k)(\omega) \geq E_k(u_k(f_{-k}, g_k)|\mathcal{H}_k)(\omega)$$

for any $\mathcal{H}_k$-measurable function $g_k : \Omega \to S_k$. □

The substantive difference between the *a posteriori* equilibrium concept and the more general subjective Aumann correlated equilibrium concept is that at an *a posteriori* equilibrium, for each player k, the strategy $f_k(\omega)$ defined by f is optimal for k at *all* states of the world, not simply those to which k assigns positive probability. Aumann (1974) coins the term "*a posteriori* equilibrium" to emphasize that each player always maximizes expected utility by conforming with the equilibrium after receiving her private information. This property does not hold for every Aumann correlated equilibrium. The correlated equilibrium (2.*xvii*) defined for the example of Figure 2.3.1 is not an *a posteriori* equilibrium, since $f_1(\omega_2) = A_2$ is not optimal for Amie. Players can have differing subjective probabilities at an *a posteriori* correlated equilibrium. In the Battle of the Sexes game of Example 2.2.1, if $\Omega = \{H, T\}$ and both players observe the coin flip, the subjective Aumann correlated equilibrium

$$f(\omega) = \begin{cases} (A_1, A_1) & \text{if } H \\ (A_2, A_2) & \text{if } T \end{cases}$$

where $\mu_1(H) = .55$ and $\mu_2(T) = .60$ is optimal at each ω for both Amie and Kay, so f is an *a posteriori* equilibrium. When the players' probabilities are consistent, the notions of Aumann correlated equilibrium and *a posteriori* equilibrium coincide.

Brandenburger and Dekel (1987) prove that there is a certain equivalence between correlated rationalizability and *a posteriori* equilibrium. Some preliminaries are needed to show this.

Definition 2.3.3. A set of strategy profiles $B \subseteq S$ is a *best reply set* iff for each $k \in N$ and each $A_{kj} \in B_k$, there is a distribution $\sigma_k \in \mathcal{P}_k(B_{-k})$ such that A_{kj} is a best response for k given σ_k.   □

Lemma 2.3.4. If $B \subseteq S$ is a best reply set, then $B \subseteq S^M$.

Proof. Suppose that for a value of m, $1 \leq m < M$, that $B \subseteq S^m$. Let $A_{kj} \in B_k$ for some $k \in N$. Then for some distribution $\sigma_k \in \mathcal{P}_k(B_{-k})$, A_{kj} is a best response for k given σ_k. By hypothesis, $B_{-k} \subseteq S^m_{-k}$, so define $\tilde{\sigma}_k$ for each $A_{-k} \in S^m_{-k}$ by

$$\tilde{\sigma}_k = \begin{cases} \sigma_k(A_{-k}) & \text{if } A_{-k} \in B_{-k} \\ 0 & \text{otherwise} \end{cases}$$

Then A_{kj} is a best response to $\tilde{\sigma}_k \in \mathcal{P}_k(S^m_{-k})$, so $A_{kj} \in S^{m+1}_k$. Since A_{kj} was chosen arbitrarily, we have $B \subseteq S^{m+1}$. By induction, $B \subseteq S^M$.   □

From this result, one can obtain an alternate characterization of rationalizability.

Corollary 2.3.5. $S^M = \bigcup\{B \subseteq S | B \text{ is a best reply set}\}$.[16]

---

[16]Brandenburger and Dekel (1987, p. 1393) *define* correlated rationalizability in terms of best reply sets. They note that their definition is equivalent to the definitions of rationalizability given in Bernheim (1984) and Pearce (1984) with probabilistic independence dropped, but they do not give a proof of this equivalence.

Proof. By Lemma 2.3.4,

$$\bigcup\{B \subseteq S | B \text{ is a best reply set}\} \subseteq S^M.$$

S^M is clearly a best reply set, since for each $A_{kj} \in S_k^M$, there is a distribution $\sigma_k \in \mathcal{P}_k(S_{-k}^M)$ to which A_{kj} is a best reply. Hence

$$S^M \subseteq \bigcup\{B \subseteq S | B \text{ is a best reply set}\}. \quad \square$$

Brandenburger and Dekel's (1987) equivalence result shows that the strategy profiles defined by the set of a game's *a posteriori* correlated equilibria coincide with the set of the game's correlated rationalizable strategy profiles. I repeat a variation of their result here.[17]

Proposition 2.3.6 (Brandenburger and Dekel, 1987). A strategy profile $A \in S$ is rationalizable iff there is an *a posteriori* equilibrium $f : \Omega \to S$ of Γ in which $f(\omega) = A$ for some $\omega \in \Omega$.

Proof. The "only if" part of the proof was proved above as Lemma 2.3.1.

To prove the "if" part, let $A^* \in S$ be given, and suppose there is an *a posteriori* equilibrium f such that $f(\omega_0) = A^*$ for some $\omega_0 \in \Omega$. By Corollary 2.3.5, it will suffice to show that A^* is a strategy profile in a best response set. For each $k \in N$, let

$$S_k^+ = \{A_{kj} \in S_k | A_{kj} = f(\omega) \text{ for some } \omega \in \Omega\}.$$

We claim that $S^+ = S_1^+ \times \cdots \times S_n^+$ is a best reply set. Suppose that $A'_{kj} \in S_k$, so that there is some $\omega' \in \Omega$ such that $f_k(\omega') = A'_{kj}$. Since f is an *a posteriori* equilibrium, and since k knows that each of his opponents will play a strategy defined by f, k's optimality condition at ω' may be written as

$$\sum_{A_{-k} \in S_{-k}^+} u_k(A'_{kj}, A_{-k})\mu_k\big[\{\omega : f_{-k}(\omega) = A_{-k}\}|\mathcal{H}_k(\omega')\big]$$

$$\geq \sum_{A_{-k} \in S_{-k}^+} u_k(A_{kj}, A_{-k})\mu_k\big[\{\omega : f_{-k}(\omega) = A_{-k}\}|\mathcal{H}_k(\omega')\big]$$

for all $A_{kj} \in S_{-k}^+$. In other words, A'_{kj} is a best response for k given the distribution $\sigma_k(A_{-k}) = \mu_k\big[\{\omega : f_{-k}(\omega) = A_{-k}\}|\mathcal{H}_k(\omega_0)\big]$ for each $A_{-k} \in S_{-k}^+$. Since A'_{kj} was chosen arbitrarily, we have shown that S^+ is a best reply set. Since $A = f(\omega_0)$, A is a strategy profile in S^+, so A is rationalizable. $\quad \square$

---

[17] Proposition 2.3.6 corresponds to Proposition 2.1 in Brandenburger and Dekel (1987). However, Brandenburger and Dekel prove their result in terms of payoff vectors, while I prove the result in terms of strategy profiles.

Since every objective Aumann correlated equilibrium is an *a posteriori* equilibrium, and since the Battle of the Sexes example shows that a game's objective Aumann correlated equilibria can be a proper subset of the game's *a posteriori* equilibria, Proposition 2.3.6 shows that in general the set of strategy profiles defined by the game's objective Aumann correlated equilibria is properly contained by the set of the game's rationalizable strategy profiles.

I now turn to the relationship between rationalizability and endogenous correlated equilibrium. In Proposition 2.3.7, I show that the endogenous correlated equilibrium concept is a refinement of correlated rationalizability when strategies are not correlated with an external event space. Brandenburger and Dekel (1988) show that in 2-player games, if the beliefs of the players are common knowledge, condition (2.*xii*) characterizes common knowledge of Bayesian rationality, and that (2.*xii*) characterizes a Nash equilibrium-in-beliefs. As they note, condition (2.*xii*) characterizes a Nash equilibrium-in-beliefs for the n-player case if the probability distributions are consistent and satisfy probabilistic independence. Proposition 2.3.7 extends Brandenburger and Dekel's result to the endogenous correlated equilibrium concept by relaxing the consistency and probabilistic independence assumptions.

Proposition 2.3.7. Assume that the probabilities

$$\mu = (\mu_1, \ldots, \mu_n) \in \mathcal{P}_1(S_{-1}) \times \cdots \times \mathcal{P}_n(S_{-n})$$

are common knowledge. Then common knowledge of Bayesian rationality is satisfied iff μ is an endogenous correlated equilibrium.

Proof. Suppose first that common knowledge of Bayesian rationality is satisfied. Then, by Proposition 2.1.3, for a given player $k \in N$, if $\mu_i(A_{kj}) > 0$ for each player $i \neq k$, then A_{kj} must be optimal for k given some distribution $\sigma_k \in \mathcal{P}_k(S_{-k})$. Since the players' distributions are common knowledge, this distribution is precisely μ_k, so (2.*xii*) is satisfied for k. (2.*xii*) is similarly established for each other player $i \neq k$, so μ is an endogenous correlated equilibrium.

Now suppose that μ is an endogenous correlated equilibrium. Then, since the distributions are common knowledge, (2.*viii*) is common knowledge, so common knowledge of Bayesian rationality is satisfied by Proposition 2.1.3. ☐

Corollary 2.3.8 (Brandenburger and Dekel, 1988). Assume in a two-player game that the probabilities

$$\mu = (\mu_1, \mu_2) \in \mathcal{P}_1(S_{-1}) \times \mathcal{P}_2(S_{-2})$$

are common knowledge. Then common knowledge of Bayesian rationality is satisfied iff μ is a Nash equilibrium.

Proof. The endogenous correlated equilibrium concept reduces to the Nash equilibrium concept in the 2-player case, so the corollary follows by Proposition 2.3.7. □

Proposition 2.3.7 shows that the endogenous correlated equilibrium concept is a refinement of correlated rationalizability, in which the players have common knowledge of one another's beliefs as well as common knowledge of Bayesian rationality. To be precise, one passes from correlated rationalizability to endogenous correlated equilibrium if, in addition to assuming

(C1) Each player knows the payoff function $u : S \to \mathbb{R}^n$,

and

(C2) Each player is Bayesian rational,

one also assumes:

(C3) Each player k knows the probability distribution $\mu_i \in \mathcal{P}_i(S_{-i})$ of each opponent i, and

(C★) Each player knows that each of her opponents knows (C1)–(C3), and she knows that her opponents know that she knows (C1)–(C3), and so on.

If the players have the common knowledge characterized by (C1)–(C3) and (C★), then by Proposition 2.3.7 they will play an endogenous correlated equilibrium strategy combination.

Conversely, one may view correlated rationalizability as a coarsening of the endogenous correlated equilibrium concept, in which players do not know one another's beliefs, but retain common knowledge that they are all Bayesian rational. If one assumes only (C1), (C2), and (C*), then by Proposition 2.1.3 the players will play a correlated rationalizable strategy profile that is not necessarily an equilibrium. For instance, as noted in §2.1, in the Stag Hunt game with payoff matrix given in Figure 2.1.1, the strategy combination (A_1, A_2) is rationalizable given the Bayes concordant system of beliefs

$$\mu_1(\text{Kay plays } A_1) = .7$$

and

$$\mu_2(\text{Amie plays } A_1) = .4,$$

but either player would defect from (A_1, A_2) if she were to learn the distribution of her opponent. On the other hand, by Proposition 2.3.7, at an endogenous correlated equilibrium it is common knowledge that each player is maximizing expected utility *given his knowledge of the others' distributions,* so an endogenous correlated equilibrium is by definition stable with respect to knowledge of the opponents' beliefs.

Both the Aumann and the endogenous correlated equilibrium concepts generalize the Nash equilibrium concept by relaxing the mathematically convenient probabilistic independence assumption in various ways. Consequently, the two correlated equilibrium concepts overlap. However, neither *objective* correlated equilibrium concept contains the other.

An objective Aumann correlated equilibrium can fail to be an endogenous correlated equilibrium. For instance, in the Battle of the Sexes game of Example 2.2.1, the joint distribution

$$(2.xviii) \qquad \mu_1(A_1, A_1) = \mu_2(A_1, A_1) = \frac{1}{2}$$

characterizes an Aumann correlated equilibrium. Each player is able to have a nondegenerate probability distribution over every strategy profile of the game, and not just the strategies of her opponent, without mixing because she pegs her strategy on the recommendation of the colleague, or on the result of the colleague's coin toss, if she observes this. The endogenous correlated equilibrium does not presuppose that the players have access either to an external signal or to an arbiter. At an endogenous correlated equilibrium, each player has a nondegenerate distribution over the acts of her opponents only, since she knows for certain that she will play a best response given what she believes about her opponents' play. Suppose that in the Battle of the Sexes game, each player ignores the recommendation from the arbiter and acts upon what she believes about her opponent only. Each player can compute her distribution over her opponent by computing the marginal distributions from (2.xviii). The players' beliefs over the opponent are defined by

$$(2.xix) \qquad \mu_1(\text{Kay plays } A_1) = \mu_1(\text{Kay plays } A_2) = \frac{1}{2}$$

$$(2.xx) \qquad \mu_2(\text{Amie plays } A_1) = \mu_2(\text{Amie plays } A_2) = \frac{1}{2}$$

If they calculate expected utilities on the basis of the marginals only, then they will miscoordinate by playing the nonequilibrium combination (A_1, A_2).[18]

---

[18] To see this, note that

$$E_1(u_1(A_1)) = \frac{1}{2} \cdot 2 + \frac{1}{2} \cdot 0 = 1 > \frac{1}{2} = \frac{1}{2} \cdot 0 + \frac{1}{2} \cdot 1 = E_1(u_1(A_2))$$

and

$$E_2(u_2(A_1)) = \frac{1}{2} \cdot 1 + \frac{1}{2} \cdot 0 = \frac{1}{2} < 1 = \frac{1}{2} \cdot 0 + \frac{1}{2} \cdot 2 = E_2(u_2(A_2)).$$

Consequently, the marginal distributions defined by (2.*xix*) cannot be an endogenous correlated equilibrium, since Amie would be assigning a positive probability to Kay's playing A_1, knowing that Kay cannot maximize expected utility by playing A_1 given her distribution (2.*xx*) over Amie's acts, and likewise Kay would be assigning a positive probability to Amie's playing A_2 knowing that A_2 is not a best response for Amie given (2.*xix*). This example shows that to sustain an Aumann correlated equilibrium, the players must maximize *conditional* expected utility. In particular, at an Aumann correlated equilibrium it is essential that each player conditions on the information she receives directly or indirectly regarding the external event, and plays her best response given the resulting conditional probability distribution.

Conversely, an objective endogenous correlated equilibrium need not be an objective Aumann correlated equilibrium. Objective Aumann correlated equilibria satisfy a stability property called *ratifiability*, which endogenous correlated equilibria do not always satisfy. As noted in the discussion following Example 2.2.1, an Aumann correlated equilibrium may be characterized in two ways. In the *lottery characterization*, introduced in Aumann (1974), the players correlate their strategies with an external event. In the *arbiter characterization*, introduced in Aumann (1987), a referee recommends a strategy to each player.[19] The players will be at Aumann correlated equilibrium if each player has no incentive to disobey the recommendation. Aumann (1987) shows that the lottery characterization and the arbiter characterization of his correlated equilibrium concept are equivalent. Now the arbiter characterization is equivalent to the following: Suppose that each player has a probability distribution η_k over the set of pure strategy profiles S. The players $k \in N$ are at Aumann correlated equilibrium if and only if for every k and for every A_{kj} such that $\eta_k(A_{kj}) > 0$, (2.*xv*) is satisfied. In other words, the players are at an Aumann correlated equilibrium iff each player is maximizing expected utility conditional on her obeying the *recommended* strategy. Maximizing expected utility conditional on one's own recommended act is an application of the principle of *ratifiability* introduced by Jeffrey (1983).

Definition 2.3.9 (Jeffrey 1983). Given that agent k can choose from the alternative acts $A_1, \ldots, A_n$, an act A_k is *ratifiable* for an agent k iff $E_k(u_k(A_k|A_k)) \geq E_k(u_k(A_j|A_k))$, $1 \leq j \leq n$. $\qquad\square$

---

[19] Again, the terms "lottery characterization" and "arbiter characterization" are mine, not Aumann's. In fact, Aumann (1987) stresses that in what I call the arbiter characterization of Aumann correlated equilibrium, each player conditions on *his own chosen strategy*, and not directly on an external signal. However, I argue below that without introducing "trembles" into the decision-making process, which would make it possible for a player to fail to play the strategy she decides to play, a player can only condition *nontrivially* on her own strategy if she pegs her strategies to the outcomes of an external event or the recommendations of an arbiter.

Shin (1991) was the first to notice the connection between ratifiability and objective Aumann correlated equilibrium. In particular, Shin proves that players engaged in a noncooperative game are at an objective Aumann correlated equilibrium if, and only if, under the arbiter characterization each player's recommended strategy is ratifiable.[20] Note that ratifiability is a nontrivial concept only when one has a nondegenerate distribution over one's own actions. If one chooses an action A_k with certainty because the act A_k maximizes one's unconditional expected utility, say because this action is one's best response to what one expects the opponents to play in a noncooperative game, then A_k is trivially ratifiable since one chooses A_k with probability one, so that

$$E_k(u_k(A_k)|A_k) = E_k(u_k(A_k)) \geq E_k(u_k(A_j)) \text{ for all } A_j.$$

Given the conventional definition of a conditional probability measure, no other action could be ratifiable, since each $A_j \neq A_k$ is a null event, so that the conditional expectation given $A_j \neq A_k$ under these conditions is undefined.[21]

To show that an endogenous correlated equilibrium can fail to be an Aumann correlated equilibrium, let us consider the 3-player game characterized by the payoff matrices in Figure 2.3.2, where Player 1 (Ron) chooses the row, Player 2 (Peter) chooses the column, and Player 3 (Paul) chooses the matrix:

A_1 $\hspace{8cm}$ A_2

	A_1	A_2
A_1	$(6,6,6)$	$(2,7,2)$
A_2	$(7,2,2)$	$(0,0,2)$

	A_1	A_2
A_1	$(2,2,7)$	$(2,0,0)$
A_2	$(0,2,0)$	$(0,0,0)$

Figure 2.3.2. 3-Player Chicken

This is a 3-player version of "Chicken." Each player has an incentive to choose A_2 if the others both choose A_1. On the other hand, if a given player plays A_2 and either of the other players decides (or both of them decide) to play A_2, then he ends up with 0, the worst possible payoff. If the players' distributions over

---

[20]To be more precise, Shin proves that players are at Aumann correlated equilibrium if, and only if, each player's distribution is *modestly ratifiable*, that is, each player allows for the possibility of "trembles" leading to playing strategies other than his chosen strategy, but believes that his opponents are not susceptible to trembles. See Theorem 8.1 in Shin (1991), p. 251.

[21]However, given the extended definition of conditional probability discussed above, some of the other acts could be ratifiable, though the chosen act can never fail to be ratifiable.

their opponents are defined by

(2.xxi) μ_1(Paul and Peter play A_1) $= \mu_2$(Ron and Peter play A_1)

$$= \mu_3(\text{Ron and Paul play } A_1) = \frac{2}{3}$$

and

(2.xxii) μ_1(Paul and Peter play A_2) $= \mu_2$(Ron and Peter play A_2)

$$= \mu_3(\text{Ron and Paul play } A_2) = \frac{1}{3}$$

then, given this system of distributions, each player's expected utilities for each act are

$$E_k(u_k(A_1)) = \sum_{\boldsymbol{A}_{-k} \in S_{-k}} u_k(A_1, \boldsymbol{A}_{-k})\mu_k(\boldsymbol{A}_{-k}) = 6 \cdot \frac{2}{3} + 2 \cdot \frac{1}{3} = \frac{14}{3}$$

and

$$E_k(u_k(A_2)) = \sum_{\boldsymbol{A}_{-k} \in S_{-k}} u_k(A_2, \boldsymbol{A}_{-k})\mu_k(\boldsymbol{A}_{-k}) = 7 \cdot \frac{2}{3} = \frac{14}{3}.$$

Hence, (μ_1, μ_2, μ_3) is a mixed endogenous correlated equilibrium, and each player can maximize expected utility by playing either A_1 or A_2. As noted in the previous paragraph, if a player chooses either pure strategy with certainty, his choice is trivially ratifiable. In this example, we can adopt the viewpoint of an arbiter, as in Aumann's framework, who has a probability distribution p over all of the act combinations $\boldsymbol{A} \in S$. From the arbiter's viewpoint,

(2.xxiii) $$\mu(A_1, A_1, A_1) = \frac{2}{3},$$

(2.xxiv) $$\mu(A_2, A_2, A_2) = \frac{1}{3}$$

and all other combinations have probability 0.[22] Hence

$$\mu(i \text{ plays } A_1 \wedge j \text{ plays } A_1 | k \text{ plays } A_1) = \frac{\frac{2}{3}}{\frac{2}{3}} = 1$$

---

[22] In fact, the distribution defined by (2.xxiii) and (2.xxiv) is the only joint distribution that is consistent with all three players' endogenous correlated equilibrium distributions. Suppose the players have a common distribution μ over the joint strategy profiles $\boldsymbol{A} \in S$ consistent with the endogenous correlated equilibrium distributions. The players will assign zero probability to all of the uncoordinated act combinations. For instance,

$$\mu(A_1, A_1, A_2) \leq \mu_k(A_1, A_2) = 0, \, k = 1, 2, 3 \text{ (by (2.xxi) and (2.xxii))}.$$

and

$$\mu(i \text{ plays } A_2 \wedge j \text{ plays } A_2 | k \text{ plays } A_2) = \frac{\frac{1}{3}}{\frac{1}{3}} = 1.$$

Note that in this example the players' probabilities are consistent. Since at equilibrium these probabilities are common knowledge, suppose that the players have the same distribution μ over all strategy combinations $\boldsymbol{A} \in S$ as the arbiter's distribution. If the players compute expected utilities conditional on their own acts, that is, they condition according to the arbiter's recommendation, then the equilibrium will break down. For instance, if Ron conditions on his choice to play A_1, then his expected utilities are

$$
\begin{aligned}
E_1(u_1(A_1|A_1)) &= \sum_{\boldsymbol{A} \in S} \mu(\boldsymbol{A}_{-1}|A_1)u_1(\boldsymbol{A}) \\
&= 6 \cdot \mu(A_1, A_1|A_1) \text{ (all other terms are zero)} \\
&= 6 \cdot 1 = 6
\end{aligned}
$$

while

$$
\begin{aligned}
E_1(u_1(A_2|A_1)) &= \sum_{\boldsymbol{A} \in S} \mu(\boldsymbol{A}_{-1}|A_1)u_1(\boldsymbol{A}) \\
&= 7 \cdot \mu(A_1, A_1|A_1) \text{ (all other terms are zero)} \\
&= 7 \cdot 1 = 7
\end{aligned}
$$

so if he were to condition on a "recommendation" to play A_1, he would want to deviate and play A_2. Similarly, if Peter and Paul believe that the distribution defined by (2.*xxiii*) and (2.*xxiv*) is the right joint distribution over the strategy profiles, and condition on their own choices, then they will also conclude that they prefer to play A_2 given this distribution if an external observer recommended that each play A_1. Hence the players would choose the nonequilibrium combination (A_2, A_2, A_2) if each computed expected utility conditional on being told to

---

Hence

$$\mu(A_1, A_1, A_1) + \mu(A_2, A_2, A_2) = 1.$$

Now by (2.*xxi*),

$$\mu(A_1, A_1, A_1) \le \mu_k(A_1, A_1) = \frac{2}{3}, \ k = 1, 2, 3,$$

and, by (2.*xxii*)

$$\mu(A_2, A_2, A_2) \le \mu_k(A_2, A_2) = \frac{1}{3}, \ k = 1, 2, 3,$$

so to obtain (2.*xxiii*) it suffices to show that $\mu(A_1, A_1, A_1) \ge \frac{2}{3}$. But if $\mu(A_1, A_1, A_1) < \frac{2}{3}$, then

$$\mu(A_1, A_1, A_1) + \mu(A_2, A_2, A_2) < \frac{2}{3} + \frac{1}{3} = 1$$

a contradiction, so (2.*xxiii*) obtains. (2.*xxiv*) follows similarly.

play A_1. By a similar argument, if each player were to calculate expected utility conditional on being told to play A_2, then each player would conclude that A_1 is the best strategy, so they would end up at the nonequilibrium point (A_1, A_1, A_1). In other words, the pure strategy choices at this endogenous correlated equilibrium are not ratifiable given the joint distribution characterized by (2.*xxiii*) and (2.*xxiv*). Consequently, the joint distribution defined by (2.*xxiii*) and (2.*xxiv*) determined by the endogenous correlated equilibrium defined by (2.*xxi*) and (2.*xxii*) is not an Aumann correlated equilibrium.

The joint distribution defined by (2.*xxiii*) and (2.*xxiv*) in the 3-player Chicken example is not an Aumann correlated equilibrium because each individual's probabilities for his own acts are both consistent with the beliefs his opponents have about him and correlated with the opponents' strategies. The endogenous correlated equilibrium concept does not require either that one's beliefs about oneself be consistent with what one's opponents believe or that one's distribution over oneself must be correlated with one's distribution over the opponents. Indeed, I suggest that, unless a player can fail to carry out his decisions, the only way that a player could have a nondegenerate distribution over his own actions that is correlated with the distribution over his opponents would be to tie his strategy to an external event or to the recommendation of a referee, which is the external structure underlying the Aumann correlated equilibrium concept. Consider Ron's position in the endogenous correlated equilibrium defined by (2.*xxi*) and (2.*xxii*). He knows that both of his opponents' marginal probabilities for his own actions are

(2.*xxv*) $$\mu_2(\text{Ron chooses } A_1) = \mu_3(\text{Ron chooses } A_1) = \frac{2}{3}$$

and

(2.*xxvi*) $$\mu_2(\text{Ron chooses } A_2) = \mu_3(\text{Ron chooses } A_2) = \frac{1}{3}.$$

Should Ron take his opponents' beliefs about himself as normative, and have a nondegenerate probability distribution over his own acts that agrees with (2.*xxv*) and (2.*xxvi*)? In fact, Ron has no reason to think that he *must* choose his strategies with nondegenerate probability. True, a mixed strategy in which Ron chooses A_1 with probability $\frac{2}{3}$ and A_2 with probability $\frac{1}{3}$ is a best response given his distribution over Peter and Paul defined by (2.*xxi*) and (2.*xxii*), but so is either pure strategy and every other possible mixed strategy. Indeed, at any equilibrium interpreted as an equilibrium-in-beliefs, players never have a positive reason to play mixed strategies, since the probabilities that are traditionally defined by mixed strategies are reinterpreted as the probabilities in the minds of the other players regarding one's own act. Given only his beliefs regarding his opponents, either pure strategy is a best response for Ron. However, suppose that Ron were to decide that his beliefs regarding his own actions ought to be consistent with his opponents' beliefs. The only way for Ron to achieve a nondegenerate distribution over his own actions, which he must do prior to actual play, is to decide to play a probabilistic strategy, which he can do by tying his strategy to an event E, such as a coin toss or a recommendation, over which he has a prior probability $\mu_1(B) = \frac{2}{3}$, so that Ron plays A_1 if B occurs and A_2 if B^c occurs.[23] In this case, exogenously correlated strategies are possible, if the players happen to peg their strategies on the same event B. However, appealing to an external event introduces more structure than the endogenous correlated equilibrium concept requires, and in fact sets the stage for Aumann's correlated equilibrium concept.

Nevertheless, there is one other way for players to have nondegenerate distributions over their own acts to consider, namely if they are able to "slip" and play strategies other than the strategies they decide to play. In other words, a player could have a nondegenerate distribution over his own acts if he distinguishes between *deciding* upon a strategy and *executing* or *actually playing* this strategy, and if he thinks he might fail to play the strategy he decides to play. Differentiating between one's decisions and one's actions is in fact the way in which Jeffrey (1983) introduced the notion of ratifiability, and it is the way that Shin (1991) characterizes ratifiability. In Shin's (1991) framework, there is a small positive probability that an individual plays a strategy other than the one he chooses. Suppose in the 3-player Chicken game that each player implements his strategy by pushing either of two buttons. If Ron *decides* to play A_1, then he might doubt that he will actually play A_1. Such doubts could arise for a variety of reasons. Ron might worry that the buttons are cross-wired by mistake. Or, if pushing the button sends a signal to a referee who announces the joint strategy combination played after receiving signals from all three players, then Ron might worry that the referee does not follow his directions all of the time. Or Ron might think that the button mechanism is completely reliable, but still worry that as he reaches to push the A_1-button, he might "tremble" because of a nervous disorder that flares up precisely when he tries to act on a decision and push the A_2-button instead. Under these conditions, ratifiability can be a nontrivial notion if a player computes the probabilities that players, including himself, follow strategies conditional on his *decision* to play a particular strategy. The strategy a player decides upon then takes the same role as the strategy an arbiter recommends in the expected utility calculation. If players differentiate between decision and performance in this

---

[23]Following the usual convention, 'B^c' denotes the complement of the event B, that is, if Ω is the sure event, then $B^c = \Omega - B$.

manner, then they can achieve an Aumann correlated equilibrium without direct reference to an external event space, but doing so introduces a different externality, namely the mechanism or condition that makes "trembles" possible, so that a player's decision is not perfectly correlated with his action. In the end, in order to justify the Aumann correlated equilibrium concept, one needs to suppose that players incorporate some externality into their reasoning, be it an external event, a recommendation, or a mechanism or condition that produces "trembles."

CHAPTER 3

Equilibrium Selection via Inductive Dynamic Deliberation

§3.0   Introduction

Equilibria in noncooperative games are characterized by the notion of joint expected utility maximization. Players are at equilibrium when each player maximizes her own expected utility given everyone's choices, that is, no player can gain a higher utility by unilaterally defecting from the equilibrium. However, it is by no means obvious that players engaged in a noncooperative game will indeed play a strategy profile that is an equilibrium, particularly when a game has multiple equilibria. How are the players to settle upon an equilibrium? One answer to this question, which I review in this section, is to exploit the common knowledge assumptions that underlie various equilibrium concepts and model the players as dynamic deliberators who adjust their beliefs about each other until they converge to an equilibrium. According to this approach, the players use their common knowledge of the game's payoff structure and their Bayesian rationality to modify their beliefs, quantified as subjective probability distributions, recursively with a common inductive rule. This process of *inductive rational deliberation* enables players to reach an equilibrium from a state of initial indecision by updating their beliefs according to an inductive learning rule. It also turns out that under certain interpretations of this *inductive dynamics*, players can converge to an equilibrium even if they initially have no common knowledge.

Throughout this chapter, I will continue to interpret all of the probabilities associated with players' strategies as subjective probabilities that players have for their opponents' actions, rather than as explicitly mixed strategies. In particular, I will continue to interpret the various equilibrium concepts as equilibrium-in-beliefs concepts. So far as I can see, the arguments of §1.6 and §2.3 favoring the "subjectivist" interpretation of mixed strategies for players in a "static" setting, where they will play their respective strategies given their beliefs, apply equally well to players who are updating their beliefs *dynamically* before play.

§3.1   The Dirichlet Rule

In most game-theoretic models, the players are assumed to be Bayesian rational. As discussed in Chapter 2, to be Bayesian rational is to choose an act that maximizes expected utility, given what one knows. However, players who maximize their expected utility naively can fail to play an equilibrium. To see this, suppose that Amie and Kay are going to play a Battle of the Sexes game with the payoff structure defined by Figure 3.1.1 as naive Bayesian expected utility maximizers.

Kay

		A_1	A_2
Amie	A_1	$(2,1)$	$(0,0)$
	A_2	$(0,0)$	$(1,2)$

Figure 3.1.1. Battle of the Sexes

Suppose further that each player believes that each of her opponent's alternative strategies is equally likely. Such beliefs are plausible, considering that every strategy profile of Battle of the Sexes is rationalizable. If each player chooses from her alternative acts simply by naively applying the Bayesian *maximize-expected-utility-principle*, or *MEU-principle*, then Amie will reason that choosing A_1 yields her an expected utility of $\frac{1}{2} \cdot 2 + \frac{1}{2} \cdot 0 = 1$ while choosing A_2 yields her an expected utility of only $\frac{1}{2} \cdot 0 + \frac{1}{2} \cdot 1 = \frac{1}{2}$, so she will choose A_1. Likewise, Kay will reason that choosing A_1 yields her an expected utility of $\frac{1}{2} \cdot 1 + \frac{1}{2} \cdot 0 = \frac{1}{2}$ and that choosing A_2 yields her an expected utility of $\frac{1}{2} \cdot 0 + \frac{1}{2} \cdot 2 = 1$, so she will choose A_2. However, the players' joint action, (A_1, A_2) is not an equilibrium. Moreover, (A_1, A_2) yields the payoff vector $(0,0)$, so paradoxically by applying the *MEU*-principle each player receives the worst possible payoff.

In this scenario, each player receives the most undesirable payoff because she applies the *MEU*-principle without taking into account the deliberations of her opponent. Suppose we modify the situation by introducing a "proto-common knowledge" assumption and having the players act accordingly: Both players are expected utility maximizers, and each player knows that her opponent is also an expected utility maximizer. In order to maximize expected utility, each player will want to take into account the deliberations of the other player as well as her own. So, beginning once more with Battle of the Sexes where each player believes that her opponents' alternative choices are equiprobable, Amie reasons that Kay will prefer A_2 and Kay reasons that Amie will prefer A_1. To maximize their respective expected utilities, Amie will now choose A_2 and Kay will now choose A_1. This joint act, (A_2, A_1), also yields the payoff vector $(0, 0)$, so again the two players could not have done worse.

Suppose we extend the situation further by assuming that the players have common knowledge of the following:

(C1) Each player knows the payoff structure of the game Γ,

(C2) Each player is Bayesian rational, and

(C3) Each player knows the beliefs of her opponents, as well as her own beliefs.

These are the same common knowledge assumptions that underpin the Nash equilibrium concept, although in this example Kay and Amie are not initially at a Nash equilibrium. Indeed, from the results of Chapter 2 we know that for Amie's and Kay's beliefs to remain out of equilibrium is incompatible with their common knowledge. They must modify their beliefs about each other somehow. Given these common knowledge assumptions, Amie realizes that, taking her use of the *MEU*-principle into account as well as Kay's own use of the *MEU*-principle, Kay will opt for A_1, so Amie will want to choose A_1. Similarly, Kay realizes that Amie will incorporate her use of the *MEU*-principle into her reasoning and choose A_2, so Kay will want to choose A_2. The players are back to the undesirable joint action (A_1, A_2) they arrived at by not taking their opponents' calculations into account at all.

Yet the story does not end here. For by their common knowledge of (C1)–(C3), each player simulates her opponent's reasoning as described in the previous paragraph and realizes that a third round of deliberation brings them to the joint action (A_2, A_1). But the players run through the deliberative process again, going to (A_1, A_2) once more, and then deliberate again, going to (A_2, A_1), and so on. Simply having the players incorporate the common knowledge assumptions (C1)–(C3) into their reasoning does not help them, for under this framework they are caught in a never-ending cycle of deliberations that oscillate between the two worst possible outcomes.

As Skyrms (1990) points out, players who naively apply their common knowledge that all players are expected utility maximizers will be subject to such pathological cycles of deliberation because such players are insufficiently cautious. Naive Bayesian deliberators assume that each round of deliberation results in everyone choosing the act that maximizes her own expected utility with probability one. However, Skyrms (1990) argues that an agent would act incoherently by simply choosing the act that maximizes expected utility at any round of deliberation if he knows that he is one of a group of common knowledge deliberators and that there is any positive probability that the process of deliberation will ultimately lead to his choosing an alternative act.[1] Hence in this Battle of the Sexes game, both players would be acting incoherently by simply choosing with certainty the alternative that maximizes expected utility at the nth round of deliberation, since both know that the next round of deliberation would carry each of them to the other alternative.

One way for players to break out of such cycles is for them to modify their probabilities for their opponent's acts according to an *inductive rule*. Players who are inductive deliberators will construct predictions of which acts their opponents will choose during a round of deliberation, and raise their probabilities for chosen acts and lower the probabilities for the acts not chosen at this round. Inductive deliberators might update their probabilities for their opponents' acts according to the *Dirichlet rule*. A Dirichlet deliberator k updates his probability distribution $\mu_k^n(\cdot)$ according the following formula: If one of m possible outcomes $A_1, \ldots, A_m$ can occur in each of n trials, and n_{A_i} is the number of times that A_i occurs in the n trials, then

$$(3.i) \qquad\qquad \mu_k^n(A_i) = \frac{n_{A_i} + \gamma_{A_i}}{n + \sum_j \gamma_{A_j}},$$

where $\gamma_{A_j} \geq 0$, $1 \leq j \leq m$ and $\sum_j \gamma_{A_j} > 0$. The value chosen for γ_{A_i} reflects the strength of k's initial conviction that A_i will occur in any given trial. Before any trials have occurred, that is, when $n = 0$, the quotient $\gamma_{A_i} / \sum \gamma_{A_j}$ determines one's *prior probability* that A_i occurs. The requirement that the sum $\sum \gamma_{A_j}$ be positive entails that at least one of the γ_{A_j}'s chosen must be greater than zero. Since one of the events $A_1, \ldots, A_m$ must occur, one's probabilities that A_i occurs cannot all be zero on pain of incoherence. Inductive deliberators who use the Dirichlet rule can control the effect of initial trials by increasing the magnitude of the γ_{A_j}'s. Since the values for the γ_{A_j}'s can be unequal, the Dirichlet rule also allows for one to have unequal prior probabilities for the given events $A_1, \ldots, A_m$. Note that if one sets $\lambda_k = \sum \gamma_{A_j}$ and denotes the prior probability distribution by $\mu_k^0(\cdot)$, then one can give an alternate formulation of

---

[1] The details of this argument are very complicated, but the leading idea is straightforward. If at any round of deliberation an agent concentrates all his probability on an act A_j, that is, $\mu_k(A_j) = 1$, then he leaves himself open to an unconditional *Dutch Book*, that is, a gamble in which he is bound to lose no matter what the outcome, unless A_j is the act that maximizes his expected utility at the end of deliberation. See Skyrms (1990), Chapter 5, especially pp. 123–124.

the Dirichlet rule:

$$(3.ii) \qquad \mu_k^n(A_i) = \frac{n_{A_i} + \lambda_k \mu_k^0(A_i)}{n + \lambda_k}.$$

The version of the Dirichlet rule given in ($3.ii$) highlights the fact that at the nth stage of the updating process, one's Dirichlet probability that A_i will occur is a *mixture* of one's prior probability and the relative frequency of A_i during the first n trials.[2] The Dirichlet rule is called *inductive* because it is an instance of the rule for inductive logic proposed by Carnap (1980). This method of updating probabilities generalizes the *method of fictitious play* introduced by Brown (1951) as a means of computing mixed Nash equilibria. In the present context, the players use the inductive rule to *learn* which strategy they ought to play given what their opponents play.

As indicated above, the cycles of inductive deliberation may be considered a sequence of *fictitious plays* of the game at hand, in which each player mentally simulates the choices everyone would make in successive rounds of the game and updates her probabilities for her opponent's choices according to the inductive rule. This is the way in which Brown (1951) interpreted inductive dynamics. To illustrate the fictitious play interpretation of the dynamics, let us return to the Battle of the Sexes example. Suppose that Kay and Amie are inductive Dirichlet deliberators who are not settled upon an equilibrium to begin with, but who do have common knowledge of (C1)–(C3). Suppose further that $\gamma_{jA_i} = 10$, $1 \leq i, j \leq 2$. Then Amie is updating her probabilities that Kay chooses A_1 or A_2, and she updates these probabilities according to the formulae

$$\mu_1^n(\text{Kay chooses } A_1) = \frac{n_{A_1} + 10}{n + 20}$$

and

$$\mu_1^n(\text{Kay chooses } A_2) = \frac{n_{A_2} + 10}{n + 20},$$

where $\mu_1^n(\cdot)$ is Amie's subjective probability measure, n_{A_1} is the number of times Kay chooses A_1, and n_{A_2} is the number of times Kay chooses A_2 in n simulated plays determined by the n rounds of deliberation. Kay updates her probabilities that Amie chooses either A_1 or A_2 according to the formulae

$$\mu_2^n(\text{Amie chooses } A_1) = \frac{n_{A_1} + 10}{n + 20}$$

---

[2] Formulations ($3.i$) and ($3.ii$) of the Dirichlet rule are of course logically equivalent, but at times one version is notationally more convenient than the other. I will switch between the two versions of the Dirichlet rule somewhat freely in this chapter, depending which version I think makes the exposition easier to follow.

and

$$\mu_2^n(\text{Amie chooses } A_2) = \frac{n_{A_2} + 10}{n + 20},$$

where $\mu_2^n(\cdot)$, n_{A_1}, and n_{A_2} are defined for Kay as they are for Amie *mutatis mutandis*. Initially

$$\mu_1^0(\text{Kay chooses } A_1) = \frac{10}{20} = \frac{1}{2}$$

$$\mu_1^0(\text{Kay chooses } A_2) = \frac{10}{20} = \frac{1}{2}$$

and

$$\mu_2^0(\text{Amie chooses } A_1) = \frac{10}{20} = \frac{1}{2}$$

$$\mu_2^0(\text{Amie chooses } A_2) = \frac{10}{20} = \frac{1}{2},$$

that is, their priors over the opponent's actions are uniform. Since they have common knowledge that both are Bayesian rational, each can compute the expected utilities of her opponent as well as her own expected utilities:

$$E_1^0(u_1(A_1)) = 2 \cdot \frac{1}{2} + 0 \cdot \frac{1}{2} = 1$$

$$E_1^0(u_1(A_2)) = 0 \cdot \frac{1}{2} + 1 \cdot \frac{1}{2} = \frac{1}{2}$$

$$E_2^0(u_2(A_1)) = 1 \cdot \frac{1}{2} + 0 \cdot \frac{1}{2} = \frac{1}{2}$$

$$E_2^0(u_2(A_2)) = 0 \cdot \frac{1}{2} + 2 \cdot \frac{1}{2} = 1$$

Since $E_1^0(u_1(A_1)) > E_1^0(u_1(A_2))$ and $E_2^0(u_2(A_2)) > E_2^0(u_2(A_1))$, Kay will reason that Amie would choose A_1 on the first round of play, and Amie will reason that Kay would choose A_2 on the first round. Hence after one round of deliberation Amie updates her probabilities for Kay's alternative strategies by applying the Dirichlet rule:

$$\mu_1^1(\text{Kay chooses } A_1) = \frac{0 + 10}{1 + 20} = \frac{10}{21}$$

$$\mu_1^1(\text{Kay chooses } A_2) = \frac{1 + 10}{1 + 20} = \frac{11}{21}$$

and Kay updates her probabilities for Amie's alternative strategies as follows:

$$\mu_2^1(\text{Amie chooses } A_1) = \frac{1 + 10}{1 + 20} = \frac{11}{21}$$

$$\mu_2^1(\text{Amie chooses } A_2) = \frac{0 + 10}{1 + 20} = \frac{10}{21}.$$

At the next round of deliberation, Kay and Amie recalculate expected utilities given the *updated* probability distributions:

$$E_1^1(u_1(A_1)) = 2 \cdot \frac{10}{21} + 0 \cdot \frac{11}{21} = \frac{20}{21}$$

$$E_1^1(u_1(A_2)) = 0 \cdot \frac{10}{21} + 1 \cdot \frac{11}{21} = \frac{11}{21}$$

$$E_2^1(u_2(A_1)) = 1 \cdot \frac{11}{21} + 0 \cdot \frac{10}{21} = \frac{11}{21}$$

$$E_2^1(u_2(A_2)) = 0 \cdot \frac{11}{21} + 2 \cdot \frac{10}{21} = \frac{20}{21}$$

Given the expected utilities defined by these distributions, Kay would maximize her expected utility by choosing A_2 once more and Amie would maximize her expected utility by choosing A_1 once more. Since the players both know this, they update their probabilities accordingly, so that after the second round of deliberation

$$\mu_1^2(\text{Kay chooses } A_1) = \frac{0 + 10}{2 + 20} = \frac{5}{11}$$

$$\mu_1^2(\text{Kay chooses } A_2) = \frac{2 + 10}{2 + 20} = \frac{6}{11}$$

and

$$\mu_2^2(\text{Amie chooses } A_1) = \frac{2 + 10}{2 + 20} = \frac{6}{11}$$

$$\mu_2^2(\text{Amie chooses } A_2) = \frac{0 + 10}{2 + 20} = \frac{5}{11}.$$

Continuing in this fashion, Amie's probability that Kay will choose A_2 will ultimately converge to $\frac{2}{3}$ and Kay's probability that Amie will choose A_2 will converge to $\frac{1}{3}$.

One can interpret the inductive deliberation of these two players geometrically. The deliberation space may be modeled as the unit square, with the horizontal axis representing Amie's possible probabilities and the vertical axis representing Kay's possible probabilities. The players' deliberation generates an orbit of beliefs about their opponents, which converges to the mixed equilibrium point $(\frac{2}{3}, \frac{1}{3})$ shown in Figure 3.1.2.

The sequence $(\boldsymbol{\mu}^m) = (\mu_1^m, \mu_2^m)$ determined by the successive applications of the Dirichlet rule forms a *dynamical system*, and consequently one may refer to Dirichlet deliberation as *Dirichlet dynamics*. A *deliberational equilibrium* of a game is a fixed point of this dynamical process. Note that the deliberational

Figure 3.1.2

Convergence to Mixed Equilibrium-in-Beliefs
in
Battle of the Sexes

Dirichlet Deliberators converge to the mixed Nash equilibrium-in-beliefs in Battle of the Sexes. $\mu_1^n(\cdot)$ is Amie's probability distribution at the nth round of deliberation, and $\mu_2^n(\cdot)$ is Kay's probability distribution at the nth round of deliberation. $(p^*, q^*) = (\frac{2}{3}, \frac{1}{3})$ is the mixed equilibrium-in-beliefs.

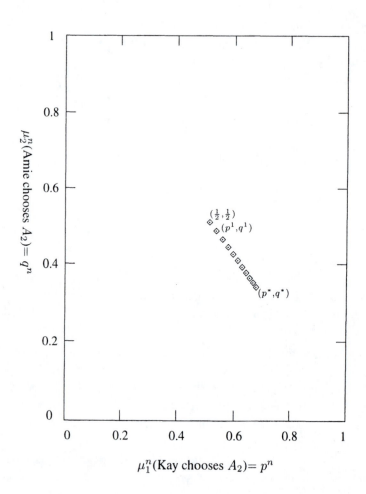

equilibrium $(\frac{2}{3}, \frac{1}{3})$ in this example is precisely the mixed Nash equilibrium-in-beliefs for this game.

One may also interpret inductive deliberation as a sequence of *actual plays* by naive Bayesians, who always play strategies that maximize expected utility given their beliefs at the moment, but who do learn from experience.[3] Such an actual play interpretation of the dynamics yields a natural explanation for how actual repeated games can lead to an equilibrium-in-beliefs. For instance, suppose that Amie and Kay are to play Battle of the Sexes every day, without knowing anything about the opponent other than what the opponent plays each day. If both are naive expected utility maximizers who update their personal probabilities according to the Dirichlet rule with $\gamma_{A_i} = 10$, then initially

$$\mu_1^0(\text{Kay chooses } A_2) = \frac{1}{2}$$

and

$$\mu_2^0(\text{Amie chooses } A_2) = \frac{1}{2}.$$

Since Amie and Kay both follow the *MEU*-principle, Amie chooses A_1 and Kay chooses A_2 on the first day. Hence after one round of play Amie updates her probability that Kay chooses A_2 to

$$\mu_1^1(\text{Kay chooses } A_2) = \frac{1 + 10}{1 + 20} = \frac{11}{21}$$

and Kay updates her probability that Amie chooses A_2 to

$$\mu_2^1(\text{Amie chooses } A_2) = \frac{10}{1 + 20} = \frac{10}{21}.$$

The next day they repeat the game, and Kay maximizes her expected utility by choosing A_2 once more and Amie maximizes her expected utility by choosing A_1 once more. The players update their probabilities accordingly, so that

$$\mu_1^2(\text{Kay chooses } A_2) = \frac{12}{22}$$

and

$$\mu_2^2(\text{Amie chooses } A_2) = \frac{10}{22}.$$

---

[3] Since these kind of Bayesians modify their beliefs regarding each other systematically by applying inductive logic (in this case, the Dirichlet rule), they are in one respect less naive than the sort of deliberators described above whose beliefs regarding each other are degenerate probability distributions, which assign probability one to a different pure strategy at every round of deliberation.

Continuing in this fashion, Amie's probability that Kay will choose A_2 will ultimately converge to $\frac{2}{3}$ and Kay's probability that Amie will choose A_2 will converge to $\frac{1}{3}$. The sequence of updated probabilities of these naive expected utility maximizers can be mapped onto the unit square, and it coincides exactly with the orbit of probabilities achieved by two rational deliberators using the same updating rule who simulate their opponents' reasoning in successive rounds of fictitious play. This sequence of actual plays generates an inductive dynamical orbit that converges to the Nash equilibrium-in-beliefs, as in fictitious play, but the deliberators in this story will not know that they have converged to equilibrium, since they do not even know each others' payoffs.

There is a third way to interpret the Dirichlet dynamics as a sequence of plays by representatives of populations. In this scenario, the "players" are entire populations, and at each round of deliberation, one member of each population is selected to represent her population. The representatives of the various populations play a single round of the game, each choosing a strategy that maximizes expected utility given the representative's current beliefs regarding what the other representatives will do, which are defined by applying the Dirichlet rule to the past history of play. After playing their round, the representatives drop out and new representatives are selected, who will repeat the process given newly updated beliefs. One might think of the representative interpretation as a "quasi-evolutionary" interpretation, since typically in evolutionary game theory, the players are individuals who are chosen at random from a population and who drop out after a single round of play. However, in evolutionary game theory, the players are usually modeled as *replicators* who are not sophisticated enough to learn inductively.[4] To illustrate the representative interpretation of Dirichlet dynamics, let us consider a variation of the Battle of the Sexes example, in which the "players" are two distinct populations, the *Tories* and the *Whigs*, as illustrated in Figure 3.1.3.

Whigs

		A_1	A_2
Tories	A_1	(2, 1)	(0, 0)
	A_2	(0, 0)	(1, 2)

Figure 3.1.3. Two Populations Matched in Battle of the Sexes

---

[4] See the classic treatment of evolutionary game theory by Maynard Smith (1982).

At the start of deliberation, the Whigs and the Tories both have a prior uniform distribution over the members of the opposing population defined by $\gamma_{A_i} = 10$, but they do not know the beliefs of the members of the opposing population or even what their opponent's payoffs are. At the first round of deliberation, a Tory and a Whig are selected. Their distributions are defined by

$$\mu_1^0(\text{a Whig chooses } A_2) = \frac{1}{2}$$

and

$$\mu_2^0(\text{a Tory chooses } A_2) = \frac{1}{2}.$$

Both representatives choose the strategy that maximizes expected utility, so the Tory chooses A_1 and the Whig chooses A_2. These representatives now both yield to new representatives, who will play the second round of deliberation. The second Tory updates her probability that a Whig will choose A_2 to

$$\mu_1^1(\text{a Whig chooses } A_2) = \frac{1 + 10}{1 + 20} = \frac{11}{21}$$

and the second Whig updates her probability that a Tory chooses A_2 to

$$\mu_2^1(\text{a Tory chooses } A_2) = \frac{10}{1 + 20} = \frac{10}{21}.$$

So at the second round the Whig maximizes her expected utility by choosing A_2 and the second Tory maximizes her expected utility by choosing A_1. They now yield in favor of a third pair of representatives, who update their probabilities accordingly, so that

$$\mu_1^2(\text{a Whig chooses } A_2) = \frac{12}{22}$$

and

$$\mu_2^2(\text{a Tory chooses } A_2) = \frac{10}{22}.$$

Continuing in this fashion, the Tory representative's probability that a Whig chooses A_2 converges to $\frac{2}{3}$ and the Whig representative's probability that a Tory chooses A_2 converges to $\frac{1}{3}$. This sequence of updated probabilities coincides exactly with the orbits of probabilities generated by fictitious players and actual players who have the same parameters defining the prior distributions. The representatives in this story will not know that they have converged to equilibrium, since neither representative knows the payoffs of the other representative.

In summary, one can interpret the Dirichlet dynamics in at least three different ways, which have different underlying common knowledge assumptions:

(1) *Fictitious Play Interpretation:* The players mentally simulate a sequence of successive plays by computing one another's expected utilities at each stage of deliberation, noting which strategy maximizes expected utility for each player, and updating probabilities according to the Dirichlet by increasing the probability of the strategy combination the opponents would have played at that stage of deliberation. This interpretation requires the deliberators to have common knowledge of (C1)–(C3), so that they can simulate one another's expected utility calculations.

(2) *Actual Play Interpretation:* The players actually play the game repeatedly, and update probabilities as functions of the frequencies of strategy combinations they observe. Each player chooses a strategy that maximizes expected utility at each round of deliberation, and updates his probabilities by observing which strategy combination his opponents play. In the actual play interpretation, a deliberator need only know the payoff structure of the game, or even just his own payoffs, the parameters that define his priors, and the frequencies of strategy combinations the opponents played in past rounds of deliberation. One crucial difference between the fictitious play and actual play interpretations of inductive Dirichlet dynamics is that in fictitious play, the deliberators will always know when they are at equilibrium, while in actual play, the deliberators can converge to an equilibrium without realizing it, since they do not even necessarily know the payoffs of the other players.

(3) *Representative Interpretation:* The n players at each stage of deliberation are representatives of n distinct populations. At each stage of deliberation, one member from each population is selected at random to play a round of the game. Each representative plays the strategy that maximizes expected utility given what the representatives in past plays have done, where probabilities for the current round are determined by the Dirichlet rule. In this interpretation, the representatives do not need to know anything about representatives from opposing populations other than the strategies they play, but all of the members of a particular population must have the same prior, and each representative must have full knowledge of the history of past plays. After playing a round of the game, each representative drops out, though the representative might be selected again at some point in the future. Again, the system might converge to equilibrium without any of the representatives realizing this.

§3.2 Inductive Deliberation with Endogenous Correlation

The deliberational dynamics account of equilibrium selection illustrated above with a 2-player game extends naturally to n-player games. Beginning at an initial state of indecision, n rational deliberators using an appropriate inductive rule, such as the Dirichlet rule, can converge to a Nash equilibrium. However, the transition from 2-player games to games having three or more players introduces an extra complication into the deliberational dynamics model. When a player has more than one opponent, he must decide whether or not to regard the strategies his opponents choose as stochastically independent events. If the players do not assume that their opponents' strategies are probabilistically independent, then inductive deliberation can carry the players to an endogenous correlated equilibrium-in-beliefs. Indeed, even if the rational deliberators have priors that satisfy probabilistic independence, *the process of deliberation can itself generate correlation in beliefs*. This phenomenon can culminate with the players converging to a correlated equilibrium.

To illustrate, let us consider how inductive deliberators would deal with the game defined by the payoff matrices in Figure 3.2.1, where Player 1 (Ron) chooses the row, Player 2 (Peter) chooses the column, and Player 3 (Paul) chooses the matrix:

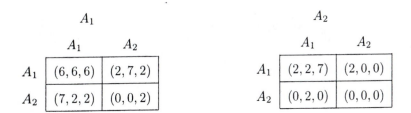

	A_1	A_2
A_1	$(6,6,6)$	$(2,7,2)$
A_2	$(7,2,2)$	$(0,0,2)$

A_1

	A_1	A_2
A_1	$(2,2,7)$	$(2,0,0)$
A_2	$(0,2,0)$	$(0,0,0)$

A_2

Figure 3.2.1. 3-Player Chicken

This is a 3-player version of "Chicken." Each player has an incentive to choose A_2 if the others both choose A_1. On the other hand, if a given player plays A_2 and either of the other players decides (or both of them decide) to play A_2, then he ends up with 0, the worst possible payoff. This particular Chicken game has three pure-strategy Nash equilibria, namely (A_1, A_1, A_2), (A_1, A_2, A_1), and (A_2, A_1, A_1), and a completely mixed Nash equilibrium where each player believes that

$$\mu_k(\text{opponent 1 plays } A_1) = \mu_k(\text{opponent 2 plays } A_1) = \sqrt{\frac{2}{3}},$$

and which yields the payoff vector $(4\frac{2}{3}, 4\frac{2}{3}, 4\frac{2}{3})$.

Now suppose that the three players are Dirichlet deliberators. As in the 2-player case, each player begins once more at an initial state of uncertainty over what his two opponents will do, and then updates his probabilities at each round of deliberation. Each player now has two opponents to worry about, and finds that he has to answer a question he would not have to consider had he only one opponent. Should he assume that the acts of his two opponents are probabilistically independent, or should he allow for the possibility that his opponents' acts might be correlated? If the opponents' moves are probabilistically independent, then an inductive deliberator can update his probabilities for each of his opponent's acts separately, and then determine the probability of each combination of his opponents' moves by taking the product of the probabilities of their individual moves. For instance, in order for Ron to calculate the expected utilities of his alternative strategies, he needs to use his probabilities for the four strategy combinations

$$
\begin{aligned}
A_{11} &= \text{(Peter plays } A_1, \text{ Paul plays } A_1), \\
A_{12} &= \text{(Peter plays } A_1, \text{ Paul plays } A_2), \\
A_{21} &= \text{(Peter plays } A_2, \text{ Paul plays } A_1), \text{ and} \\
A_{22} &= \text{(Peter plays } A_2, \text{ Paul plays } A_2).
\end{aligned}
$$

If Ron has initial probabilities $\mu_1^0(\text{Peter plays } A_2) = \frac{1}{3}$ and $\mu_1^0(\text{Paul plays } A_1) = \frac{1}{3}$, and assumes that his opponents' moves are probabilistically independent, then he can compute

$$\mu_1^0(A_{21}) = \mu_1^0(\text{Peter plays } A_2) \cdot \mu_1^0(\text{Paul plays } A_1) = \frac{1}{3} \cdot \frac{1}{3} = \frac{1}{9}.$$

On the other hand, if Ron does not assume probabilistic independence, then he cannot determine the probability of the act combination A_{21} simply by multiplying the probabilities of each opponent's individual acts. If Ron admits the possibility that the strategies Peter and Paul choose might be correlated, then he will need to compute the probabilities of each of the four possible strategy combinations Peter and Paul might play and update each probability separately. For instance, in the fictitious play framework when Ron updates his probability for the combination A_{21} at the $n+1$st round of deliberation, he must simulate his opponents' calculations of expected utility and consider A_{21} to have occurred if and only if *both* Peter's expected utility of playing A_2 strictly exceeds his expected utility of playing A_1 and Paul's expected utility of playing A_1 strictly exceeds his expected utility of playing A_2. In other words, given that Peter's and Paul's strategies might be correlated, Ron will update his probabilities for Peter's and Paul's strategy *combinations* according to the Dirichlet rule:

$$\mu_1^n(A_{ij}) = \frac{n_{A_{ij}} + \gamma_{A_{ij}}}{n + \sum \gamma_{A_{ij}}}$$

where $n_{A_{ij}}$ is the number of times during the first n trials that $E_2^m(u_2(A_i)) > E_2^m(u_2(A_j))$ and $E_3^m(u_3(A_j)) > E_3^n(u_3(A_i))$ have held together. At the $n+1$st round of deliberation, Ron determines that

$$\mu_1^{n+1}(A_{21}) = \frac{n_{A_{21}} + 1 + \gamma_{A_{21}}}{n + 1 + \sum \gamma_{A_{ij}}}$$

if both $E_2^{n+1}(u_2(A_2)) > E_2^{n+1}(u_2(A_1))$ *and* $E_3^{n+1}(u_3(A_1)) > E_3^{n+1}(u_3(A_2))$.

Most of the literature on fictitious play has the players assuming probabilistic independence for mathematical convenience. This assumption implies that a limit of the fictitious play process will be a Nash equilibrium. Inductive deliberational dynamics which allow for the possibility of correlated strategies (hereafter referred to as *correlation-dynamics*) can converge to correlated equilibria that cannot be reached by an inductive dynamics that assumes probabilistic independence (hereafter referred to as *independence-dynamics*). In particular, by applying correlation-dynamics, rational deliberators find that they can converge to correlated equilibria that are not Nash equilibria.

Returning to 3-player Chicken, if the players are dynamic independence-deliberators, then a player may model his belief space that one of his opponents plays A_2 as a unit interval, in which the numbers from 0 to 1 inclusive represent his possible probabilities that the opponent plays A_2. Since the player is an independence deliberator, his probability measure for the joint action of his two opponents is the product measure of his probability measures over each of his opponent's acts, and his belief space may be modeled by the unit square, where the point $(1, 1)$ represents his belief that both opponents play A_2 with probability one. If each player begins his deliberations with a uniform prior distribution over his opponents' strategies, then the deliberation of each player traces an orbit in the unit square, as shown in Figure 3.2.2. Starting from uniform priors, the players' probability distributions converge to the mixed Nash equilibrium-in-beliefs.

If the three players now turn to playing Chicken as correlation-deliberators with uniform priors, then they will converge to a correlated equilibrium that

Figure 3.2.2

Orbit of Independence-Deliberation in 3-Player Chicken

Player 1 (Ron) converges to his end of the mixed Nash equilibrium in belief in 3-player Chicken as a Dirichlet independence-deliberator. $\mu_1^n(\cdot)$ is Ron's probability distribution at the nth round of deliberation. $(p^*, q^*) = (1 - \sqrt{\frac{2}{3}}, 1 - \sqrt{\frac{2}{3}})$ is Ron's end of the mixed equilibrium-in-beliefs.

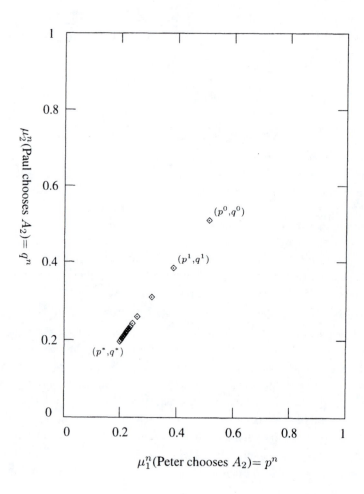

does not correspond to any of the Nash equilibria. Now each player must update separately the probabilities of the act combinations

$$
\begin{aligned}
A_{11} &= \text{(opponent 1 plays } A_1, \text{ opponent 2 plays } A_1), \\
A_{12} &= \text{(opponent 1 plays } A_1, \text{ opponent 2 plays } A_2), \\
A_{21} &= \text{(opponent 1 plays } A_2, \text{ opponent 2 plays } A_1), \text{ and} \\
A_{22} &= \text{(opponent 2 plays } A_2, \text{ opponent 2 plays } A_2).
\end{aligned}
$$

His belief space may be modeled as a tetrahedron, with vertices corresponding to A_{11}, A_{12}, A_{21}, and A_{22}.

Suppose that the three players begin with uniform prior probabilities for their opponents' act combinations defined by $\gamma_{A_{ij}} = \frac{1}{4}$ for $1 \leq k \leq 3, 1 \leq i, j \leq 2$, that is, at the beginning of deliberation $\mu_k^0(A_{ij}) = \frac{1}{4}$, and in the mixture version (3.*ii*) of the Dirichlet rule, $\lambda_k = 1$, $1 \leq k \leq 3$. Then at the first round of deliberation, Player 1 calculates the expected utilities for his opponents' alternative strategies as follows:

$$
\begin{aligned}
E_2^0(u_2(A_1)) &= \frac{1}{4} \cdot 6 + \frac{1}{4} \cdot 2 + \frac{1}{4} \cdot 2 + \frac{1}{4} \cdot 2 = 3, \\
E_2^0(u_2(A_2)) &= \frac{1}{4} \cdot 7 + \frac{1}{4} \cdot 0 + \frac{1}{4} \cdot 0 + \frac{1}{4} \cdot 0 = 1\frac{3}{4}, \\
E_3^0(u_3(A_1)) &= \frac{1}{4} \cdot 6 + \frac{1}{4} \cdot 2 + \frac{1}{4} \cdot 2 + \frac{1}{4} \cdot 2 = 3, \\
E_3^0(u_3(A_2)) &= \frac{1}{4} \cdot 7 + \frac{1}{4} \cdot 0 + \frac{1}{4} \cdot 0 + \frac{1}{4} \cdot 0 = 1\frac{3}{4}.
\end{aligned}
$$

Since *both* of Player 1's opponents would maximize expected utility by playing A_1 given their priors, Player 1 concludes that the opponents would play the strategy combination A_{11}, since he knows that both opponents are Bayesian rational. Player 1 updates his probabilities with the Dirichlet rule accordingly:

$$
\begin{aligned}
\mu_1^1(A_{11}) &= \frac{1}{1+1} \cdot \frac{1}{1} + \frac{1}{1+1} \cdot \frac{1}{4} = \frac{5}{8}, \\
\mu_1^1(A_{12}) &= \frac{1}{1+1} \cdot \frac{0}{1} + \frac{1}{1+1} \cdot \frac{1}{4} = \frac{1}{8}, \\
\mu_1^1(A_{21}) &= \frac{1}{1+1} \cdot \frac{0}{1} + \frac{1}{1+1} \cdot \frac{1}{4} = \frac{1}{8}, \\
\mu_1^1(A_{22}) &= \frac{1}{1+1} \cdot \frac{0}{1} + \frac{1}{1+1} \cdot \frac{1}{4} = \frac{1}{8}.
\end{aligned}
$$

Since this game has a symmetric payoff structure, and since each player has a uniform prior over her opponents' strategy combinations, Players 2 and 3 update their probabilities at the first stage of deliberation using calculations similar to Player 1's. At the end of the first round of deliberation, the players have the updated beliefs:

$$\mu_k^1(A_{11}) = \frac{5}{8}, \qquad\qquad \mu_k^1(A_{12}) = \frac{1}{8},$$

$$\mu_k^1(A_{21}) = \frac{1}{8}, \qquad\qquad \mu_k^1(A_{22}) = \frac{1}{8}, \ 1 \le k \le 3.$$

Note that since Bayesian rationality and the priors are common knowledge, each player knows what her opponents' updated probabilities are, as well as her own probabilities.

At the second round of deliberation, each player repeats the updating process using the updated probabilities calculated during the first round of deliberation. Player 1 computes the expected utilities of his opponents once more:

$$
\begin{aligned}
E_2^1(u_2(A_1)) &= \frac{5}{8} \cdot 6 + \frac{1}{8} \cdot 2 + \frac{1}{8} \cdot 2 + \frac{1}{8} \cdot 2 = 4\frac{1}{2}, \\
E_2^1(u_2(A_2)) &= \frac{5}{8} \cdot 7 + \frac{1}{8} \cdot 0 + \frac{1}{8} \cdot 0 + \frac{1}{8} \cdot 0 = 4\frac{3}{8}, \\
E_3^1(u_3(A_1)) &= \frac{5}{8} \cdot 6 + \frac{1}{8} \cdot 2 + \frac{1}{8} \cdot 2 + \frac{1}{8} \cdot 2 = 4\frac{1}{2}, \\
E_3^1(u_3(A_2)) &= \frac{5}{8} \cdot 7 + \frac{1}{8} \cdot 0 + \frac{1}{8} \cdot 0 + \frac{1}{8} \cdot 0 = 4\frac{3}{8}.
\end{aligned}
$$

Once again, Player 1 determines that both of his opponents would play A_1 given these beliefs, so Player 1 updates his probabilities with the Dirichlet rule accordingly:

$$
\begin{aligned}
\mu_1^2(A_{11}) &= \frac{2}{2+1} \cdot \frac{2}{2} + \frac{1}{2+1} \cdot \frac{1}{4} = \frac{3}{4}, \\
\mu_1^2(A_{12}) &= \frac{2}{2+1} \cdot \frac{0}{2} + \frac{1}{2+1} \cdot \frac{1}{4} = \frac{1}{12}, \\
\mu_1^2(A_{21}) &= \frac{2}{2+1} \cdot \frac{0}{2} + \frac{1}{2+1} \cdot \frac{1}{4} = \frac{1}{12}, \\
\mu_1^2(A_{22}) &= \frac{2}{2+1} \cdot \frac{0}{2} + \frac{1}{2+1} \cdot \frac{1}{4} = \frac{1}{12}.
\end{aligned}
$$

Again by symmetry Players 2 and 3 update their probabilities similarly, so that at the end of the second round of deliberation, the players have the beliefs:

$$\mu_k^2(A_{11}) = \frac{3}{4}, \qquad\qquad \mu_k^2(A_{12}) = \frac{1}{12},$$

$$\mu_k^2(A_{21}) = \frac{1}{12}, \qquad\qquad \mu_k^2(A_{22}) = \frac{1}{12}, \ 1 \le k \le 3.$$

At the third stage of Dirichlet deliberation, each player calculates utilities and uses the information gained from his calculations to update his probabilities a third time. Once again, Player 1 computes his opponents' expected utilities for their strategy alternatives given the current system of beliefs:

$$E_2^2(u_2(A_1)) = \frac{3}{4} \cdot 6 + \frac{1}{12} \cdot 2 + \frac{1}{12} \cdot 2 + \frac{1}{12} \cdot 2 = 5,$$

$$E_2^2(u_2(A_2)) = \frac{3}{4} \cdot 7 + \frac{1}{12} \cdot 0 + \frac{1}{12} \cdot 0 + \frac{1}{12} \cdot 0 = 5\frac{1}{4},$$

$$E_3^2(u_3(A_1)) = \frac{3}{4} \cdot 6 + \frac{1}{12} \cdot 2 + \frac{1}{12} \cdot 2 + \frac{1}{12} \cdot 2 = 5,$$

$$E_3^2(u_3(A_2)) = \frac{3}{4} \cdot 7 + \frac{1}{12} \cdot 0 + \frac{1}{12} \cdot 0 + \frac{1}{12} \cdot 0 = 5\frac{1}{4}.$$

Note that this time, both of Player 1's opponents maximize expected utility by playing A_2. Player 1, knowing that his opponents are Bayesian rational, concludes that they would play the strategy combination A_{22} given their current beliefs, and updates his probabilities accordingly:

$$\mu_1^3(A_{11}) = \frac{2}{3+1} \cdot \frac{2}{3} + \frac{1}{3+1} \cdot \frac{1}{4} = \frac{9}{16},$$

$$\mu_1^3(A_{12}) = \frac{3}{3+1} \cdot \frac{0}{3} + \frac{1}{3+1} \cdot \frac{1}{4} = \frac{1}{16},$$

$$\mu_1^3(A_{21}) = \frac{3}{3+1} \cdot \frac{0}{3} + \frac{1}{3+1} \cdot \frac{1}{4} = \frac{1}{16},$$

$$\mu_1^3(A_{22}) = \frac{3}{3+1} \cdot \frac{1}{3} + \frac{1}{3+1} \cdot \frac{1}{4} = \frac{5}{16}.$$

By symmetry, at the end of the third round of deliberation, the players' probabilities are:

$$\mu_k^3(A_{11}) = \frac{9}{16}, \qquad \mu_k^3(A_{12}) = \frac{1}{16},$$

$$\mu_k^3(A_{21}) = \frac{1}{16}, \qquad \mu_k^3(A_{22}) = \frac{5}{16}, \ 1 \leq k \leq 3.$$

As the stages of deliberation progress, the players' beliefs converge to the endogenous correlated equilibrium characterized by the distributions

$$\mu_k^*(A_{11}) = \frac{2}{3},$$

$$\mu_k^*(A_{12}) = \mu_k^*(A_{21}) = 0, \text{ and}$$

$$\mu_k^*(A_{22}) = \frac{1}{3}, \ 1 \leq k \leq 3.$$

Figure 3.2.3.

Orbit of Correlation-Deliberation in 3-Player Chicken

Player 1 (Ron) converges from the uniform prior to his end of the endogenous correlated equilibrium distribution

$$\mu_k(A_{11}) = \frac{2}{3}, \ \mu_k(A_{12}) = \mu_k(A_{21}) = 0, \ \mu_k(A_{22}) = \frac{1}{3}, \ k = 1, 2, 3,$$

of 3-player Chicken as a Dirichlet correlation-deliberator.

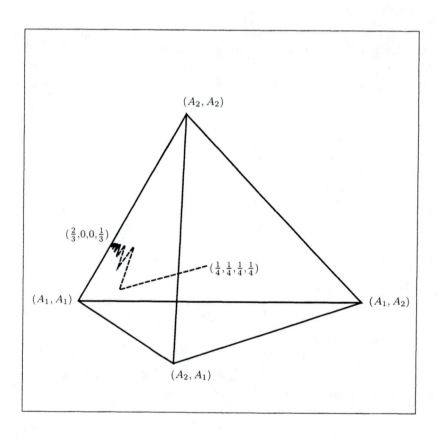

The path of deliberation of one of these players in the tetrahedron representing his belief space is depicted in Figure 3.2.3. A quick calculation of product probabilities shows both that this correlated equilibrium cannot be attained under independence-deliberation and that this equilibrium is not a Nash equilibrium.[5] At these probability distributions, the players are at a mixed equilibrium-in-beliefs, for

$$
\begin{aligned}
E_k(u_k(A_1)) &= 6\mu_k^*(A_{11}) + 2\mu_k^*(A_{12}) + 2\mu_k^*(A_{21}) + 2\mu_k^*(A_{22}) \\
&= 6 \cdot \frac{2}{3} + 2 \cdot \frac{2}{3} = 4\frac{2}{3}
\end{aligned}
$$

and

$$
E_k(u_k(A_2)) = 7\mu_k^*(A_{11}) = 7 \cdot \frac{2}{3} = 4\frac{2}{3}
$$

so that each player maximizes expected utility by choosing either of his pure strategies. This correlated equilibrium happens to yield each player the same expected payoff of $4\frac{2}{3}$ as does the mixed Nash equilibrium. However, this example is surprising because the prior probabilities $\mu_k^0(A_{ij}) = \frac{1}{4}$ satisfy the formula

$$
\mu_k^0(A_{ij}) = \mu_k^0(\text{opponent 1 plays } A_2) \cdot \mu_k^0(\text{opponent 2 plays } A_2),
$$

that is, the initial distributions satisfy probabilistic independence. Hence inductive deliberators can start with probability distributions satisfying probabilistic independence and converge to an equilibrium with correlated probabilities for their opponents' strategies. *Correlation in beliefs emerges spontaneously during the deliberation process.*

Of course, if the players begin with non-uniform prior probabilities for their opponents' act combinations, then they may well arrive at different correlated

---

[5]To see this, we note that in any round of independence deliberation,

(1) $\mu_k^n(A_{12}) = \mu_k^n(\text{opponent 1 plays } A_1) \cdot \mu_k^n(\text{opponent 2 plays } A_2),$

while at this equilibrium

$$
\mu_k^n(\text{opponent 1 plays } A_1) = \mu_k^n(A_{11}) + \mu_k^n(A_{12}) = \frac{2}{3} + 0 = \frac{2}{3}
$$

and

$$
\mu_k^n(\text{opponent 2 plays } A_2) = \mu_k^n(A_{12}) + \mu_k^n(A_{22}) = 0 + \frac{1}{3} = \frac{1}{3},
$$

so that

$$
\mu_k^n(\text{opponent 1 plays } A_1) \cdot \mu_k^n(\text{opponent 2 plays } A_2) = \frac{2}{3} \cdot \frac{1}{3} \neq 0 = \mu_k^n(A_{12}).
$$

Hence at no round of independence-deliberation can the players attain this correlated equilibrium. This argument also shows that the equilibrium is not Nash, for any Nash equilibrium for this game must satisfy (1).

equilibria. For instance, suppose that each player begins deliberations with the prior probability distribution

$$\mu_k^0(A_{11}) = \mu_k^0(A_{22}) = .01, \mu_k^0(A_{12}) = \mu_k^0(A_{21}) = .49$$

determined by $\gamma_{A_{11}} = \gamma_{A_{22}} = 1, \gamma_{A_{12}} = \gamma_{A_{21}} = 49$. Given these values for each γ_{ij}, Dirichlet correlation-deliberation converges to the equilibrium at which

$$\mu_k^*(A_{11}) = \frac{2}{3}, \mu_k^*(A_{12}) = \mu_k^*(A_{21}) = \frac{1}{6}, \mu_k^*(A_{22}) = 0, 1 \le k \le 3,$$

and where each player has an expected payoff of $4\frac{2}{3}$.

As a final example, we consider a variation of 3-player Chicken in which the payoff structure is given in Figure 3.2.4:

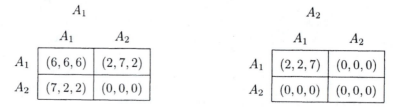

Figure 3.2.4. **Public Good Provision**

In this game, which the reader may recall as the Public Good Provision game of §1.4, the payoffs are symmetric, but now all three players suffer the worst possible outcome if any two of them (or all three) play A_2. This game belongs to a class of games that model social arrangements where a suboptimal equilibrium results when a certain *threshold number* of individuals fail to contribute toward an outcome desirable for all. These social situations can be modeled as n-player games, in which each player may choose either to *cooperate* by contributing toward the mutually beneficial outcome, or to *defect* by not contributing. Such *cooperation games* are characterized by two features: *(a)* every player does better if all cooperate than if all defect, and *(b)* every player has an incentive to defect from the strategy combination of universal cooperation. In most cooperation games, if the number of defectors is less than a certain threshold number, then the players are at an equilibrium at which the cooperators enjoy some benefit of cooperation.[6] When the number of defectors reaches the threshold number, no player

---

[6]The Prisoners' Dilemma is the one cooperation game which has no equilibria at which some players benefit by cooperating. This is because in the Prisoners' Dilemma, defecting is strictly

can gain by cooperating, and the players will then be at equilibrium only if all defect. For instance, in this 3-player variation of Chicken the threshold number is two. If strategy A_1 is interpreted as "cooperate" and strategy A_2 as "defect," then in this game the strategy combination of universal cooperation Pareto-dominates the strategy combination of universal defection, but each player is tempted to defect unilaterally from (A_1, A_1, A_1). Should one player defect and the other two cooperate, then the players are at an equilibrium that is clearly advantageous to the defector, but still better for all players than the equilibrium (A_2, A_2, A_2). If, say, Ron defects unilaterally, then Peter and Paul will cooperate, since cooperation is still beneficial to both of them despite Ron's defection. However, if two players defect, the third player gains nothing from cooperating unilaterally, that is, any benefits of cooperation disappear if the number of defectors in this game is two or higher. If both Peter and Paul defect, then Ron might as well defect, too.

This variation of 3-player Chicken has four pure strategy equilibria, namely (A_1, A_1, A_2), (A_1, A_2, A_1), (A_2, A_1, A_1), and (A_2, A_2, A_2). This game also has the single mixed Nash equilibrium at which each player has probabilities

$$\mu_k^*(\text{opponent 1 plays } A_1) = \mu_k^*(\text{opponent 2 plays } A_1) = \frac{4}{5},$$

and at this equilibrium each player has an expected payoff of $4\frac{12}{25} = 4.48$. Independence-deliberation using the Dirichlet rule with uniform priors for each player will carry the players to the mixed Nash equilibrium. If the players discard the independence assumption, then correlation-deliberation given a variety of choices for the $\gamma_{A_{ij}}$'s may converge to any of the pure strategy equilibria or to the mixed Nash equilibrium. However, suppose that each of the three players begins with $\gamma_{A_{11}} = \gamma_{A_{12}} = \gamma_{A_{21}} = 33$ and $\gamma_{A_{22}} = 1$, that is, he initially believes the cases in which both of his opponents play A_1 or in which only one opponent plays A_2 to be equally likely, but believes it unlikely that both of his opponents will play A_2. Then correlation-deliberation will carry the players to the equilibrium characterized by the probability distribution

$$\mu_k^*(A_{11}) = \frac{2}{3}, \mu_k^*(A_{12}) = \mu_k^*(A_{21}) = \frac{1}{6}, \mu_k^*(A_{22}) = 0, \; k = 1, 2, 3.$$

At this correlated equilibrium, each player's expected payoff is $4\frac{2}{3}$, which is a greater payoff than the payoff he may expect at the mixed Nash equilibrium.

---

dominant for each player, so the only equilibrium is the strategy combination at which each player defects. One might regard the Prisoners' Dilemma as a degenerate cooperation game, in which the threshold number is zero.

Consequently, this example shows that *correlation-deliberation can converge to a correlated equilibrium point that Pareto-dominates the mixed Nash equilibrium reached by independence-deliberation.*

The Formal Model

I now formally define the notions of Dirichlet correlation-deliberation and deliberational correlated equilibrium, and discuss some of their elementary properties. The notations of Chapter 2 remain in force here. In particular, $\Gamma = (N, S, \boldsymbol{u})$ denotes an n-player game in strategic form, and $\mathcal{P}_k(S_{-k})$ denotes the of probability distributions over the pure strategy combinations S_{-k}.

I first give a general definition of inductive deliberational dynamics, and then define the Dirichlet dynamics.

Definition 3.2.1. Given a game $\Gamma = (N, S, \boldsymbol{u})$, we say that the players $1, \ldots, n$ are *inductive dynamic deliberators* iff

(1) Each player begins with a probability distribution $\mu_k^0 : S_{-k} \mapsto [0, 1]$ for the act combinations of his opponents, and

(2) The players apply a common rule φ that maps the distribution μ_k^{m-1} to a new distribution μ_k^m at the end of the mth stage of deliberation, that is, $\mu_k^m = \varphi(\mu_k^{m-1})$.

The n players are *independence-deliberators* iff for every $k \in N$ and every $m \in \mathbb{N}$,

$$(3) \quad \mu_k^m(\boldsymbol{A}_{-k}) = \mu_k^m(A_{1j_1}) \cdots \mu_k^m(A_{k-1j_{k-1}}) \cdot \mu_k^m(A_{k+1j_{k+1}}) \cdots \mu_k^m(A_{nj_n})$$

for each $\boldsymbol{A}_{-k} \in S_{-k}$. If condition (3) does not obtain at every round of deliberation, then the players are *correlation-deliberators*. We extend the definition of the dynamical rule φ to the distribution vector $\boldsymbol{\mu}^m$ which results from the players' updating in the obvious way: Given the vector of distributions $\boldsymbol{\mu}^{m-1} = (\mu_1, \ldots, \mu_n)$,

$$\varphi(\boldsymbol{\mu}^{m-1}) = \boldsymbol{\mu}^m = (\mu_1^m, \ldots, \mu_n^m) = (\varphi(\mu_1^{m-1}), \ldots, \varphi(\mu_n^{m-1})).$$

We say that the players $1, \ldots, n$ are at a *deliberational equilibrium-in-beliefs* iff $\varphi(\boldsymbol{\mu}^m) = \boldsymbol{\mu}^m$, and in this case $\boldsymbol{\mu}^m$ is called a *deliberational equilibrium*.   □

As we have argued above, in general players engaged in a game have no *a priori* reason to suppose that the independence condition 3.2.1(3) obtains for the distributions of their opponents' act combinations. Moreover, we have seen in the examples that even if independence is initially satisfied, that is, even if μ^0 satisfies 3.2.1(3), correlation in beliefs may emerge spontaneously among dynamic deliberators, so that they converge to an equilibrium distribution for which independence fails. For these reasons, we suggest that in general the theory of inductive dynamic deliberation should be developed under the assumption that agents are correlation-deliberators.

The players use the dynamical rule as a method for selecting one of their possible distributions for their opponents' act combinations. In the examples we have seen a number of different cases in which the sequence of distribution vectors generated by Dirichlet deliberation converges to an equilibrium distribution. Now we formally define the Dirichlet dynamics.

Definition 3.2.2. Given a game $\Gamma = (N, S, u)$, we say that the players $1, \ldots, n$ are *inductive Dirichlet deliberators* iff the dynamical rule φ they apply is defined as follows:

(1) At the start of deliberation, each Player k assigns a value $\gamma_{A_{-k}}$ to each $A_{-k} \in S_{-k}$. For every $A_{-k} \in S_{-k}$, $\gamma_{A_{-k}} \geq 0$ and for at least one $A_{-k} \in S_{-k}$, $\gamma_{A_{-k}} > 0$. The initial distribution $\mu_k^0(\cdot)$ that Player k has for the act combinations of his opponents in S_{-k} is determined by the formula

$$\mu_k^0(A_{-k}) = \frac{\gamma_{A_{-k}}}{\sum\limits_{B_{-k} \in S_{-k}} \gamma_{B_{-k}}}.$$

(2) Initially Player k sets $n_{A_{-k}} = 0$ for each $A_{-k} \in S_{-k}$. At the $m + 1$st round of deliberation, Player k updates his probabilities according to the rule

$$\mu_k^m(A_{-k}) = \frac{n_{A_{-k}} + \theta + \gamma_{A_{-k}}}{m + 1 + \sum \gamma_{B_{-k}}}$$

where $n_{A_{-k}}$ is the number of times that $A_{-k} \in S_{-k}$ has been played during the first m rounds of deliberation, and where

(a) $\theta = 1$ if for each opponent's strategy $A_{ij_i} \in A_{-k}$,

$$E_i^{m-1}(u_i(A_{ij_i})) > E_i^{m-1}(u_i(A_{il_i})) \text{ for } j_i \neq l_i,$$

(b) $\theta = \frac{\mu_k^m(A_{-k})}{\sum \mu_k^m(B_{il_i})}$ if for each opponent's strategy $A_{ij_i} \in A_{-k}$,

$$E_i^{m-1}(u_i(A_{ij_i})) \geq E_i^{m-1}(u_i(A_{il_i})) \text{ for } j_i \neq l_i,$$

and for some act $A_{ij_i} \in \mathbf{A}_{-k}$ and some acts $B_{il_i} \in S_i$ such that $A_{ij_i} \neq B_{il_i}$,

$$E_i^{m-1}(u_i(A_{ij_i})) = E_i^{m-1}(u_i(B_{il_i})),$$

and

(c) $\theta = 0$ otherwise, that is, if for any opponent's strategy $A_{ij_i} \in \mathbf{A}_{-k}$, for some $l_i \neq j_i$ we have

$$E_i^{m-1}(u_i(A_{il_i})) > E_i^{m-1}(u_i(A_{ij_i})). \quad \square$$

In other words, each player increases his $n_{\mathbf{A}_{-k}}$ by 1 if and only if each of his opponents maximizes expected utility by choosing her end of the strategy combination $\mathbf{A}_{-k} \subseteq \mathbf{A}$. If any opponent can gain a higher expected utility by playing some strategy other than her end of $\mathbf{A}_{-k}$, then $n_{\mathbf{A}_{-k}}$ remains as it was at the nth round of deliberation, and consequently $\mu_k^{m+1}(\mathbf{A}_{-k}) < \mu_k^m(\mathbf{A}_{-k})$. Part (*b*) of the definition of θ gives the rule for dealing with ties, when all opponents maximize expected utility by playing their end of $\mathbf{A}_{-k}$, but some opponents can also maximize expected utility by playing an alternative strategy. The $\gamma_{\mathbf{A}_{-k}}$'s of the Dirichlet dynamics are set over the opponents' act combinations, and the player updates his probabilities of opponents' act combinations. Hence, deliberators who update according to the Dirichlet rule as defined here are inductive correlation-deliberators.

The Dirichlet rule is defined in terms of the *fictitious play* interpretation of the dynamics. Each player updates her probabilities at each round by computing the expected utilities of each opponent and modifying the probabilities of each act combination the opponents might play accordingly. However, as noted above, one can also regard Dirichlet deliberators as naive players who update according to the results of actual repeated play or as a series of representatives of populations, such that each representative plays the game once and then yields to a new representative. Under both the actual play and the representative interpretations, each player chooses a strategy that maximizes his expected utility at each round of deliberation, and updates his probabilities by observing which strategy combination his opponents play. Such deliberators need only know the payoff structure of the game, or even just their own payoffs, and what each opponent has played at each previous round of deliberation. As noted above, one crucial difference between the fictitious play and the actual play and representative interpretations of inductive Dirichlet dynamics is that in fictitious play, the deliberators will *know* when they are at correlated equilibrium, while in the other two interpretations, the deliberators can converge to a correlated equilibrium without knowing they are at equilibrium, since they do not even necessarily know the payoffs of the other players. The definition of Dirichlet dynamics still makes sense for the actual play and representative interpretations, if one regards all of the expected utilities in the definition as computed by an "ideal observer" who knows the payoff structure of the game and who knows that every player is a Dirichlet deliberator with certain parameters.

We now show that *when the players engaged in a game are inductive Dirichlet deliberators, the notions of endogenous correlated equilibrium and deliberational equilibrium are equivalent.*

Proposition 3.2.3. Given that the players engaged in a game Γ are Dirichlet deliberators, a system of beliefs μ^* is a deliberational equilibrium iff it is an endogenous correlated equilibrium.

Proof. Suppose that μ^* is not an endogenous correlated equilibrium. Then condition (2.*xii*) fails,[7] so some player k has a distribution μ_k^* over S_{-k} such that, for some strategy $A_{ij_i} \in S_i$, $i \neq k$, $\mu_k^*(A_{ij_i}) > 0$ and A_{ij_i} does not maximize i's expected utility. Hence, if A'_{-k} is any act combination in S_{-k} such that $A_{ij_i} \in A'_{-k}$, then by the definition of the Dirichlet rule, $\varphi(\mu_k^*(A'_{-k})) < \mu_k^*(A'_{-k})$. Hence, μ^* is not a deliberational equilibrium. By contraposition, if μ^* is a deliberational equilibrium, then μ^* is an endogenous correlated equilibrium.

Now suppose that μ^* is not a deliberational equilibrium. Then $\varphi(\mu^*) \neq \mu^*$, so the probability of at least one act combination of some player's opponents is lowered, that is, there is some $A'_{-k} \in S_{-k}$ such that $\varphi(\mu_k^*(A'_{-k})) < \mu_k^*(A'_{-k})$. By the definition of the Dirichlet rule, for at least one $i \neq k$, $A_{ij_i} \in A'_{-k}$ does not maximize i's expected utility. Since $\mu_k^*(A_{ij_i}) \geq \mu_k^*(A'_{-k}) > \varphi(\mu_k^*(A'_{-k})) \geq 0$, condition (2.*xii*) is violated, so μ^* is not an endogenous correlated equilibrium. Applying contraposition again, if μ^* is an endogenous correlated equilibrium, then μ^* is a deliberational equilibrium. $\square$

A variety of results are known about the convergence properties of Dirichlet dynamics, but the dynamics do not always converge to equilibrium. Robinson (1951) proved that fictitious play always converges to a Nash equilibrium for 2-player zero-sum games. Miyasawa (1961) showed that fictitious play converges to a Nash equilibrium for 2-player non-zero-sum games if the players each have two alternative strategies. Monderer and Shapley (1993) proved that fictitious play always converges to a Nash equilibrium in games in which players have identical payoffs at every strategy combination. Shapley (1964) showed that fictitious play can fail to converge to an equilibrium with an example of a 2-player

---

[7] See Definition 2.2.1., on p. 78.

game in which the probability distributions of fictitious play deliberators cycle around the game's Nash equilibrium without ever reaching it. Richards (1993) proves that for a certain class of noncooperative games, the fictitious play dynamics will be *chaotic*. These results all generalize to Dirichlet dynamics. The most general conditions under which inductive dynamics converge either to a Nash equilibrium or a correlated equilibrium remain unknown.

Convergence in Strategies

The Dirichlet dynamics defines a sequence of the deliberators' probabilities over their opponents' actions, updated over time. A limit point of this sequence is a distribution vector that characterizes an equilibrium of the game. At each stage of Dirichlet deliberation, every deliberator chooses a strategy that is a best response given her beliefs at the time. Hence, the Dirichlet dynamics also defines a sequence of best response strategy profiles that parallel the sequence of updated distributions. This best response strategy profile sequence motivates an alternate convergence concept for the Dirichlet dynamics, namely *convergence in strategies*.

To illustrate convergence in strategies, let us suppose that Amie and Kay are Dirichlet deliberators engaged in a Battle of the Sexes game with payoff structure defined by Figure 3.2.5, and that their priors are defined by $\gamma_{1A_1} = 3$, $\gamma_{1A_2} = 4$, and $\gamma_{2A_1} = \gamma_{2A_2} = 3$.

Kay

		A_1	A_2
Amie	A_1	$(\sqrt{2}, 1)$	$(0, 0)$
	A_2	$(0, 0)$	$(1, \sqrt{2})$

Figure 3.2.5. Battle of the Sexes *II*

Under the actual play interpretation, at the start of deliberation,

$$E_1^0(u_1(A_1)) = \sqrt{2} \cdot \frac{3}{7} + 0 \cdot \frac{4}{7} = \frac{3\sqrt{2}}{7} > \frac{4}{7} = 0 \cdot \frac{3}{7} + 1 \cdot \frac{4}{7} = E_1^0(u_1(A_2))$$

$$E_2^0(u_2(A_1)) = 1 \cdot \frac{1}{2} + 0 \cdot \frac{1}{2} = \frac{1}{2} < \frac{\sqrt{2}}{2} = 0 \cdot \frac{1}{2} + \sqrt{2} \cdot \frac{1}{2} = E_2^0(u_2(A_2))$$

and so the deliberators play the nonequilibrium profile (A_1, A_2) and update their probabilities thus:

$$\mu_1^1(A_1) = \frac{3}{1+7} = \frac{3}{8}$$

$$\mu_1^1(A_2) = \frac{1+4}{1+7} = \frac{5}{8}$$

$$\mu_2^1(A_1) = \frac{1+3}{1+6} = \frac{4}{7}$$

$$\mu_2^1(A_2) = \frac{3}{1+6} = \frac{3}{7}$$

At the second round of deliberation,

$$E_1^1(u_1(A_1)) = \sqrt{2} \cdot \frac{3}{8} + 0 \cdot \frac{5}{8} = \frac{3\sqrt{2}}{8} < \frac{5}{8} = 0 \cdot \frac{3}{8} + 1 \cdot \frac{5}{8} = E_1^1(u_1(A_2))$$

$$E_2^1(u_2(A_1)) = 1 \cdot \frac{4}{7} + 0 \cdot \frac{3}{7} = \frac{4}{7} < \frac{3\sqrt{2}}{7} = 0 \cdot \frac{4}{7} + \sqrt{2} \cdot \frac{3}{7} = E_2^1(u_2(A_2))$$

so this time the deliberators coordinate on the equilibrium profile (A_2, A_2) and update their probabilities thus:

$$\mu_1^2(A_1) = \frac{3}{2+7} = \frac{1}{3}$$

$$\mu_1^2(A_2) = \frac{2+4}{2+7} = \frac{2}{3}$$

$$\mu_2^2(A_1) = \frac{1+3}{2+6} = \frac{1}{2}$$

$$\mu_2^2(A_2) = \frac{1+3}{2+6} = \frac{1}{2}$$

At the third round of deliberation,

$$E_1^2(u_1(A_1)) = \sqrt{2} \cdot \frac{1}{3} + 0 \cdot \frac{5}{8} = \frac{\sqrt{2}}{3} < \frac{2}{3} = 0 \cdot \frac{1}{3} + 1 \cdot \frac{2}{3} = E_1^2(u_1(A_2))$$

$$E_2^2(u_2(A_1)) = 1 \cdot \frac{1}{2} + 0 \cdot \frac{1}{2} = \frac{1}{2} < \frac{\sqrt{2}}{2} = 0 \cdot \frac{1}{2} + \sqrt{2} \cdot \frac{1}{2} = E_2^2(u_2(A_2))$$

so Amie and Kay again play the equilibrium (A_2, A_2). As shall be proved presently, since (A_2, A_2) is a strict equilibrium, once the deliberators start to play (A_2, A_2), at each subsequent stage of deliberation the Dirichlet rule reinforces each deliberator's updated probabilities that the opponent will play her end of the equilibrium, so that over time they never deviate from (A_1, A_2) and their updated probabilities converge to the Nash equilibrium characterized by the belief distributions $\mu_1^*(A_2) = \mu_2^*(A_2) = 1$. The equilibrium (A_2, A_2) is a fixed profile of Dirichlet deliberation with these priors.

The sequence $(\mathbf{A}^m)$ of best response strategy combinations determined by Dirichlet dynamics forms another dynamical system. The terms of the sequence $(\mathbf{A}^m)$ are uniquely determined by the updated sequence of distributions (μ^m) up to tie-breaking cases.[8] We can define a fixed point of this dynamical system.

Definition 3.2.4. Given a set of Dirichlet deliberators engaged in a game $\Gamma = (N, S, \mathbf{u})$, a *fixed profile* of Dirichlet dynamics is a strategy profile $\mathbf{A}^{m_0} \in S$ such that, for all $m > m_0$, $\mathbf{A}^m = \mathbf{A}^{m_0}$. The system of Dirichlet deliberation is said to *converge in strategies* iff the sequence $(\mathbf{A}^m)$ converges to a fixed profile.   □

In the remainder of this section, I prove some elementary results regarding convergence in strategies. In the following lemma, I will make use of the identity

$$(3.iii) \qquad \mu_k^{m+1}(\mathbf{A}_{-k}) = \frac{\theta}{m + 1 + \lambda_k} + \frac{m + \lambda_k}{m + 1 + \lambda_k} \cdot \mu_k^m(\mathbf{A}_{-k})$$

which emphasizes the recursive nature of the Dirichlet dynamics. [9]

Lemma 3.2.5. If Dirichlet deliberators play a strict equilibrium $\mathbf{A}^*$ at any round of deliberation, then they will play $\mathbf{A}^*$ at the subsequent round of deliberation.

---

[8] In cases in which a player's best pure strategy response is not uniquely determined by the player's current probability distribution, one can either update the sequence $(\mathbf{A}^m)$ by including the opponent's distributions over the player's best replies, as if the player were going to play a mixed strategy, or by recording the pure strategy they actually observe the player play. Clearly, the former option better reflects a fictitious play interpretation of the dynamics, while the latter reflects an actual repeated play or a representative interpretation.

[9] This identity is easy to derive. We have

$$\mu_k^m(\mathbf{A}_{-k}) = \frac{n_{\mathbf{A}_{-k}} + \lambda_k \mu_k^0(\mathbf{A}_{-k})}{m + \lambda_k}$$

and

$$
\begin{aligned}
\mu_k^{m+1}(\mathbf{A}_{-k}) &= \frac{n_{\mathbf{A}_{-k}} + \theta + \lambda_k \mu_k^0(\mathbf{A}_{-k})}{m + 1 + \lambda_k} \\
&= \frac{\theta}{m + 1 + \lambda_k} + \frac{1}{m + 1 + \lambda_k} \cdot (n_{\mathbf{A}_{-k}} + \lambda_k \mu_k^0(\mathbf{A}_{-k})) \\
&= \frac{\theta}{m + 1 + \lambda_k} + \frac{m + \lambda_k}{m + 1 + \lambda_k} \cdot \left(\frac{1}{m + \lambda_k} (n_{\mathbf{A}_{-k}} + \lambda_k \mu_k^0(\mathbf{A}_{-k})) \right) \\
&= \frac{\theta}{m + 1 + \lambda_k} + \frac{m + \lambda_k}{m + 1 + \lambda_k} \cdot \mu_k^m(\mathbf{A}_{-k})
\end{aligned}
$$

Recall that $\lambda_k = \Sigma \gamma_{\mathbf{B}_{-k}}$, so that $\gamma_{\mathbf{A}_{-k}} = \gamma_{\mathbf{A}_{-k}} \cdot \frac{\lambda_k}{\lambda_k} = \lambda_k \cdot \mu_k^0(\mathbf{A}_{-k})$.

Proof. If the players play $A^* = (A_1^*, \ldots, A_n^*)$ at round m of deliberation, then necessarily for each $k \in N$,

$$E_k^{m-1}(u_k(A_k^*)) \geq E_k^{m-1}(u_k(A_{kj})) \text{ for all } A_{kj} \neq A_k^*$$

which implies that

(1) $$\sum_{\boldsymbol{A}_{-k} \in S_{-k}} [u_k(A_k^*, \boldsymbol{A}_{-k}) - u_k(A_{kj}, \boldsymbol{A}_{-k})]\mu_k^m(\boldsymbol{A}_{-k}) \geq 0$$

Now note that at the $m + 1$st round of deliberation, for all $A_{kj} \neq A_k^*$,

(2) $E_k^m(u_k(A_k^*)) - E_k^m(u_k(A_{kj}))$

$= [u_k(A_k^*, \boldsymbol{A}_{-k}^*) - u_k(A_{kj}, \boldsymbol{A}_{-k}^*)]\mu_k^{m+1}(\boldsymbol{A}_{-k}^*)$

$\qquad + \displaystyle\sum_{\boldsymbol{A}_{-k} \neq \boldsymbol{A}_{-k}^*} [u_k(A_k^*, \boldsymbol{A}_{-k}) - u_k(A_{kj}, \boldsymbol{A}_{-k})]\mu_k^{m+1}(\boldsymbol{A}_{-k})$

$= [u_k(A_k^*, \boldsymbol{A}_{-k}^*) - u_k(A_{kj}, \boldsymbol{A}_{-k}^*)]$

$\qquad \cdot \left(\dfrac{1}{m+1+\lambda_k} + \dfrac{m+\lambda_k}{m+1+\lambda_k} \cdot \mu_k^m(\boldsymbol{A}_{-k}^*) \right)$

$\qquad + \displaystyle\sum_{\boldsymbol{A}_{-k} \neq \boldsymbol{A}_{-k}^*} [u_k(A_k^*, \boldsymbol{A}_{-k}) - u_k(A_{kj}, \boldsymbol{A}_{-k})]$

$\qquad \cdot \left(\dfrac{m+\lambda_k}{m+1+\lambda_k} \cdot \mu_k^m(\boldsymbol{A}_{-k}) \right) \qquad$ [by (3.*iii*)]

$= \dfrac{1}{m+1+\lambda_k} \cdot [u_k(A_k^*, \boldsymbol{A}_{-k}^*) - u_k(A_{kj}, \boldsymbol{A}_{-k}^*)] + \dfrac{m+\lambda_k}{m+1+\lambda_k}$

$\qquad \cdot \displaystyle\sum_{\boldsymbol{A}_{-k} \in S_{-k}} [u_k(A_k^*, \boldsymbol{A}_{-k}) - u_k(A_{kj}, \boldsymbol{A}_{-k})]\mu_k^m(\boldsymbol{A}_{-k})$

The first term of the rightmost member of equation (2) is strictly positive because A^* is a strict equilibrium, and the second term is nonnegative by (1). Hence $E_k^m(u_k(A^*)) > E_k^m(u_k(A_{kj}, \boldsymbol{A}_{-k}^*))$ given $\mu_k^{m+1}(\cdot)$, so k will play A_k^* at round $m + 1$. Since k was chosen arbitrarily from N, we see that every player strictly prefers to play his end of A^* at round $m + 1$. $\qquad\qquad\qquad\square$

In the following proposition it is shown that a strict Nash equilibrium A^* is an absorbing process of the Dirichlet dynamics.

Proposition 3.2.6 (Absorption Theorem). If A^* is a strict Nash equilibrium and Dirichlet deliberators play A^* at any round of deliberation, they will play A^* at all future rounds of deliberation.[10]

Proof. Suppose that Dirichlet deliberators play a strict Nash equilibrium A^* at the mth round of deliberation and at each of l rounds after round m, $l \geq 0$. By Lemma 3.2.5, since the deliberators play A^* at round $m + l$, the updated distribution vector $\boldsymbol{\mu}^{m+l+1} = (\mu_1^{m+l+1}, \ldots, \mu_n^{m+l+1})$ is such that for each $k \in N$, $A_k^* \in A^*$ is k's unique best response to μ_k^{m+l+1}. Hence the deliberators will play A^* at round $m + l + 1$, so the corollary follows by complete induction. $\square$

Note that the Absorption Theorem is not a trivial consequence of Proposition 3.2.3, which implies that if the deliberators' beliefs are at equilibrium, so that $\mu_k^m(A_{-k}^*) = 1$, then the players will play the equilibrium A^* at all rounds following m. Rather, the Absorption Theorem proves that if Dirichlet deliberators play a strict equilibrium once, they will never deviate from this equilibrium, even if their beliefs have not yet converged to the deliberational equilibrium corresponding to this equilibrium. It is easy to show that, once the deliberators' sequence of plays settles upon a strict Nash equilibrium, their beliefs do indeed converge to this equilibrium.

Proposition 3.2.7. If Dirichlet deliberators begin to play a strict Nash equilibrium A^*, then $\boldsymbol{\mu}^m \to \boldsymbol{\mu}^*$ as $m \to \infty$, where $\boldsymbol{\mu}^*$ is the vector of distributions which characterizes A^*.

Proof. The Nash equilibrium distribution vector $\boldsymbol{\mu}^* = (\mu_1^*, \ldots, \mu_n^*)$ for A^* is defined by

$$\mu_k^*(A_{-k}) = \begin{cases} 1 & \text{if } A_{-k} = A_{-k}^* \\ 0 & \text{if } A_{-k} \neq A_{-k}^* \end{cases}, k \in N.$$

By the Absorption Theorem, if Dirichlet deliberators play A^* for the first time at round m_1 of deliberation, then they play A^* at all rounds that follow m_1. Hence, for player $k \in N$, for $m \geq m_1$,

$$\mu_k^{m+1}(A_{-k}^*) = \frac{n_{A_{-k}^*} + 1 + \gamma_{A_{-k}^*}}{m + 1 + \sum \gamma_{B_{-k}}}$$

$$= \frac{m - m_1 + 1 + \gamma_{A_{-k}^*}}{m + 1 + \sum \gamma_{B_{-k}}} \uparrow 1 \text{ as } m \to \infty,$$

---

[10] This result for fictitious play with probabilistic independence has been known among game theorists for some time. Fudenberg and Kreps (1991, 22) state this result without proof. However, to my knowledge I gave the first proof in the literature in §3.2 of Vanderschraaf (1995). I call Proposition 3.2.6 the "Absorption Theorem" because it says that a strict Nash equilibrium is an absorbing state of the dynamical process (A^m) defined by the Dirichlet dynamics.

and for $A_{-k} \neq A^*_{-k}$,

$$0 \leq \mu_k^{m+1}(A_{-k}) = \frac{n_{A_{-k}} + \gamma_{A_{-k}}}{m+1+\sum \gamma_{B_{-k}}}$$

$$\leq \frac{m_1 - 1 + \gamma_{A_{-k}}}{m+1+\sum \gamma_{B_{-k}}} \downarrow 0 \text{ as } m \to \infty,$$

so $\mu_k^m(A_{-k}) \to 0$ as $m \to \infty$ by the Sandwich theorem for sequential limits. Hence $\mu_k^m \to \mu_k^*$ as $m \to \infty$. □

In other words, convergence in strategies implies convergence in distribution. The converse of this result fails. To see this, suppose that Kay and Amie are Dirichlet deliberators engaged in the Battle of the Sexes game of Figure 3.2.5, this time with uniform priors defined by $\gamma_{iAj} = 1, i, j = 1, 2$. In this case, the sequence of plays determined by the dynamics is

$$(A_1, A_2), (A_2, A_1), (A_1, A_2), (A_2, A_1), (A_1, A_2), (A_2, A_1),$$
$$(A_1, A_2), (A_1, A_2), (A_2, A_1), (A_1, A_2), (A_1, A_2), (A_2, A_1), \dots$$

so Amie and Kay miscoordinate at every round of deliberation, never reaching a fixed profile. However, the sequence of distributions defined by the dynamics converges to the mixed Nash equilibrium characterized by

$$\mu_1^*(A_1) = \frac{1}{1+\sqrt{2}}, \mu_2^*(A_1) = \frac{\sqrt{2}}{1+\sqrt{2}}.$$

Consequently, convergence in strategies is a stronger mode of convergence than convergence in distribution.

§3.3 Correlating with "States of the World"

The model of inductive deliberation described above can be generalized in several ways. We will consider one such generalization here. Under the fictitious play interpretation of the inductive dynamics of the previous section, the players have common knowledge of the game's payoff structure and their Bayesian rationality, and know nothing else. In this section, we will consider the consequences of giving the players more information. In particular, at each stage of deliberation, the players will receive a signal generated from some external event. By incorporating their signals into the deliberative process, inductive deliberators can learn to play correlated equilibria of the kind introduced in Aumann (1974, 1987). *We give examples that show that inductive deliberators can converge to* an Aumann correlated equilibrium from initially weakly correlated beliefs, and even from priors that satisfy probabilistic independence.

In this new model, each player k has an *information partition* $\mathcal{H}_k$ of a sure event Ω. The elementary events $\omega \in \Omega$ are known as the "states of the world." Both $\mathcal{H}_k$ and Ω are fixed for all rounds of play. At each round of play, k learns that an event $H_{kj}(\omega) \in \mathcal{H}_k$ has occurred, though k does not in general know which $\omega \in \Omega$ has occurred. The elementary event ω that occurs at any particular round of deliberation is stochastically independent of the elementary events that occur at other rounds of deliberation. Ω is the external event space or "lottery" that underpins Aumann's (1974, 1987) correlated equilibrium concept. However, we do not assume that players have agreed to play an Aumann correlated equilibrium to begin with. Player k updates *conditional* probabilities of the opponents' strategy combinations according to the following variation of the Dirichlet rule:

$$(3.iv) \qquad \mu_k^m(A_{-k}|H_{kj}) = \frac{n_{A_{-k} \wedge H_{kj}} + \gamma_{A_{-k} \wedge H_{kj}}}{n_{H_{kj}} + \sum \gamma_{B_{-k} \wedge H_{kj}}}$$

where $n_{A_{-k} \wedge H_{kj}}$ is the number of times the opponents play A_{-k} *and* H_{kj} has occurred, $n_{H_{kj}}$ is the number of times that H_{kj} has occurred, and the $\gamma_{B_{-k} \wedge H_{kj}}$'s are nonnegative numbers that determine k's conditional priors over the opponents' strategy combinations given that H_{kj} has occurred.

We apply this model first to the Battle of the Sexes game of Figure 3.1.1. As we saw in §2.2, in this game Amie and Kay can achieve an Aumann correlated equilibrium that is a mixture of the two pure strategy Nash equilibria if they agree to ask their friend Ron to toss a fair penny, and to both play A_1 if the penny lands heads-up ("H") and to both play A_2 if the penny lands tails-up ("T"). Then the combinations (A_1, A_1) and (A_2, A_2) are each played with probability $\frac{1}{2}$, and the uncoordinated strategy combinations are played with probability zero. Setting

$$f(\omega) = \begin{cases} (A_1, A_1) & \text{if } \omega = H \\ (A_2, A_2) & \text{if } \omega = T \end{cases}$$

both players have an overall expected payoff of $\frac{1}{2} \cdot 2 + \frac{1}{2} \cdot 1 = \frac{3}{2}$ if they follow the correlated equilibrium f. As noted in §2.2, the payoff vector $(\frac{3}{2}, \frac{3}{2})$ Pareto-dominates the payoff vector $(\frac{2}{3}, \frac{2}{3})$ of the mixed Nash equilibrium, and moreover by following f, Amie and Kay are sure to coordinate.

Suppose the situation is modified so that Kay and Amie are to play Battle of the Sexes repeatedly without being allowed to communicate, though they still know the result of a coin flip at each round of play. They cannot explicitly agree to play the correlated equilibrium strategy of playing (A_1, A_1) if H and (A_2, A_2)

if T, but if they are conditional Dirichlet deliberators, they can learn to play the correlated equilibrium, given the right priors. In this case, $\Omega = \{H, T\}$, and $\mathcal{H}_1 = \mathcal{H}_2 = \{\{H\}, \{T\}\}$. At each round of play, Ron tells Amie and Kay whether H occurred or T occurred. Kay uses (3.*iv*) to update her probabilities:

$$\mu_2^m(\text{Amie chooses } A_1|H) \;=\; \frac{n_{\text{Amie chooses } A_1 \wedge H} + \gamma_{\text{Amie chooses } A_1 \wedge H}}{n_H + \sum \gamma(H)}$$

$$\mu_2^m(\text{Amie chooses } A_2|H) \;=\; \frac{n_{\text{Amie chooses } A_2 \wedge H} + \gamma_{\text{Amie chooses } A_2 \wedge H}}{n_H + \sum \gamma(H)}$$

$$\mu_2^m(\text{Amie chooses } A_1|T) \;=\; \frac{n_{\text{Amie chooses } A_1 \wedge T} + \gamma_{\text{Amie chooses } A_1 \wedge T}}{n_T + \sum \gamma(T)}$$

$$\mu_2^m(\text{Amie chooses } A_2|T) \;=\; \frac{n_{\text{Amie chooses } A_2 \wedge T} + \gamma_{\text{Amie chooses } A_2 \wedge T}}{n_T + \sum \gamma(T)}$$

Amie updates her conditional probabilities similarly. Note that Kay and Amie have not explicitly agreed to tie their strategies to the coin toss, and (in lieu of such an agreement) Ron does not recommend strategies to either Amie or Kay. If they are conditional Dirichlet deliberators who begin with uniform priors over the opponent's acts, then Kay and Amie will converge to the mixed Nash equilibrium. In other words, for this game conditional Dirichlet deliberation with uniform priors yields the same results as unconditional Dirichlet deliberation given uniform priors. On the other hand, if Kay and Amie each have priors that indicate their individual beliefs that the opponent will be predisposed to correlate her strategy choice to the coin flip in the same way, then the dynamics converge almost surely to a deliberational correlated equilibrium with the same payoff vector and distribution of plays as the Aumann correlated equilibrium. For instance, suppose that Kay's gammas are:

$$\gamma_{\text{Amie plays } A_1 \wedge H} \;=\; 51,$$

$$\gamma_{\text{Amie plays } A_2 \wedge H} \;=\; 49,$$

$$\gamma_{\text{Amie plays } A_1 \wedge T} \;=\; 49,$$

$$\gamma_{\text{Amie plays } A_2 \wedge T} \;=\; 51.$$

Then Kay's priors are

$$\mu_2^0(\text{Amie plays } A_1 | H) \;=\; \frac{51}{51 + 49} = .51,$$

$$\mu_2^0(\text{Amie plays } A_2 | H) \;=\; \frac{49}{51 + 49} = .49,$$

$$\mu_2^0(\text{Amie plays } A_1 | T) \;=\; \frac{49}{51 + 49} = .49,$$

$$\mu_2^0(\text{Amie plays } A_2 | T) \;=\; \frac{51}{51 + 49} = .51.$$

If, similarly, Amie's prior probabilities are

$$\mu_1^0(\text{Kay plays } A_1 | H) \;=\; .51,$$

$$\mu_1^0(\text{Kay plays } A_2 | H) \;=\; .49,$$

$$\mu_1^0(\text{Kay plays } A_1 | T) \;=\; .49, \text{ and}$$

$$\mu_1^0(\text{Kay plays } A_2 | T) \;=\; .51,$$

then, almost surely, the conditional Dirichlet dynamics converges to the distribution vector $\mu^* = (\mu_1^*, \mu_2^*)$, where

$$\mu_1^*(\text{Kay plays } A_1 | H) \;=\; 1,$$

$$\mu_1^*(\text{Kay plays } A_2 | H) \;=\; 0,$$

$$\mu_1^*(\text{Kay plays } A_1 | T) \;=\; 0,$$

$$\mu_1^*(\text{Kay plays } A_2 | T) \;=\; 1.$$

$$\mu_2^*(\text{Amie plays } A_1 | H) \;=\; 1,$$

$$\mu_2^*(\text{Amie plays } A_2 | H) \;=\; 0,$$

$$\mu_2^*(\text{Amie plays } A_1 | T) \;=\; 0,$$

$$\mu_2^*(\text{Amie plays } A_2 | T) \;=\; 1,$$

which is the distribution that characterizes the Aumann correlated equilibrium f. This example shows that an Aumann correlated equilibrium can be an attractor of the conditional Dirichlet rule.

Almost sure convergence is guaranteed for this example because the two deliberators receive the same signal at each round of deliberation. Consequently, the rounds of conditional Dirichlet deliberation may be divided into two subsequences of deliberation, one corresponding to the H outcome and the other corresponding to the T outcome of the coin flip. Moreover, the H and T subsequences of deliberation taken separately trace the same orbits as would have been traced had the deliberators been *unconditional* deliberators starting with the priors determined by the γ's at one of the two outcomes of the coin flip. The H subsequence starts at $\mu_1^0(A_1|H) = \mu_2^0(A_1|H) = .51$, which is in the basin of attraction of (A_1, A_1) for unconditional Dirichlet deliberation. Similarly, the T subsequence starts in basin of attraction of (A_2, A_2) for unconditional Dirichlet deliberation. Consequently, conditional Dirichlet deliberation converges to (A_1, A_1) if H and (A_2, A_2) if T, which is the Aumann correlated equilibrium, unless either H or T occurs only finitely many times in the sequence of coin flips, in which case one of the subsequences of conditional deliberation will stop short of its attractor. By the Borel-Cantelli lemma,[11] with probability one H and T both occur infinitely often in a sequence of flips of a fair coin, so the conditional deliberation converges to the Aumann correlated equilibrium with probability one.

The next example shows that conditional inductive deliberators can spontaneously converge to an Aumann correlated equilibrium even if the players begin with priors that satisfy probabilistic independence. In (1991b), Skyrms considers a variation of a 3-player example given in Aumann (1974) with payoff structure given by the matrices in Figure 3.3.1. Here Amie chooses the row, Kay chooses

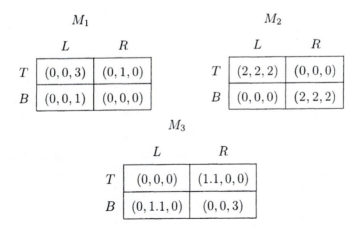

Figure 3.3.1. Skyrms' 3-Player Example

---

[11] The relevant special case of the Borel-Cantelli lemma in probability theory can be stated as follows: In an infinite sequence of independent trials of an experiment with outcomes $B_1, \ldots, B_m$, if $\mu(B_i) > 0$ at one (and therefore any) trial, then $\mu(\{B_i \text{ occurs infinitely often in the sequence}\}) = 1$.

the column, and Ron chooses the matrix. The players are at an Aumann correlated equilibrium with payoff vector $(2, 2, 2)$ if Amie and Kay observe a coin
flip and play (T, L) if the coin comes up H and (B, R) if the coin comes up T,
and Ron (who doesn't know the outcome of the coin flip) plays M_2. As Aumann
(1974) points out, Ron would not even want to know the outcome of the coin flip,
since if he did, he would break for either M_1 or M_3, which would drive Kay and
Amie to play (B, L) or (T, R). In this example,

$$\mathcal{H}_{\text{Kay}} = \mathcal{H}_{\text{Amie}} = \{\{H\}, \{T\}\}$$

and

$$\mathcal{H}_{\text{Ron}} = \{H, T\} = \Omega,$$

the trivial partition.

Suppose that Kay, Ron and Amie aren't at a correlated equilibrium to begin
with, but that they do modify their probability distributions over their opponents'
acts conditional on their information partitions with the Dirichlet rule. Again, the
players learn at each round that a certain event in their information partition has
occurred, but they are not told how they ought to play given their information.
If the players begin with uniform priors over their opponents' actions, they can
converge to an Aumann correlated equilibrium. Interestingly, starting from uniform priors, the players can converge either to the equilibrium already described
or to the following correlated equilibrium: (B, R, M_2) if the coin comes up H
and (T, L, M_2) if the coin comes up T. Both of these correlated equilibria have
the players playing either (B, R, M_2) or (T, L, M_2) according to the result of
the coin flip, and they both yield the payoff vector $(2, 2, 2)$, but the players can
learn to correlate their choices to the value of the coin flip *either* way, that is, they
can learn to always play (T, L, M_2) if the coin comes up H or they can learn to
always play (B, R, M_2) if the coin comes up T. The correlated equilibrium distribution the players settle upon is determined by the early sequence of coin flips
the players observe. *Once again, correlation emerges spontaneously among de-*
liberators who begin with priors that satisfy probabilistic independence, though
in this extended model the correlation is exogenous rather than endogenous.

Why would players who do not communicate with one another condition
their probabilities on their information partitions? Aumann (1974, 1987) does not
give an account of how players would come to peg their strategies on an external
event. Consequently, Aumann's theory does not give an account of how players
come to select a particular Aumann correlated equilibrium. Conditional inductive dynamics gives one possible resolution of the equilibrium selection problem,
and also an account of how players would come to correlate their strategies with

an external event. Players who modify their probability distributions by conditioning on their information partitions are simply using all of the information at their disposal when they update. If the information a player receives from the external event turns out to have no bearing on the results of play, the updated probability will be the same as if he had updated unconditionally. On the other hand, if the player notices a correlation between his opponents' strategies and his signals, he can incorporate this correlation into his deliberations with a rule like the conditional Dirichlet rule. Suppose that Kay is engaged in a repeated game with Amie and Ron. In the beginning Kay knows nothing other than the payoff structure of the game, although at each round of play she learns what Amie and Ron play. If Ron and Amie have the same information, that is, each player knows the game's payoff structure and what the opponents play, and if all are Dirichlet deliberators who do not assume probabilistic independence, then they might eventually converge to an endogenous correlated equilibrium. But suppose that Kay is given one more bit of information: before each round of deliberation Kay observes the outcome of a coin flip. Kay gets no recommended strategy to play, and does not know whether or not Amie and/or Ron have received any information regarding this coin flip. However, Kay decides to update according to the conditional Dirichlet rule and to see what happens. By conditioning, Kay simply uses the "rule of thumb" that one ought to use all of the information at one's disposal in making one's decision at each round of deliberation.[12] If the information from the coin flip turns out to be statistically irrelevant to the sequence of her opponents' strategy combinations, then Kay is no worse off for having conditioned on it, since the result of the conditional updating will be the same as the result of unconditional updating. On the other hand, conditioning on her signal could be to Kay's advantage, since, as the previous 3-player example shows, conditional Dirichlet deliberation can converge to an Aumann correlated equilibrium at which Kay gains her highest possible payoff.

   This justification of conditional inductive deliberation is similar to the justification Woodford (1990) gives for having the agents in his model condition on "sunspots" in order to learn how to play *"sunspot equilibria,"* although Woodford applies this equilibrium concept to macroeconomic models rather than to noncooperative games, and the "sunspots" in Woodford's model are states of a Markov process, while the sequence of signals in our model is a stochastically independent sequence. Woodford argues that agents might as well condition their dynamic updating on external events nicknamed "sunspots," even though these sunspots apparently have nothing to do with the economy. Even if the sunspots

---

[12] Skyrms discusses the role of information in updating one's probabilities much more thoroughly in Chapter 4 of Skyrms (1990), entitled "The Value of Knowledge."

play no direct role in the economy, conditioning on the "extraneous" information they provide makes sense, since this information could influence the agents'
expectations regarding the state of the economy, and in turn influence their dynamic updating. If conditioning on the sunspots has an effect on their dynamics,
the agents can achieve a sunspot equilibrium different from any equilibrium they
can achieve without conditioning. On the other hand, if it turns out that conditioning on the sunspots has no effect on their dynamics, the agents will eventually
learn this and be no worse off for having considered the sunspots.

The Formal Model

In order to give the formal definition of conditional Dirichlet deliberation,
we extend the model by introducing an external event space and a system of
information partitions on this space. To the game $\Gamma = (N, S, u)$, we add a finite
probability space Ω together with the information partitions $\mathcal{H}_k$, $k \in N$.

Definition 3.3.1. Let $\Gamma = (N, S, u)$, Ω, and the partitions $\mathcal{H}_k$ of Ω be given,
and let an elementary event $\omega \in \Omega$ occur at each round of deliberation. The
players $1, \ldots, n$ are *conditional Dirichlet deliberators* iff the dynamical rule φ
they apply is defined as follows:

(1) At the start of deliberation, each player k assigns a value $\gamma_{A_{-k} \wedge H_{kj}} \geq 0$ to
   each $A_{-k} \in S_{-k}$ and each $H_{kj} \in \mathcal{H}_k$. For every $H_{kj} \in \mathcal{H}_k$, $\gamma_{B_{-k} \wedge H_{kj}} >$
   0 for at least one least one $B_{-k} \in S_{-k}$. The prior conditional distribution
   $\mu_k^0(\cdot | \mathcal{H}_k)$ that each player has for the act combinations of his opponents in
   S_{-k} is defined by

$$\mu_k^0(A_{-k} | H_{kj}) = \frac{\gamma_{A_{-k} \wedge H_{kj}}}{\sum\limits_{B_{-k} \in S_{-k}} \gamma_{B_{-k} \wedge H_{kj}}}, \ H_{kj} \in \mathcal{H}_k.$$

(2) For each $H_{kj} \in \mathcal{H}_k$ and each $A_{-k} \in S_{-k}$,

$$n_{H_{kj}} = \sum_{t=1}^{m} 1_{H_{kj}}(\omega^t)^{13}$$

---

[13]Following the usual convention, the indicator function $1_B : \Omega \rightarrow \{0, 1\}$ is defined as

$$1_B(\omega) = \begin{cases} 1 & \text{if } \omega \in B \\ 0 & \text{if } \omega \notin B \end{cases}$$

and

$$n_{\boldsymbol{A}_{-k} \wedge H_{kj}} = \sum_{t=1}^{m} 1_{\boldsymbol{A}_{-k} \wedge H_{kj}}(\omega^t)$$

that is, $n_{H_{kj}}$ is the number of times that H_{kj} has occurred during the first m rounds of deliberation, and $n_{\boldsymbol{A}_{-k} \wedge H_{kj}}$ is the number of times that $\boldsymbol{A}_{-k}$ and H_{kj} have both occurred during the first m rounds of deliberation. At the $m + 1$st round of deliberation, Player k updates his probability distribution $\mu_k^m(\cdot | \mathcal{H}_k)$ according to the rule

$$\mu_k^{m+1}(\boldsymbol{A}_{-k} | H_{kj}) = \mu_k^m(\boldsymbol{A}_{-k} | H_{kj})$$

if H_{kj} did not occur at the $m + 1$st round of deliberation, and, if H_{kj} occurred at the $m + 1$st round of deliberation, then

$$\mu_k^{m+1}(\boldsymbol{A}_{-k} | H_{kj}) = \frac{n_{\boldsymbol{A}_{-k} \wedge H_{kj}} + \theta + \gamma_{\boldsymbol{A}_{-k} \wedge H_{kj}}}{n_{H_{kj}} + 1 + \sum \gamma_{\boldsymbol{B}_{-k} \wedge H_{kj}}}$$

where

(a) $\theta = 1$ if for each opponent's strategy $A_{ij_i} \in \boldsymbol{A}_{-k}$,

$$E_i^m(u_i(A_{ij_i}) | \mathcal{H}_i)(\omega) > E_i^m(u_i(A_{il_i}) | \mathcal{H}_i)(\omega) \text{ for } j_i \neq l_i,$$

(b) $\theta = \frac{\mu_k^m(\boldsymbol{A}_{-k} | H_{kj})}{\Sigma \mu_k^m(\boldsymbol{B}_{il_i} | H_{kj})}$ if for each opponent's strategy $A_{ij_i} \in \boldsymbol{A}_{-k}$,

$$E_i^m(u_i(A_{ij_i}) | \mathcal{H}_i)(\omega) \geq E_i^m(u_i(A_{il_i}) | \mathcal{H}_i)(\omega) \text{ for } j_i \neq l_i,$$

and for some act $A_{ij_i} \in \boldsymbol{A}_{-k}$ and some acts $B_{il_i} \in S_i$ such that $A_{ij_i} \neq B_{il_i}$,

$$E_i^m(u_i(A_{ij_i}) | \mathcal{H}_i)(\omega) = E_i^m(u_i(B_{il_i}) | \mathcal{H}_i)(\omega), \text{ and}$$

(c) $\theta = 0$ otherwise, that is, if for any opponent's strategy $A_{ij_i} \in \boldsymbol{A}_{-k}$, for some $l_i \neq j_i$ we have

$$E_i^m(u_i(A_{il_i}) | \mathcal{H}_i)(\omega) > E_i^m(u_i(A_{ij_i}) | \mathcal{H}_i)(\omega).$$

The sequence of updated distributions is denoted by

$$\mathfrak{P}^m = (\mu_1^m(\cdot | \mathcal{H}_1), \ldots, \mu_n^m(\cdot | \mathcal{H}_n)).$$

The players are at a *conditional Dirichlet deliberational equilibrium* iff, for each $\omega \in \Omega$,

$$(\mu_1^{m+1}(\cdot | \mathcal{H}_1), \ldots, \mu_n^{m+1}(\cdot | \mathcal{H}_n)) = (\mu_1^m(\cdot | \mathcal{H}_1), \ldots, \mu_n^m(\cdot | \mathcal{H}_n))$$

and in this case the vector

$$\mathfrak{P}^* = (\mu_1^*(\cdot|\mathcal{H}_1), \ldots, \mu_n^*(\cdot|\mathcal{H}_n)) = (\mu_1^m(\cdot|\mathcal{H}_1), \ldots, \mu_n^m(\cdot|\mathcal{H}_n))$$

is called a *conditional Dirichlet equilibrium*.   □

As with unconditional Dirichlet deliberation, this definition is given in terms of a fictitious play interpretation of the dynamics. Under the fictitious play interpretation, the following need to be common knowledge: (*i*) the Bayesian rationality of all the players, (*ii*) the payoff structure of the game, and (*iii*) the partitions $\mathcal{H}_k$. While no player gets to know the signals his opponents receive, they all must know the *partitions* of every player in order to compute the expected utilities of the other players. Under the fictitious play interpretation, each player mentally simulates the expected utility calculations of the others at every round of deliberation for each $\omega \in \Omega$. Again, part (*b*) of the definition of θ gives the players a method for dealing with ties. Of course, the common knowledge assumptions for the *actual play* interpretation of this dynamics are much weaker. In actual play, the players observe an actual event in their information partition, and update their conditional probabilities by observing the actual plays of their opponents. Such deliberators can converge to an Aumann correlated equilibrium knowing only their own payoffs and their own private event $H_{kj} \in \mathcal{H}_k$ at each round of deliberation. However, as in the case of such naive unconditional Dirichlet deliberators, naive conditional deliberators can converge to a correlated equilibrium without realizing they are at equilibrium.

We now consider how deliberational correlated equilibria and Aumann correlated equilibria are related. As with endogenous correlated equilibria, the vector of probability distributions $(\sigma_1(\cdot|\mathcal{H}_1), \ldots, \sigma_n(\cdot|\mathcal{H}_n))$ that determines the expectations in (2.*xiv*) characterizes the Aumann correlated equilibrium. However, the Aumann and the conditional deliberational correlated equilibrium concepts are not equivalent. Note that by part (*b*) of Definition 2.2.3, in order for the players to know they are at an Aumann correlated equilibrium, they must have common knowledge of the function $f : \Omega \to S$ as well as common knowledge of Bayesian rationality, the game's payoff structure, and the partitions $\mathcal{H}_k$, $k \in N$. These common knowledge assumptions are stronger than those underlying the fictitious play interpretation of deliberational equilibria, and are a principal reason why the Aumann and the conditional deliberational correlated equilibrium concepts fail to be equivalent. There are elementary examples of games in which an Aumann correlated equilibrium fails to be a deliberational equilibrium, and *vice versa*.

To show that an Aumann correlated equilibrium can fail to be a deliberational equilibrium, we return to the 3-player game of Figure 3.3.1 proposed by

Skyrms (1991b). If the three players are at the Aumann correlated equilibrium at which they play (T, L, M_2) if the coin comes up H and (B, R, M_2) if the coin comes up T, then Ron's probability distribution over Amie's and Kay's strategy combinations is

$$\mu_3^0(T, L) = \frac{1}{2}$$
$$\mu_3^0(T, R) = 0$$
$$\mu_3^0(B, L) = 0$$
$$\mu_3^0(B, R) = \frac{1}{2}$$

If Amie, Kay and Ron are conditional Dirichlet deliberators, then if deliberation starts at this Aumann equilibrium and the coin comes up H, Kay and Amie will play (T, L), so Ron, who does not see the coin flip, modifies his probabilities thus:

$$\mu_3^1(T, L) = \frac{1+1}{1+2} = \frac{2}{3}$$
$$\mu_3^1(T, R) = 0$$
$$\mu_3^1(B, L) = 0$$
$$\mu_3^1(B, R) = \frac{1}{1+2} = \frac{1}{3}$$

Since $\mu_3^0 \neq \mu_3^1$, this Aumann correlated equilibrium is not a deliberational equilibrium.

To show that a deliberational correlated equilibrium can fail to be an Aumann correlated equilibrium, let us consider 3-player Chicken once again. As noted above, the players are at deliberational equilibrium if

$$\mu_1(A_{11}) = \mu_2(A_{11}) = \mu_3(A_{11}) = \frac{2}{3}$$

and

$$\mu_1(A_{22}) = \mu_2(A_{22}) = \mu_3(A_{22}) = \frac{1}{3},$$

and each player can maximize expected utility by playing either A_1 or A_2. One may consider this unconditional deliberational equilibrium a special case of a conditional deliberational equilibrium, in which the players condition on the trivial partition of a probability space Ω. In order for this deliberational equilibrium to be an Aumann correlated equilibrium, there must be a function $f : \Omega \rightarrow S$

that satisfies (2.*xiv*) for each $\omega \in \Omega$ and such that, for $k = 1, 2, 3$,

(3.*v*)
$$\mu_k\big(\{\omega | f_{-k}(\omega) = (A_1, A_1)\}\big) = \frac{2}{3}$$

and

(3.*vi*)
$$\mu_k\big(\{\omega | f_{-k}(\omega) = (A_2, A_2)\}\big) = \frac{1}{3}$$

However, the only function f satisfying (3.*v*) and (3.*vi*) is $f : \Omega \to S$ such that, for $k = 1, 2, 3$,

$$\mu_k\big(\{\omega | f(\omega) = (A_1, A_1, A_1)\}\big) = \frac{2}{3}$$

and

$$\mu_k\big(\{\omega | f(\omega) = (A_2, A_2, A_2)\}\big) = \frac{1}{3}.^{14}$$

In other words, each player assigns positive probability only to the act combinations where all three players perform the same act. This function is not an Aumann correlated equilibrium, since each player will be tempted to defect from f at particular values of $\omega \in \Omega$. For instance, if ω is such that $f(\omega) = (A_1, A_1, A_1)$, then

$$E_1(u_1 \circ f | \Omega)(\omega) = E_1(u_1(A_1, A_1, A_1)) = 6$$

while

$$E_1(u_1 \circ (A_2, f_{-1}) | \Omega)(\omega) = E_1(u_1(A_2, A_1, A_1)) = 7$$

so (2.*iv*) fails. At this unconditional deliberational equilibrium, under the fictitious play interpretation the players have common knowledge only of the payoffs and each player's *beliefs*, and given this information, each player can maximize expected utility by playing either A_1 or A_2. By adding the probability space Ω and the function $f : \Omega \to S$ that characterize Aumann correlated equilibrium to the deliberational model, under the fictitious play interpretation the *choices* the players would make given their beliefs become common knowledge, and with this additional knowledge the players are no longer at equilibrium.

The relationship between Aumann and deliberational correlated equilibria is not yet fully understood. Nevertheless, we can show that a certain special class of Aumann correlated equilibria are fixed points of conditional Dirichlet deliberation. Following Aumann (1987), we call the states of the world *public* if each player has the same information partition $\mathcal{H}$, since in this case each player

---

[14]Recall the derivation given in §2.3.

receives the same information. We now show that if the states of the world are public, then players at an Aumann correlated equilibrium are at a conditional deliberational equilibrium.

Proposition 3.3.2. If each player has the information partition $\mathcal{H}$ of Ω, and f is an Aumann correlated equilibrium with respect to $\mathcal{H}$, then players who play f are at a conditional Dirichlet deliberational correlated equilibrium with respect to $\mathcal{H}$.

Proof. Suppose that $\mathfrak{S} = (\sigma_1(\cdot|\mathcal{H}), \ldots, \sigma_n(\cdot|\mathcal{H}))$ is the vector of probability distributions that characterizes the correlated equilibrium $f : \Omega \to S$, and that the n players are conditional Dirichlet deliberators. The Dirichlet dynamics are defined in terms of the fictitious play interpretation, so we may assume that the distributions that make up $\mathfrak{S}$ are common knowledge. Since each player receives the same signal at each round of deliberation, any sequence $\mathfrak{S}^n$ of deliberation can be divided into subsequences of *unconditional* Dirichlet deliberation corresponding to each element of $\mathcal{H}$. Hence it will suffice to show that, for a fixed $H_k \in \mathcal{H}$, if deliberation starts at the system of beliefs $\mathfrak{S}$, then $(\sigma_1(\cdot|H_k), \ldots, \sigma_n(\cdot|H_k))$ is an unconditional deliberational equilibrium of the subsequence $\mathfrak{S}^n_{H_k}$ of rounds of deliberation that are generated by the deliberators when they observe H_k. Now suppose that $\omega \in H_k$ occurs. Then, by (2.*xiv*), for each $k \in N$,

$$(1) \quad \sum_{A_{-k} \in S_{-k}} \sigma_k(A_{-k}|H_k)u_k(f_k(\omega), A_{-k})$$

$$\geq \sum_{A_{-k} \in S_{-k}} \sigma_k(A_{-k}|H_k)u_k(A_{kj_k}, A_{-k})$$

for all $A_{kj_k} \in S_k$.

(1) is simply the Bayesian rationality condition that characterizes endogenous correlated equilibrium, that is, given that the players all observe H_k, if their distributions are all common knowledge, then by (1) and Proposition 2.3.7, $(\sigma_1(\cdot|H_k), \ldots, \sigma_n(\cdot|H_k))$ will be an endogenous correlated equilibrium. Then by Proposition 3.2.3, $(\sigma_1(\cdot|H_k), \ldots, \sigma_n(\cdot|H_k))$ is an unconditional deliberational equilibrium. $\square$

The converse of this proposition fails, since, as demonstrated above, in 3-player Chicken with each player having the degenerate information partition, the players can be at a deliberational equilibrium that is not an Aumann correlated equilibrium.

Convergence in Strategies
for Aumann Correlated Equilibrium

Deliberational equilibria for conditional Dirichlet deliberation have been defined in terms of the deliberators' distributions over opponents' strategy combinations, but there is an alternate way to characterize fixed points of Dirichlet deliberation, in terms of the sequence of plays the dynamics determines. At the start of deliberation, each player k determines for each $\omega_j \in \Omega$ a strategy $A_k(\omega_j)$ that maximizes k's expected utility conditional on the cell $H_{kj}(\omega_j) \in \mathcal{H}_k$ given k's conditional priors. At each tth stage of deliberation, if $\omega^t \in \Omega$ occurs, then deliberators choose a strategy combination $A(\omega^t)$ such that each player k maximizes expected utility conditional on the cell $H_{kj}(\omega^t) \in \mathcal{H}_k$. Given the strategy combination the deliberators observe at time t, each updates her conditional probabilities and determines which strategy $f_k(\omega_j)$ maximizes expected utility at each $\omega_j \in \Omega$. This process determines a sequence (f^t) of exogenously correlated strategy combinations.

Notice that the value ω^t that occurs at time t determines the values for f^t at the elements of Ω that *do not* occur at time t. For instance, recall the 3-player game of Figure 3.3.1. Again, Amie chooses the row, Kay chooses the column, and Ron chooses the matrix, and their respective information partitions are $\mathcal{H}_1 = \mathcal{H}_2 = \{\{H\}, \{T\}\}$ and $\mathcal{H}_3 = \Omega$. If they each have uniform conditional priors defined by

$$\gamma_{(A_{2i},A_{3j}) \wedge \omega} = 1, \; \omega \in \Omega,$$
$$\gamma_{(A_{1i},A_{3j}) \wedge \omega} = 1, \; \omega \in \Omega, \text{ and}$$
$$\gamma_{(A_{1i},A_{2j})} = 1,$$

then, for each $\omega \in \Omega$,

$$E_1^0(u_1(T)|\omega) = 0 \cdot \frac{1}{6} + 2 \cdot \frac{1}{6} + 0 \cdot \frac{1}{6} + 0 \cdot \frac{1}{6} + 0 \cdot \frac{1}{6} + 1.1 \cdot \frac{1}{6} = \frac{31}{60}$$

$$E_1^0(u_1(B)|\omega) = 1 \cdot \frac{1}{6} + 0 \cdot \frac{1}{6} + 0 \cdot \frac{1}{6} + 0 \cdot \frac{1}{6} + 2 \cdot \frac{1}{6} + 0 \cdot \frac{1}{6} = \frac{1}{2}$$

$$E_2^0(u_2(L)|\omega) = 0 \cdot \frac{1}{6} + 2 \cdot \frac{1}{6} + 0 \cdot \frac{1}{6} + 0 \cdot \frac{1}{6} + 0 \cdot \frac{1}{6} + 1.1 \cdot \frac{1}{6} = \frac{31}{60}$$

$$E_2^0(u_2(R)|\omega) = 1 \cdot \frac{1}{6} + 0 \cdot \frac{1}{6} + 0 \cdot \frac{1}{6} + 0 \cdot \frac{1}{6} + 2 \cdot \frac{1}{6} + 0 \cdot \frac{1}{6} = \frac{1}{2}$$

$$E_3^0(u_3(M_1)) = 3 \cdot \frac{1}{4} + 0 \cdot \frac{1}{4} + 0 \cdot \frac{1}{4} + 0 \cdot \frac{1}{4} = \frac{3}{4}$$

$$E_3^0(u_3(M_2)) = 2 \cdot \frac{1}{4} + 0 \cdot \frac{1}{4} + 0 \cdot \frac{1}{4} + 2 \cdot \frac{1}{4} = 1$$

$$E_3^0(u_3(M_3)) = 0 \cdot \frac{1}{4} + 0 \cdot \frac{1}{4} + 0 \cdot \frac{1}{4} + 3 \cdot \frac{1}{4} = \frac{3}{4}$$

Hence f^0 is defined by $f^0(\omega) = (T, L, M_2)$. If $\omega^1 = H$, the deliberators play $A(\omega^1) = (T, L, M_2)$, and they recalculate conditional expected utilities, taking into account what they observed at round 1. The conditional expected utilities for Amie and Kay given $\omega = T$ are unchanged, since they did not observe T. Their conditional expected utilities given $\omega = H$ are now:

$$E_1^1(u_1(T)|H) = 0 \cdot \frac{1}{1+6} + 2 \cdot \frac{1+1}{1+6} + 0 \cdot \frac{1}{1+6}$$

$$+ 0 \cdot \frac{1}{1+6} + 0 \cdot \frac{1}{1+6} + 1.1 \cdot \frac{1}{1+6} = \frac{51}{70}$$

$$E_1^1(u_1(B)|H) = 1 \cdot \frac{1}{1+6} + 0 \cdot \frac{1+1}{1+6} + 0 \cdot \frac{1}{1+6}$$

$$+ 0 \cdot \frac{1}{1+6} + 2 \cdot \frac{1}{1+6} + 0 \cdot \frac{1}{1+6} = \frac{3}{7}$$

$$E_2^1(u_2(L)|H) = 0 \cdot \frac{1}{1+6} + 2 \cdot \frac{1+1}{1+6} + 0 \cdot \frac{1}{1+6}$$

$$+ 0 \cdot \frac{1}{1+6} + 0 \cdot \frac{1}{1+6} + 1.1 \cdot \frac{1}{1+6} = \frac{51}{70}$$

$$E_2^1(u_2(R)|H) = 1 \cdot \frac{1}{1+6} + 0 \cdot \frac{1+1}{1+6} + 0 \cdot \frac{1}{1+6}$$

$$+ 0 \cdot \frac{1}{1+6} + 2 \cdot \frac{1}{1+6} + 0 \cdot \frac{1}{1+6} = \frac{3}{7}$$

and Ron, who observed only that Amie and Kay combined to play (T, L) on the first round of deliberation, computes his new expected utilities:

$$E_3^1(u_3(M_1)) = 3 \cdot \frac{1+1}{1+4} + 0 \cdot \frac{1}{1+4} + 0 \cdot \frac{1}{1+4} + 0 \cdot \frac{1}{1+4} = \frac{6}{5}$$

$$E_3^1(u_3(M_2)) = 2 \cdot \frac{1+1}{1+4} + 0 \cdot \frac{1}{1+4} + 0 \cdot \frac{1}{1+4} + 2 \cdot \frac{1}{1+4} = \frac{6}{5}$$

$$E_3^1(u_3(M_3)) = 0 \cdot \frac{1+1}{1+4} + 0 \cdot \frac{1}{1+4} + 0 \cdot \frac{1}{1+4} + 3 \cdot \frac{1}{1+4} = \frac{3}{5}.$$

Ron can maximize expected utility either at M_1 or at M_2. Suppose that Ron selects M_1.[15] Hence f^1 is defined by $f^1(\omega) = (T, L, M_2) = f^0(\omega)$. If $\omega = H$ again at round 2, the deliberators play $(A(H)) = (T, L, M_2)$, and they recalculate conditional expected utilities. Once again, the conditional expected utilities given that $\omega = T$ are unchanged, since Amie and Kay have not observed T as of yet. The updated conditional expected utilities given that $\omega = H$ are[16]

$$E_1^2(u_1(T)|H) = 0 \cdot \frac{\frac{1}{2}+1}{2+6} + 2 \cdot \frac{\frac{3}{2}+1}{2+6} + 0 \cdot \frac{1}{2+6} + 0 \cdot \frac{1}{2+6}$$

$$+ 0 \cdot \frac{1}{2+6} + 1.1 \cdot \frac{1}{2+6} = \frac{61}{80}$$

$$E_1^2(u_1(B)|H) = 1 \cdot \frac{\frac{1}{2}+1}{2+6} + 0 \cdot \frac{\frac{3}{2}+1}{2+6} + 0 \cdot \frac{1}{2+6} + 0 \cdot \frac{1}{2+6}$$

$$+ 2 \cdot \frac{1}{2+6} + 0 \cdot \frac{1}{2+6} = \frac{35}{80}$$

$$E_2^2(u_2(L)|H) = 0 \cdot \frac{\frac{1}{2}+1}{2+6} + 2 \cdot \frac{\frac{3}{2}+1}{2+6} + 0 \cdot \frac{1}{2+6} + 0 \cdot \frac{1}{2+6}$$

$$+ 0 \cdot \frac{1}{2+6} + 1.1 \cdot \frac{1}{2+6} = \frac{61}{80}$$

$$E_2^2(u_2(R)|H) = 1 \cdot \frac{\frac{1}{2}+1}{2+6} + 0 \cdot \frac{\frac{3}{2}+1}{2+6} + 0 \cdot \frac{1}{2+6} + 0 \cdot \frac{1}{2+6}$$

$$+ 2 \cdot \frac{1}{2+6} + 0 \cdot \frac{1}{2+6} = \frac{35}{80}$$

while Ron's updated expected utilities are:

$$E_3^2(u_3(M_1)) = 3 \cdot \frac{2+1}{2+4} + 0 \cdot \frac{1}{2+4} + 0 \cdot \frac{1}{2+4} + 0 \cdot \frac{1}{2+4} = \frac{3}{2}$$

$$E_3^2(u_3(M_2)) = 2 \cdot \frac{2+1}{2+4} + 0 \cdot \frac{1}{2+4} + 0 \cdot \frac{1}{2+4} + 2 \cdot \frac{1}{2+4} = \frac{4}{3}$$

$$E_3^2(u_3(M_3)) = 0 \cdot \frac{2+1}{2+4} + 0 \cdot \frac{1}{2+4} + 0 \cdot \frac{1}{2+4} + 3 \cdot \frac{1}{2+4} = \frac{1}{2}.$$

Consequently, at the second stage of deliberation, Amie and Kay still maximize

---

[15] Ron could maximize expected utility by playing a mixed strategy, but as argued in §1.6, he has no decisive reason to do this. I assume that if for some reason Ron indeed mixes explicitly, then Amie and Kay observe only the pure strategy that Ron actually plays based upon the outcome of his randomizing device.

[16] Since Ron can maximize expected utility by playing either M_1 or M_2, Amie and Kay use the tie-breaking rule in their updating.

expected utility by playing T and L respectively, whether the coin comes up H or T, but Ron now maximizes his expected utility by playing M_1, so f^2 is defined by $f(\omega) = (T, L, M_1)$. Note that the sequence of observed plays determines what the deliberators will choose at both $\omega = H$ and $\omega = T$, even though $\omega = T$ has not been observed as of yet.

As this example illustrates, conditional Dirichlet deliberation defines both a sequence of conditional probabilities and a sequence $(f^t(\omega^t)) = (f^t(\omega_1), \ldots, f^t(\omega_M))$ such that each deliberator maximizes expected utility by playing $f_k^t(\omega_k) \in f^t(\omega_k)$ for each $\omega_k \in \Omega$ at each stage t of deliberation. The sequence (f^t) of strategy combinations determined by conditional Dirichlet dynamics forms a dynamical system. The terms of the sequence (f^t) are uniquely determined by the distributions $(\mathfrak{P}^n)$ up to tie breaking cases.[17] In the special case in which deliberators all condition on the partition $\mathcal{H}$, the conditional probabilities on the cells in $\mathcal{H}$ that did not occur at time t remain unchanged, so if $\omega_i \neq \omega^t$, then the strategy combination $f^{t-1}(\omega_i)$ is the combination that maximizes expected utility for each $k \in N$ at round t. That is, if deliberators all condition on a common partition $\mathcal{H}$, then

$$f^t(\omega^t) = \begin{cases} A \in S & \text{such that } A_{kj} \in A \text{ is a best response to} \\ & \mu_k^t(\cdot|H(\omega_i)) \text{ if } \omega^t = \omega_i \\ f^{t-1}(\omega_i) & \text{if } \omega^t \neq \omega_i. \end{cases}$$

We can define a fixed point of this dynamical system.

Definition 3.3.3. An *almost sure stationary point* of the dynamics is a vector f^{t_0} such that for all $t \geq t_0$, the event $\{f^{t_0} = f^t\}$ occurs with probability one (from the perspective of any agent). ☐

We define a stationary point of the dynamics as an "almost sure" concept because the sequence (f^t) is a stochastic process, so that we need to rule out as stationary sequences such that for $t > t_0$, $f^{t_0}(\omega^{t_0})) = f^t(\omega^t)$ if $\omega^t = \omega^{t_0}$, but $f^{t_0}(\omega^{t_0})) \neq f^t(\omega^t)$ if $\omega^t \neq \omega^{t_0}$.

Proposition 3.3.4. If f is an almost sure stationary point of conditional Dirichlet deliberation, then f is an Aumann correlated equilibrium.

Proof. Suppose that $f = f^0$ is not an Aumann correlated equilibrium. Then for some $k \in N$ and some $\omega_j \in \Omega$,

$$E_k(u_k \circ f|\mathcal{H}_k)(\omega_j) < E_k(u_k \circ (g_k, f_{-k})|\mathcal{H}_k)(\omega_j)$$

---

[17] As mentioned in note 8, in cases in which a player has more than one best response, one has the option of updating the sequence (A^m) either by including the opponent's conditional distributions over the player's best replies or by including the pure strategy they actually observe the player play.

for some $g_k \neq f_k$. Hence at the first round of deliberation, k will prefer $g_k(\omega_j)$ over $f_k(\omega_j)$, so $f^1 \neq f^0$. Hence for all $t \geq 0$, the event $\{f^0 = f^t\}$ occurs with probability 0, so f is not an almost sure stationary point of the dynamics. The proposition follows by contraposition.   □

The converse of this proposition fails. Consider again the 3-player example in Skyrms (1991b) summarized by Figure 3.3.1 If the players' priors this time are defined by

$$\gamma_{(L,M_2)\wedge H} = \gamma_{(R,M_2)\wedge T} = 1, \qquad \gamma_{(A_2,A_3)\wedge \omega} = 0 \text{ otherwise,}$$
$$\gamma_{(T,M_2)\wedge H} = \gamma_{(B,M_2)\wedge T} = 1, \qquad \gamma_{(A_1,A_3)\wedge \omega} = 0 \text{ otherwise, and}$$
$$\gamma_{TL} = \gamma_{BR} = 1, \qquad \gamma_{TR} = \gamma_{BL} = 0$$

then they are at the Aumann correlated equilibrium f defined by

$$f(\omega) = \begin{cases} (T, L, M_2) & \text{if } \omega = H, \\ (B, R, M_2) & \text{if } \omega = T \end{cases}$$

Suppose a sequence of conditional Dirichlet deliberation begins from these priors, and that $\omega^1 = \omega^2 = H$. Then the deliberators will play (T, L, M_2) twice, and so at the third round of deliberation, Ron's updated probabilities are

$$\mu_3^3(T, L) = \frac{2+1}{2+2} = \frac{3}{4}.$$
$$\mu_3^3(B, R) = \frac{0+1}{2+2} = \frac{1}{4},$$
$$\mu_3^3(T, R) = \mu_3^3(B, L) = \frac{0+0}{2+2} = 0.$$

Given this distribution, Ron's expected utilities are

$$E_3^3(u_3(M_1)) = 3 \cdot \frac{3}{4} + 0 \cdot 0 + 0 \cdot 0 + 0 \cdot \frac{1}{4} = \frac{9}{4}$$
$$E_3^3(u_3(M_2)) = 2 \cdot \frac{3}{4} + 0 \cdot 0 + 0 \cdot 0 + 2 \cdot \frac{1}{4} = 2$$
$$E_3^3(u_3(M_3)) = 0 \cdot \frac{3}{4} + 0 \cdot 0 + 0 \cdot 0 + 3 \cdot \frac{1}{4} = \frac{3}{4}$$

so Ron will change his strategy to M_1, breaking down the correlated equilibrium.

We can demonstrate a more limited converse to this proposition, assuming that the deliberators have a common information partition and that the correlated equilibrium is strict.

Proposition 3.3.5. If deliberators have a common information partition $\mathcal{H}$, and if $f : \Omega \rightarrow S$ is a strict Aumann correlated equilibrium, then f is an almost sure stationary point of Dirichlet deliberation.

Proof. Suppose that f is a strict Aumann correlated equilibrium, and that players begin deliberation with their priors defined by the distributions which characterize f. Since f is measurable with respect to $\mathcal{H}$, for each $k \in N$ and each $\omega_j \in \Omega$,

$$\mu_k^0(A_{-k}|H_j(\omega_j)) = \begin{cases} 1 & \text{if } A_{-k} = f_{-k}(\omega_j) \\ 0 & \text{otherwise} \end{cases}$$

If $\omega^1 = \omega_j$, $f_k(\omega_j)$ is k's unique best response to $f_{-k}(\omega_j)$ given $\mu_k^0(\cdot|H_j(\omega_j))$, so k will play $f_k(\omega_j)$ on the first round of deliberation. If $\omega^1 \neq \omega_j$, then $f_k^1(\omega_j) = f(\omega_j)$ by definition. Hence $f^1 = f$. The proposition follows from the Absorption Theorem. $\qquad\square$

§3.4 Dirichlet Dynamics with Imperfect Memory

In this section, I consider a variation of Dirichlet deliberation in which the deliberators have *incomplete recall* of the sequence of past plays. More specifically, each player k will "remember" which strategy profiles have been played for a certain number η_k^t of the most recent stages of play, where η_k^t is a random variable. This type of *random recall conditional Dirichlet dynamics* (RRC-Dirichlet dynamics) is similar to the *stochastic adaptive dynamics* of Young (1993), but is motivated by a somewhat different intuitive framework. RRC-Dirichlet deliberation can converge to Aumann correlated equilibria in cases where Dirichlet deliberation with *complete recall* can converge only to the mixed Nash equilibrium, if at all.

Once more, I use Battle of the Sexes with payoff structure defined by the matrix in Figure 3.1.1 to illustrate this type of inductive dynamics. If Kay and Amie have the common partition $\mathcal{H} = \{\{H\}, \{T\}\}$ of the event space $\Omega = \{H, T\}$, and each starts with uniform conditional priors defined by

$$\gamma_{A_{ij} \wedge \omega}^0 = 1, \ i, j \in \{1, 2\}, \ \omega \in \{H, T\},$$

then as we saw above conditional Dirichlet deliberation with complete recall converges to the mixed Nash equilibrium characterized by the distributions

$$\mu_1^*(\text{Kay plays } A_2) = \mu_2^*(\text{Amie plays } A_1) = \frac{2}{3}$$

and with payoff vector $(\frac{2}{3}, \frac{2}{3})$.

These deliberators can do better if they each recall only a *subset* of the most recent rounds of deliberation, and update their probabilities for their opponent's strategies on the basis of what they can remember, rather than the full sequence of plays. Suppose that Kay and Amie begin conditional Dirichlet deliberation with uniform priors as before, that both have complete recall for the first 16 rounds of deliberation, and that afterward they start to forget some of the early history of play. The first 16 rounds of play are summarized in Table 3.4.1. Now suppose that on the 17th round of deliberation, the coin comes up H and Amie can recall 6 of the most recent rounds (including round 17) which she observed H, while Kay can recall only 5 of the most recent rounds (including round 17) in which she observed H. Each will update her probabilities by using the frequencies of past opponent's plays she can recall:

$$\mu_1^{17}(\text{Kay plays } A_1 | H) \quad = \quad \frac{2+1}{6+2} = \frac{3}{8}$$

$$\mu_1^{17}(\text{Kay plays } A_2 | H) \quad = \quad \frac{4+1}{6+2} = \frac{5}{8}$$

$$\mu_2^{17}(\text{Amie plays } A_1 | H) \quad = \quad \frac{4+1}{5+2} = \frac{5}{7}$$

$$\mu_2^{17}(\text{Amie plays } A_2 | H) \quad = \quad \frac{1+1}{5+2} = \frac{2}{7}$$

Each computes the conditional expected utilities given her updated probabilities:

$$E_1^{17}(u_1(A_1)|H) \quad = \quad \frac{3}{8} \cdot 2 + \frac{5}{8} \cdot 0 = \frac{3}{4},$$

$$E_1^{17}(u_1(A_2)|H) \quad = \quad \frac{3}{8} \cdot 0 + \frac{5}{8} \cdot 1 = \frac{5}{8},$$

$$E_2^{17}(u_2(A_1)|H) \quad = \quad \frac{5}{7} \cdot 1 + \frac{2}{7} \cdot 0 = \frac{5}{7},$$

$$E_2^{17}(u_2(A_2)|H) \quad = \quad \frac{5}{7} \cdot 0 + \frac{2}{7} \cdot 2 = \frac{4}{7}.$$

Both strictly prefer to play A_1 given their probabilities, so they have successfully coordinated on the equilibrium point (A_1, A_1). Moreover, in subsequent rounds of deliberation the two players will repeat this strategy combination every time they observe H, so long as they can recall at least one round of previous play.

Table 3.4.1

Battle of the Sexes

Played by RRC-Dirichlet Deliberators*

t	ω^t	s_1	s_2
1	H	A_1	A_2
2	T	A_1	A_2
3	H	A_1	A_2
4	T	A_1	A_2
5	H	A_2	A_1
6	T	A_2	A_1
7	H	A_1	A_2
8	T	A_1	A_2
9	H	A_1	A_2
10	T	A_1	A_2
11	H	A_2	A_1
12	T	A_2	A_1
13	H	A_1	A_2
14	T	A_1	A_2
15	H	A_1	A_2
16	T	A_1	A_2

---

*At each round t of deliberation, s_1 is the strategy that Amie plays and s_2 is the strategy that Kay plays.

This is because, given these values for the $\gamma^0_{A_{ij} \wedge \omega}$'s, if the players can recall that they have coordinated on (A_1, A_1) at the most recent round of play at which they observed H, then their distributions will be in the basin of attraction of the conditional distribution vector corresponding to (A_1, A_1) given H.

Now suppose that on the 18th round of deliberation, the coin comes up T, and at this round Kay can recall the 6 most recent rounds at which she observed T (including round 18), while Amie can recall only the 5 most recent rounds at which she observed T (including round 18). Then their updated conditional probabilities are:

$$\mu_1^{18}(\text{Kay plays } A_1|T) = \frac{1+1}{5+2} = \frac{2}{7}$$

$$\mu_1^{18}(\text{Kay plays } A_2|T) = \frac{4+1}{5+2} = \frac{5}{7}$$

$$\mu_2^{18}(\text{Amie plays } A_1|T) = \frac{4+1}{6+2} = \frac{5}{8}$$

$$\mu_2^{18}(\text{Amie plays } A_2|H) = \frac{2+1}{6+2} = \frac{3}{8}$$

Given these updated probabilities, their conditional expectations are

$$E_1^{18}(u_1(A_1)|H) = \frac{2}{7} \cdot 2 + \frac{5}{7} \cdot 0 = \frac{4}{7},$$

$$E_1^{18}(u_1(A_2)|H) = \frac{2}{7} \cdot 0 + \frac{5}{7} \cdot 1 = \frac{5}{7},$$

$$E_2^{18}(u_2(A_1)|H) = \frac{5}{8} \cdot 1 + \frac{3}{8} \cdot 0 = \frac{5}{8}, \text{ and}$$

$$E_2^{18}(u_2(A_2)|H) = \frac{5}{8} \cdot 0 + \frac{3}{8} \cdot 2 = \frac{3}{4}.$$

Hence, both players will prefer A_2, so they coordinate on the equilibrium point (A_2, A_2). Once more, given these values for the $\gamma^0_{A_{ij} \wedge \omega}$'s, so long as each player remembers at least one previous round of play at which T occurred, they will play this equilibrium each time they observe T in the future. Consequently, deliberation with random recall in this instance converges to the strict correlated equilibrium $f : \Omega \to S$ defined by

$$f(\omega) = \begin{cases} (A_1, A_1) & \text{if } \omega = H \\ (A_2, A_2) & \text{if } \omega = T \end{cases}$$

Of course, the outcome of this type of "random recall" dynamics will depend heavily upon the memories of the deliberators at early stages of deliberation. Suppose that Kay and Amie start to play Battle of the Sexes all over again as conditional Dirichlet deliberators, that the initial sequence of plays is again summarized by Table 3.4.1, and that the players again start forgetting some of the early history of play after the 16th round of play. Suppose that once again on the 17th round of deliberation, the coin comes up H, Amie can recall the 6 most recent rounds of deliberation corresponding to $\omega = H$, and Kay can recall the 5 most recent rounds of deliberation corresponding to $\omega = H$. Then Amie and Kay will coordinate on the strict equilibrium (A_1, A_1), and thus will coordinate on (A_1, A_1) for the remainder of the subsequence of deliberation at which $\omega^m = H$. However, suppose that this time on the 18th round of deliberation, the coin comes up T, and at this round Amie can now recall the 6 most recent rounds corresponding to $\omega = T$ and Kay now recall the 5 most recent rounds corresponding to $\omega = T$. Then their updated conditional probabilities are:

$$\mu_1^{18}(\text{Kay plays } A_1|T) = \frac{2+1}{6+2} = \frac{3}{8}$$

$$\mu_1^{18}(\text{Kay plays } A_2|T) = \frac{4+1}{6+2} = \frac{5}{8}$$

$$\mu_2^{18}(\text{Amie plays } A_1|T) = \frac{4+1}{5+2} = \frac{5}{7}$$

$$\mu_2^{18}(\text{Amie plays } A_2|H) = \frac{1+1}{5+2} = \frac{2}{7}$$

Given these updated probabilities, their conditional expectations are

$$E_1^{18}(u_1(A_1)|H) = \frac{3}{8} \cdot 2 + \frac{5}{8} \cdot 0 = \frac{3}{4},$$

$$E_1^{18}(u_1(A_2)|H) = \frac{3}{8} \cdot 0 + \frac{5}{8} \cdot 1 = \frac{5}{8},$$

$$E_2^{18}(u_2(A_1)|H) = \frac{5}{7} \cdot 1 + \frac{2}{7} \cdot 0 = \frac{5}{7}, \text{ and}$$

$$E_2^{18}(u_2(A_2)|H) = \frac{5}{7} \cdot 0 + \frac{2}{7} \cdot 2 = \frac{4}{7}.$$

Hence Amie and Kay will coordinate on (A_1, A_1) at this round of deliberation, and they will continue to coordinate on (A_1, A_1) for all subsequent rounds of play in which the coin comes up T. Consequently, in this case the dynamics will settle upon the strict Nash equilibrium (A_1, A_1).

This example shows that RRC-Dirichlet deliberators can become locked into an equilibrium that is "unfair" to some, if they settle upon a strict equilibrium with asymmetric payoffs early in the sequence of plays. This is not a defect of the model. Indeed, this random recall model of deliberation can account for the emergence and persistence of certain "unfair" equilibria as the result of precedents, which the players might not even remember over the stretch of time.

A model of inductive deliberation in which the players have random recall of the sort outlined above is not hard to justify intuitively. In an actual play interpretation of RRC-Dirichlet deliberation, one can easily imagine that Amie and Kay can each recall only a certain number of the most recent plays, and that the numbers of plays that each can recall will vary somewhat at each round of play. After all, humans have imperfect memories, tend to remember recent events and to forget events long past, and at some instances will be able to recall more of the immediate past than at other instances. If one interprets the deliberators as representatives of populations selected at random to play a single round of the game, then one can explain random recall as the result of representatives each being able to observe only a certain number of the most recent plays, which can vary between representatives, before actually participating in the game.

The RRC-Dirichlet dynamics is similar in spirit to the *stochastic adaptive dynamics* developed in Young (1993), but also differs from Young's stochastic adaptive dynamics in several important respects. Stochastic adaptive deliberators play their best response given their probabilities at each round of deliberation, same as Dirichlet deliberators. They also have imperfect histories of past plays, as in random recall Dirichlet dynamics. However, while random recall Dirichlet deliberators each remember a number of the *most recent* past plays, which varies at each round of deliberation, stochastic adaptive deliberators update their probabilities from *random samples* of past opponents' plays, which need not have been the most recent plays. Also, stochastic adaptive deliberators all sample the same number of past opponents' plays, though they need not sample the same past plays, while random recall Dirichlet deliberators each recall a random number of the most recent past plays, which is stochastically independent of the random numbers of the most recent past plays their opponents recall, so that the numbers of most recent past plays the various deliberators recall can differ. One can motivate this difference using representative interpretations of the different dynamics. In Young's framework, at each round of deliberation a representative from each of several populations is selected at random and matched against the other representatives. Before play, each representative can "ask around" in her own population and learn what the representatives of the other populations did at k previous rounds of play. Each representative samples k members of her own population, though the information each player obtains need not come from the same plays corresponding to his opponents' samples. In the representative interpretation of RRC-Dirichlet dynamics, at each round of play a representative from each population is selected and told in advance when she will be playing. Each representative can observe some of the plays that precede her turn, but she cannot in general observe the whole history of plays or the same set of plays each of her opponents observes prior to her turn.

Finally, the model of stochastic adaptive dynamics developed in Young (1993) does not incorporate external signals, unlike random recall conditional Dirichlet dynamics. Due to this last difference, the research on stochastic adaptive dynamics has focused on identifying sufficient conditions under which the dynamics converge to Nash equilibrium, while here I am introducing RRC-Dirichlet dynamics as one means of explaining the emergence of Aumann correlated equilibrium.

Making the players' memories imperfect can improve their results because doing so introduces a source of *asymmetry* in the players' knowledge. One might find it somewhat paradoxical that allowing the players less information in the random recall model than they would have in the complete recall model can result in their doing better. This "paradox" can be explained away if one notes that at any particular round of deliberation, one player can have more information with which to update her probabilities than her opponent. Of course, the amount of information each player has might change at the next round, so that in this round the other player has more information. This information asymmetry can drive the sequence of updated conditional distributions into the conditional basin of attraction of a pure strategy equilibrium, so that the dynamics eventually converge to an Aumann correlated equilibrium of the game, which might be one of the game's pure strategy Nash equilibria.

I now give the definition of RRC-Dirichlet deliberation. As with conditional Dirichlet deliberation with full recall, I begin with a game $\Gamma = (N, S, \boldsymbol{u})$, and add a finite probability space Ω together with information partitions $\mathcal{H}_k$, $k \in N$. Note that the priors are defined as functions of *initial prior states*, which deliberators can eventually forget. In an actual play interpretation, it seems plausible to suppose that if deliberators can forget part of the past history of play, they will not be able to remember indefinitely the states that defined their priors before they began play. Also, in the representative interpretation, it seems plausible that the representatives gradually forget the states that determine the priors. In any event, the following definition is fairly general, and covers both cases in which deliberators always recall the priors and in which deliberators ultimately forget the priors.

Definition 3.4.1. Let $\Gamma = (N, S, \boldsymbol{u})$, Ω, and the partitions $\mathcal{H}_k$ of Ω be given, and let an elementary event $\omega^t \in \Omega$ occur at each round of deliberation. The players are *RRC-Dirichlet deliberators* iff the sequence of probability distributions $(\boldsymbol{\mathfrak{P}}^t)$,

$$\boldsymbol{\mathfrak{P}}^t = (\mu_1^t(\cdot|\mathcal{H}_1), \ldots, \mu_n^t(\cdot|\mathcal{H}_n))$$

of the players' probabilities over their opponents' strategy combinations is defined recursively as follows:

(1) At the start of deliberation, Player k associates an *initial weight* $\gamma_{i\boldsymbol{A}_{-k} \wedge H_{kj}} \geq 0$ with each of $\tau_{\boldsymbol{A}_{-k} \wedge H_{kj}}$ *initial states.* Player k's initial weight for the conjunction $\boldsymbol{A}_{-k} \wedge H_{kj}$, $\gamma^0_{\boldsymbol{A}_{-k} \wedge H_{kj}}$ is defined by

$$\gamma^0_{\boldsymbol{A}_{-k} \wedge H_{kj}} = \sum_{i=1}^{\tau_{\boldsymbol{A}_{-k} \wedge H_{kj}}} \gamma_{i\boldsymbol{A}_{-k} \wedge H_{kj}}.$$

Player k's conditional prior distribution $\mu_k^0(\cdot|\mathcal{H}_k)$ is defined by

$$\mu_k^0(\boldsymbol{A}_{-k}|H_{kj}) = \frac{\gamma^0_{\boldsymbol{A}_{-k} \wedge H_{kj}}}{\sum\limits_{\boldsymbol{B}_{-k} \in S_{-k}} \gamma^0_{\boldsymbol{B}_{-k} \wedge H_{kj}}} , \; H_{kj} \in \mathcal{H}_k$$

(2) For round t of deliberation and for each player k, let η_k^t be a random variable with range $\{1, 2, \ldots, M_k^t\}$, $1 \leq M_k^t \leq t$, and let τ_k^t be a random variable with range $\{1, 2, \ldots, N_k^t\}$, $1 \leq N_k^t \leq t$. For each $H_{kj} \in \mathcal{H}_k$, and each $\boldsymbol{A}_{-k} \in S_{-k}$

$$\kappa^t_{H_{kj}} = \sum_{i=\eta_k^t}^{t} 1_{H_{kj}}(\omega^i)$$

and

$$\kappa^t_{\boldsymbol{A}_{-k} \wedge H_{kj}} = \sum_{i=\eta_k^t}^{t} 1_{\boldsymbol{A}_{-k} \wedge H_{kj}}(\omega^i)$$

that is, $\kappa^t_{H_{kj}}$ and $\kappa^t_{\boldsymbol{A}_{-k} \wedge H_{kj}}$ are the number of times that H_{kj} has occurred and the number of times that $\boldsymbol{A}_{-k}$ and H_{kj} have both occurred, respectively, during the last $t - \eta_k^t$ of the first t rounds of deliberation. At the $t + 1$st round of deliberation, Player k updates his probability distribution $\mu_k^t(\cdot|\mathcal{H}_k)$ according to the rule

$$\mu_k^{t+1}(\boldsymbol{A}_{-k}|H_{kj}) = \mu_k^t(\boldsymbol{A}_{-k}|H_{kj})$$

if H_{kj} did not occur at the $t + 1$st round of deliberation, and, if H_{kj} occurred at the $t + 1$st round of deliberation, then

$$\mu_k^{t+1}(A_{-k}|H_{kj}) = \frac{\kappa_{A_{-k} \wedge H_{kj}}^t + \theta + \gamma_{A_{-k} \wedge H_{kj}}^t}{\kappa_{H_{kj}}^t + 1 + \sum \gamma_{B_{-k} \wedge H_{kj}}^t}$$

where

(a)
$$\gamma_{B_{-k} \wedge H_{kj}}^t = \sum_{i=t-\tau_k^t+1}^{\tau_{B_{-k} \wedge H_{kj}}} \gamma_{iB_{-k} \wedge H_{kj}}$$

that is, $\gamma_{B_{-k} \wedge H_{kj}}^t$ is the sum of the initial weights that k can recall at time t, and θ is defined as in conditional Dirichlet deliberation with complete recall. □

As the reader will note, this definition resembles the definition of conditional Dirichlet deliberation with full memory, but differs from that definition in two important respects:

(1) If N_k^t is constant, so that k's recall of the initial states is bounded, then as $t \to \infty$, the number of prior states that enter into the calculation of $\gamma_{B_{-k} \wedge H_{kj}}^t$ diminishes, until the prior states finally make no contribution at all to the calculation of $\mu_k^{t+1}(A_{-k}|H_{kj})$. Condition 3.4.1(a) formalizes the intuition that each RRC-deliberator can eventually forget the values of the priors.

(2) Each deliberator k updates her conditional probabilities based upon past frequencies of the most recent η_k^t plays rather than all t past plays.

τ_k^t, the random variable that determines how many initial states player k recalls at round t, is for the sake of generality defined independently of η_k^t. In words, Definition 3.4.1 says that at time t, deliberator k can recall the results of the η_k^t most recent rounds of play and, if $t - \tau_k^t < \tau_{B_{-k} \wedge H_{kj}}$, then k can also recall $\tau_{B_{-k} \wedge H_{kj}} - t - \tau_k^t$ of the initial states that define k's priors. If one regards η_k^t and τ_k^t as degenerate random variables, then conditional Dirichlet deliberation with full memory is a special case of RRC-Dirichlet deliberation, where $\eta_k^t = \tau_k^t = t$ and $\gamma_{B_{-k} \wedge H_{kj}}^t = \gamma_{B_{-k} \wedge H_{kj}}^0$ for all $k \in N$ and all $t \geq 1$.

However, unlike the previous Dirichlet dynamics with full memory, I believe that RRC-Dirichlet dynamics does not admit of a plausible fictitious play interpretation. Definition 3.4.1 is given above in terms of an "ideal observer" who calculates every player's expected utilities at every round of deliberation given what each player knows, and then updates probabilities accordingly. Individual players would not be able to update their own probabilities by mentally simulating each others' decisions at each round of play, even if they could all receive private information from a signaling device while they were updating. In order for each player to mentally simulate his opponents' deliberations in this model, he would have to know how much each opponent *remembers* at every round of deliberation. I for one do not think that fictitious players would be able to read one another's minds and learn what everyone remembers. Additionally, even if all memories were somehow to become common knowledge, then the players would all have equally complete memories of the sequence of past plays, when the underlying motivation for this kind of dynamics is to introduce knowledge asymmetries by having deliberators remember *different* recent histories of the past plays.

On the other hand, as hinted above one can interpret this kind of dynamics very plausibly either as a sequence of actual plays by individuals with imperfect memories, or in representative terms. If one interprets the deliberators to be naive expected utility maximizers who play the game repeatedly and who update their probabilities by applying the conditional Dirichlet rule, one can easily imagine that they might not be able to remember the entire history of plays, but that they are able to remember what their opponents did at a number of the most recent plays. As noted already, if one interprets the deliberators to be representatives of populations who play the game once and then drop out, then it makes sense to suppose that each representative can observe some of the sequence of plays immediately preceding her turn at the game, but not necessarily the entire history of the game or the same set of recent past plays observed by the representatives she will oppose.

Note that Definition 3.4.1 does not set any distributional restrictions on the random variables η_k^t and τ_k^t, $1 \leq k \leq n$, that determine how much of the past history of plays each player can use in updating probabilities. In particular, Definition 3.4.1 does not include any assumptions regarding stochastic dependence or independence, either across players or across the sequence of plays. One natural choice for the joint distribution of the η_k^t's is the uniform distribution over $\{1, 2, \ldots, t\}^n$, but this is not the only distribution one might plausibly set over the history of past plays. In most of the examples considered here, we will make the following assumptions regarding the sequence of random vectors $(\boldsymbol{\eta}^t)$, where $\boldsymbol{\eta}^t = (\eta_1^t, \ldots, \eta_n^t)$:

(i) For $i \neq k$, η_i^t and η_k^t are stochastically independent. In words, the *memories* of the players, unlike their strategies, are uncorrelated at each round of deliberation.

(ii) For each $k \in N$, there are constants L_k and M_k such that if $t > L_k$, $L_k \leq \eta_k \leq M_k$. In words, each deliberator's memory is *bounded* below by L_k and above by M_k, so the player will recall at least L_k, but not more than M_k, rounds of play corresponding to $H_{kj} \in \mathcal{H}_k$ no matter how many rounds of play have occurred.

These assumptions are fairly modest. Assumption (i) says simply that what one player can remember is not evidence for what any other player can remember. Assumption (ii) reflects the intuition that each player's memory capacity remains constant throughout the sequence of plays.

The fixed points of RRC-Dirichlet dynamics have some of the same elementary properties as the fixed points of conditional Dirichlet dynamics with full memory. The proofs of the following results are the same as the proofs of similar results for conditional Dirichlet dynamics with full memory, *mutatis mutandis*.

Proposition 3.4.2. If f is an almost sure stationary point of RRC-Dirichlet deliberation, then f is an Aumann correlated equilibrium.

Proof. Similar to the proof of Proposition 3.3.4. □

Proposition 3.4.3. If deliberators have a common information partition $\mathcal{H}$, and if $f : \Omega \to S$ is a strict Aumann correlated equilibrium, then f is an almost sure stationary point of RRC-Dirichlet deliberation.

Proof. Similar to the proof of Proposition 3.3.5. □

In the remainder of this section, I will give a general convergence result for RRC-Dirichlet deliberation. Given certain appropriate boundaries on the deliberators' memories, in the special case of 2×2 games with two Nash equilibrium conventions, RRC-deliberation converges almost surely to a strict Aumann correlated equilibrium of the game. This result is analogous to Theorem 1 in Young (1993), which gives sufficient conditions for the convergence of stochastic adaptive dynamics to a strict Nash equilibrium.

Every strict Nash equilibrium of a game is such that, if a Dirichlet deliberator k's opponents play their end of this equilibrium often enough, then k will want to play his end of the equilibrium. More precisely, if A^* is a strict Nash equilibrium of a game Γ, then for each player k, there is a value $\beta_{kA_{k^*}}$ such that if k's opponents play A^*_{-k} at least $\beta_{kA_{k^*}}$ times consecutively, then $E_k(u_k(A^*_k)) > E_k(u_k(A_{kj}))$ for all $A_{kj} \neq A^*_k$. In other words, if k's opponents play their end of a strict Nash equilibrium A^* consistently, then the relative frequency of their playing A^*_{-k} will eventually overwhelm any of k's earlier probabilities that the opponents will play some strategy combination other than A^*_{-k}, with the result that A_k^* will eventually be k's best response given k's beliefs. We call $\beta_{k A_k^*}$ player k's *transition frequency* for A_k^*. Since the number of players and the number of the game's strict Nash equilibria are finite, we can set

$$\beta_{A^*} = \max\{\beta_{k A_k^*} | k \in N\}$$

and

$$\beta_\Gamma = \max\{\beta_{A^*} | A^* \text{ is a strict Nash equilibrium of } \Gamma\}.$$

which we call the *absorption frequencies* of the equilibrium A^* and of the strict equilibria of Γ, respectively.

Lemma 3.4.4. Let Γ be a 2×2 game Γ with two strict Nash equilibria, let the players be RRC-Dirichlet deliberators with a common partition $\mathcal{H}$ of Ω, and let $H_k \in \mathcal{H}$ be given. If each deliberator k recalls at least $\min\{t, \beta_\Gamma\}$ rounds, and at most $2\beta_\Gamma$ rounds, of the H_k-subsequence of deliberation at every round, then for each round $t \geq \beta_\Gamma$ of RRC-Dirichlet deliberation there is a constant positive probability that the deliberators will coordinate on a strict equilibrium of Γ.

Proof. Without loss of generality, let (A_1, A_1) and (A_2, A_2) be the strict Nash equilibria of this 2×2 game, and consider only rounds of deliberation in which $\omega^t \in H_k$ occurs. Note that, for any $N \geq 1$, the H_k-subsequence of plays $(A^t)_{t=N}^{N+\beta}$ determined by Dirichlet deliberation with full memory is fixed, and must satisfy one of the following:

(1) For some value η, $1 \leq \eta \leq \beta_\Gamma$, the deliberators coordinate on either (A_1, A_1) or (A_2, A_2) on round $N + \eta$,

(2) The deliberators play the nonequilibrium strategy combinations (A_1, A_2), (A_2, A_1) at each round of deliberation between $N + 1$ and $N + \beta_\Gamma$ inclusive, and switch from one nonequilibrium strategy combination to the other at least once.

If the deliberators fail to coordinate on either (A_1, A_1) or (A_2, A_2), then they must switch between (A_1, A_2) and (A_2, A_1) at least once. If, for instance, the deliberators miscoordinate on (A_2, A_1) for the first $\beta_{1 A_1} - 1 \leq \beta_{2 A_2} - 1$ rounds of deliberation after round N, then on the $N + \beta_{1 A_1}$th round, Player 1 will switch strategies to A_1, in which case either they will coordinate on (A_1, A_1), or Player 2 will also switch, so that they will miscoordinate on (A_1, A_2).

Now apply the above reasoning with $N = \beta_\Gamma$. If (1) is the case, then at round t there is a positive probability p that $\eta_1^t = \eta_2^t = \beta_\Gamma + \eta$, so that players coordinate on round t. If (2) is the case, then if τ, $\beta_\Gamma < \tau \leq 2\beta_\Gamma$ is a round at which deliberators with full memory would switch from one nonequilibrium strategy combination to the other, then at round t there is a positive probability p that $\eta_1 = \beta_\Gamma + \tau$ and $\eta_2 = \beta_\Gamma + \tau - 1$. Player 1 recalls enough rounds of deliberation to switch her strategy, say from A_2 to A_1. However, Player 2 does not recall enough rounds of deliberation to switch his strategy from A_1 to A_2. This is because at the $\beta_\Gamma + \tau - 1$st round of deliberation with full memory, the frequency of Player 1's playing A_1 over the sequence $(A_1^{\beta_\Gamma}, \ldots, A_1^{\beta_\Gamma + \tau - 1})$ is great enough to make A_1 Player 2's best response, so that if Player 2 can only recall the most recent $\beta_\Gamma + \tau - 1$ rounds at round $\beta_\Gamma + \tau$, then Player 2 will compute the relative frequency of Player 1's playing A_1 over the sequence $(A_1^{\beta_\Gamma + 1}, \ldots, A_1^{\beta_\Gamma + \tau - 1}, A_1)$, which must be at least as high as the frequency of A_1's over the sequence $(A_1^{\beta_\Gamma}, \ldots, A_1^{\beta_\Gamma + \tau - 1})$. Hence, if $\eta_2 = \beta_\Gamma + \tau - 1$, then A_1 is Player 2's best reply, so the players will coordinate on (A_1, A_1). Hence, we see that if (1) is the case, then there is a positive probability that the deliberators will coordinate.

Hence, in either case, there is a constant positive probability that at round t, the deliberators will coordinate on either (A_1, A_1) or (A_2, A_2), and this probability is at least p. □

The proof of the following lemma is inspired by the proof of Theorem 1 in Young (1993).

Lemma 3.4.5. If there is a value T such that for every $t \geq T$, there is a positive probability that RRC-Dirichlet deliberators with the information and memory restrictions of Lemma 3.4.4 coordinate on a strict equilibrium of Γ when $\omega^t \in H_k \in \mathcal{H}$, then the H_k-subsequence of RRC- Dirichlet dynamics converges almost surely to a strict equilibrium of Γ.

Proof. By hypothesis, for each $t \geq T$, there is a positive probability $p^* > 0$ that the following occur together:

(1) $\omega^t \in H_k$ occurs and random recall deliberators coordinate on coordinate on a strict equilibrium $\boldsymbol{A}^*$ of Γ.

(2) For each of the next $\beta_\Gamma + 1$-rounds, $\omega^t \in H_k$,

(3) From rounds t through rounds $t + \beta_\Gamma$, each deliberator recalls the previous $\eta_k^t + m$ rounds of deliberation, $1 \leq m \leq \beta_\Gamma$, and

(4) On the $t + \beta_\Gamma + 1$st round, they forget all but the most recent β_Γ-rounds.

If (1)–(3) occur, then by the Absorption Theorem the deliberators play $\boldsymbol{A}^*$ at each of the $t + m$ rounds, $0 \leq m \leq \beta_\Gamma$. If (4) also occurs, then they will forget having ever played anything other than A^* when H_k occurs over β_Γ rounds, which "locks" the deliberators onto A^* when H_k occurs from then on.

Now the probability that, for any given run of $\beta_\Gamma + 2$ rounds of deliberation after T, the deliberators do *not* coordinate on a strict equilibrium and then lock onto this equilibrium permanently as described in the previous paragraph is $1 - p^*$. Hence the probability that the deliberators *never* lock onto a strict equilibrium over $r(\beta_\Gamma + 2)$ rounds of deliberation after round T is at most $(1 - p^*)^r \to 0$ as $r \to \infty$. $\qquad\qquad\qquad\qquad\qquad\qquad\qquad\qquad\qquad\qquad\qquad\qquad\qquad\qquad\square$

Proposition 3.4.6. In a 2×2 game Γ with two strict Nash equilibria where β_Γ is the absorption frequency of the strict Nash equilibria of Γ, if the players are RRC-Dirichlet deliberators with the information and memory restrictions of Lemma 3.4.4, then deliberation converges almost surely to a strict Aumann correlated equilibrium.

Proof. Let H_j be a cell of $\mathcal{H}$. The hypotheses of Lemma 3.4.4 are satisfied, so by Lemma 3.4.5, the subsequence (f^{t_u}) of RRC-Dirichlet deliberation defined by t_u such that $\omega^{t_u} \in H_j$ converges almost surely to one of the strict Nash equilibria of Γ. Since $H_j \in \mathcal{H}$ was chosen arbitrarily, the entire system (f^t) converges almost surely to a strict Aumann correlated equilibrium f. $\qquad\qquad\qquad\square$

Proposition 3.4.6 is analogous to Miyasawa's (1961) theorem, which guarantees that fictitious play always converges to a Nash equilibrium in an arbitrary 2×2 game. However, the almost sure limit of RRC-Dirichlet deliberation in a 2×2 game with two strict Nash equilibria is a strict correlated equilibrium, while the limit of fictitious play in an arbitrary 2×2 game need not be a strict equilibrium.

One may also regard Proposition 3.4.6 as complementary to a main convergence theorem in Young (1993). Young (1993) proves that, given certain restrictions on the deliberators' memories, stochastic adaptive dynamics always converges to a strict Nash equilibrium if the game is *weakly acyclic*. The class of weakly acyclic games is much more general than the class of 2×2 games with two strict Nash equilibria. One natural extension of Young's model would be to introduce external signals, as in RRC-Dirichlet deliberation, in such a way that stochastic adaptive deliberators can converge to strict Aumann correlated equilibria. Such a generalization of stochastic adaptive dynamics would yield a more general convergence theorem than Proposition 3.4.6, but at a certain price. The only plausible interpretation of the stochastic adaptive dynamics, and the only interpretation Young gives, is the representative interpretation. An actual play interpretation of stochastic adaptive dynamics would rely upon the counterintuitive assumption that an individual's memory at any given time is a random sample of the events she has experienced. Moreover, the proof of Young's result depends crucially upon the possibility that at certain rounds of deliberation, the deliberator recalls information from disjoint samples of previous plays. Since RRC-Dirichlet deliberators all recall subsets of the most recent plays, there is always some overlap in their samples, and consequently convergence results for the RRC-Dirichlet dynamics are much harder to prove than analogous convergence results for stochastic adaptive dynamics. With these caveats in mind, I will consider a variation of RRC-Dirichlet deliberation very similar to Young's model in the next section, namely, *random sampling conditional Dirichlet dynamics* (RSC-Dirichlet dynamics).

§3.5   Random Sampling Dirichlet Deliberation

In this section, I consider a variation of random recall Dirichlet deliberation, namely, Dirichlet deliberation in which deliberators update their probabilities by using information taken from *random samples* of past plays. Given appropriate restrictions on sample sizes, this *random sampling Dirichlet deliberation* (RS-Dirichlet deliberation) always converges for a fairly general class of games, namely, *weakly acyclic games*. However, RS-Dirichlet dynamics has the disadvantage of only making sense under interpretations like the "quasi-evolutionary" interpretation in which the "deliberators" are members of populations selected and matched for one round of play, who update their beliefs based on what other members of the populations have experienced in the past.[17]

I will first present a model of RS-Dirichlet deliberation without external signals, since this model closely resembles Young's (1993) stochastic adaptive dynamics. As usual, I will introduce this variant of Dirichlet deliberation with a motivating example. Suppose that Amie and Kay are to play a round of Chicken, with payoff structure given in Figure 3.5.1:

Kay

		A_1	A_2
Amie	A_1	$(6, 6)$	$(2, 7)$
	A_2	$(7, 2)$	$(0, 0)$

Figure 3.5.1. Chicken

---

[17] See the discussion at the end of §3.4, and below on p. 165.

In contrast with previous models of deliberation, Kay and Amie will not be re-peating this game, at least not against each another. In this model, Kay and Amie each enter into the game as a *representative* of a particular population to which she belongs. For concreteness, let us call Amie's population the Tories and Kay's population the Whigs, as in the Battle of the Sexes example of Figure 3.1.3. At various times, corresponding to rounds of deliberation, a Whig and a Tory meet and play Chicken. Being Bayesian rational, each representative will play the strategy that maximizes her expected utility given her beliefs regarding her opponent. To form their beliefs, Kay and Amie each communicate with a sample of the members of their respective populations who have played Chicken in the past, and learn what happened in the rounds that the representatives of their samples played. Their respective probabilities for their opponents' strategies are the relative frequencies of strategies that opposing representatives from the sam-pled rounds have played. For instance, suppose that before Amie plays Kay, she "asks around" among her Tory confederates, and learns that 5 of the Tories who have already played met a Whig who played A_2 and 2 of the Tories who have already played met a Whig who played A_1. Then Amie's probabilities for Kay's alternative strategies are

$$\mu_1^t(A_1) = \frac{5}{7}, \quad \mu_2^t(A_2) = \frac{2}{7}.$$

Similarly, suppose that Kay samples 9 Whigs who have already played Chicken, and that 7 of them met a Tory who played A_2. Then Kay's probabilities for Amie's alternative strategies are

$$\mu_1^t(A_1) = \frac{2}{9}, \quad \mu_2^t(A_2) = \frac{7}{9}.$$

Given their respective distributions,

$$
\begin{aligned}
E_1^t(u_1(A_1)) &= 6 \cdot \frac{5}{7} + 2 \cdot \frac{2}{7} = \frac{34}{7} \\
&< \frac{35}{7} = 7 \cdot \frac{5}{7} + 0 \cdot \frac{2}{7} \\
&= E_1^t(u_1(A_2)),
\end{aligned}
$$

and

$$
\begin{aligned}
E_2^t(u_2(A_1)) &= 6 \cdot \frac{2}{9} + 2 \cdot \frac{7}{9} = \frac{26}{9} \\
&> \frac{14}{9} = 7 \cdot \frac{2}{9} + 0 \cdot \frac{7}{9} \\
&= E_2^t(u_2(A_2))
\end{aligned}
$$

and so when Amie and Kay meet and play Chicken, they play the Nash equilibrium strategy combination (A_2, A_1). After their encounter, they each return to their respective parties, and new representatives are selected to play the next round. Of course, if at the next round of play the new representatives of the Whigs and the Tories draw different samples of the past rounds of play, they might play a different strategy combination. However, given certain restrictions on the representatives' sampling, it is possible to give conditions under which the beliefs of deliberators in this RS-Dirichlet model converge, so that they remain at a fixed strategy profile of the game. For instance, suppose that the Tories and the Whigs can sample only from the 20 most recent rounds of play, and that over the stretch of time there is a run of 20 consecutive rounds at which the representatives play the Nash equilibrium (A_1, A_2). Suppose further that Kay and Amie are selected right after this run to be the representatives of the Whigs and the Tories once more. Since they can each sample from only the 20 most recent rounds of play, all of the Tories in Amie's sample will have observed the opponent playing A_2, and all of the Whigs in Kay's sample will have observed the opponent playing A_1. Hence, at this round $\mu_1^t(A_2) = \mu_2^t(A_1) = 1$, and Amie and Kay will play (A_1, A_2). Consequently, at the next round of deliberation, the new representatives will also sample over a run of 20 consecutive plays of (A_1, A_2), and so $\mu_1^{t+1}(A_2) = \mu_2^{t+1}(A_1) = 1$ and they will again play (A_1, A_2), and so on. No one in any of the populations will be able to recall ever having played a strategy profile other than the Nash equilibrium (A_1, A_2), and so (A_1, A_2) is an *absorbing state* of this stochastic process.

As I noted briefly in the previous section, I think that the only interpretation that makes sense for random sample Dirichlet deliberation, with or without external signals, is some sort of *population representative* interpretation like the quasi-evolutionary interpretation. The intuition behind such a population representative interpretation is that representatives of the various populations are matched for a single play of a game without having witnessed all of the previous plays, but have communicated with a number of confederates who have already played the game and who are willing to share their experiences with an ally. In this framework, it is plausible both that a player about to enter the game will be able to glean information only from a subset of the past plays, and that the plays she learns about need not necessarily be the most recent plays. On the other hand, random sample Dirichlet deliberation does not admit of either a fictitious play or an actual repeated play interpretation. As with random recall Dirichlet deliberation, random sample Dirichlet deliberation allows for players to have different memories of the history of past play, which does not make sense if players are mentally simulating each others' strategy choices. As for the actual play interpretation, I do not find it intuitively plausible that actual players could recall only a subset of past plays that includes rounds from several points backward in time, but not the most recent round of play.

The reader may have noted that in the motivating example, the deliberators did not enter into the game with prior probability distributions. This is because, like the RRC-Dirichlet model, I assume that random sample Dirichlet deliberators might eventually forget the states that determine the distributions of the early representatives. Indeed, the results proved below presume that the recall of the deliberators is *bounded*, in which case the deliberators must reach a point where none can remember any of the states that determined the prior probability distributions of the early representatives. Consequently, in the formal definitions of random sample Dirichlet deliberation with and without signals given below, the updating rule is such that the deliberators can forget the priors eventually, just as in the definition of RRC-Dirichlet deliberation.

I now give the formal definition for RS-Dirichlet deliberation without external signals.

Definition 3.5.1. Let $\Gamma = (N, S, \boldsymbol{u})$ be given. The players are *random sample Dirichlet deliberators* (RS-Dirichlet deliberators) iff the sequence of probability distributions $(\boldsymbol{\mu}^t) = (\mu_1^t, \dots, \mu_n^t)$, of the players' probabilities over their opponents' strategy combinations is defined recursively as follows:

(1) At the start of deliberation, Player k associates an initial weight $\gamma_{i\boldsymbol{A}_{-k}} \geq 0$ with each of $\tau_{\boldsymbol{A}_{-k}}$ initial states, $\boldsymbol{A}_{-k} \in S_{-k}$. Player k's initial weight for the strategy combination $\boldsymbol{A}_{-k} \in S_{-k}$, $\gamma_{\boldsymbol{A}_{-k}}^0$ is defined by

$$\gamma_{\boldsymbol{A}_{-k}}^0 = \sum_{i=1}^{\tau_{\boldsymbol{A}_{-k}}} \gamma_{i\boldsymbol{A}_{-k}}$$

Player k's *prior distribution* $\mu_k^0(\cdot) \in \mathcal{P}_k(S_{-k})$ is defined by

$$\mu_k^0(\boldsymbol{A}_{-k}) = \frac{\gamma_{\boldsymbol{A}_{-k}}^0}{\sum\limits_{\boldsymbol{B}_{-k} \in S_{-k}} \gamma_{\boldsymbol{B}_{-k}}^0}$$

(2) For round t of deliberation and for each player k, let κ_k^t be a random variable with range $\{1, 2, \dots, \beta_k^t\}$, let $\boldsymbol{\eta}_k^t$ be a random sample of size κ_k^t drawn without replacement from $\{M_k^t, M_k^t + 1, \dots, t\}$, $1 \leq M_k^t \leq t$, and let τ_k^t be a random variable with range $\{1, 2, \dots, N_k^t\}$, $1 \leq N_k^t \leq t$. For each $\boldsymbol{A}_{-k} \in S_{-k}$

$$\kappa_{\boldsymbol{A}_{-k}}^t = \sum_{i_k \in \boldsymbol{\eta}_k^t} 1_{\boldsymbol{A}_{-k} \wedge i_k}$$

that is, $\kappa^t_{A_{-k}}$ is the number of times that A_{-k} was played in the sampled rounds of play. At the $t + 1$st round of deliberation, player k updates his probability distribution $\mu^t_k(\cdot)$ as follows:

$$\mu^{t+1}_k(A_{-k}) = \frac{\kappa^t_{A_{-k}} + \theta + \gamma^t_{A_{-k}}}{\kappa^t_k + 1 + \sum \gamma^t_{B_{-k}}}$$

where

$$\gamma^t_{B_{-k}} = \sum_{i=t-\tau^t_k+1}^{\tau_{B_{-k}}} \gamma_{iB_{-k}}$$

and where θ is defined as in the definition of unconditional Dirichlet deliberation. $\qquad\qquad\square$

If N^t_k is fixed, so that τ^t_k is *bounded*, then k eventually cannot recall the states that define k's priors. If β^t_k is fixed, then the range of k's sampling is bounded. Note that if, for $k \in N$, κ^t_k, M^t_k, and N^t_k are degenerate random variables, such that $\kappa^t_k = M^t_k = N^t_k = t$ for all $t \in \mathbb{N}$, then each deliberator k "samples" the entire sequence of plays at each round and always recalls all of the states that determine k's priors, so unconditional Dirichlet deliberation can be considered a special case of RS-Dirichlet deliberation. Note also that no restrictions are placed on the distributions of the random samples $\eta^t_k = (i_k, \ldots, i_{k\kappa^t_k})$ other than the range $\{M^t_k, M^t_k + 1, \ldots, t\}$ of rounds that might be sampled. One might think it natural to assume that samples are stochastically independent across players and across times, but for the sake of generality I follow Young (1993) in not assuming this explicitly in the definition.

RS-Dirichlet dynamics resemble the stochastic adaptive dynamics presented in Young (1993) even more closely than RRC-Dirichlet dynamics. As in stochastic adaptive dynamics, RS-Dirichlet deliberators each use the information they obtain from taking a sample of the past history of play, which need not include the most recent plays, in making their decisions at the current round of play. Nevertheless, Young's approach and the RS-Dynamics introduced here differ in two important respects:

(*i*) Stochastic adaptive deliberators all draw the *same sample size* of past plays at each round of deliberation, while in the RS-Dirichlet model, deliberators can have unequal sample sizes. Young's restriction on sample sizes enables him to prove fairly general convergence results with very sharp bounds on the deliberators' memories. Nevertheless, I think that this restriction is somewhat hard to explain in light of the "quasi-evolutionary" representative interpretation of stochastic adaptive dynamics. If at round t the representatives of each population engaged in the game can communicate with a sample of their confederates who have played the game recently, why shouldn't some representatives be able to communicate with more of their confederates than some of the other representatives can? In any event, the deliberators' memory bounds in the results of this section are certainly less sharp than in corresponding results in Young's work, but the RS-Dirichlet model is more general than Young's model with respect to sample sizes.

(*ii*) In Young's model, the deliberators take the set of all sequences of pure strategy combinations in S of length m, the range of past history over which they each sample, to be a Markov chain, with fixed transition probabilities from one state to another defined in terms of the possible sample sizes of size k each deliberator draws. In RS-Dirichlet dynamics, on the other hand, each deliberator's probability distribution over the opponents' strategy combinations varies at each stage of deliberation, since this distribution is a function of the frequencies of strategy combinations that were played in the sample that k draws, and of course these samples will vary across time.

I now turn to the proofs of some of the elementary properties of RS-Dirichlet dynamics. In the remainder of this chapter, the full history of plays will be denoted by $\zeta(t)$, that is, $\zeta(t) = (A^1, \ldots, A^t)$.

Lemma 3.5.2. If RS-Dirichlet deliberators' sample sizes are bounded by β_Γ and $2\beta_\Gamma$ of the most recent rounds of past play, that is, $\beta_\Gamma \leq \eta_k^t \leq 2\beta_\Gamma$, and they cannot recall any of the states that determine the priors after some round K, then for each run of β_Γ rounds of deliberation after round $M = \max\{K, 2\beta_\Gamma\}$ there is a positive probability of β_Γ consecutive plays of the same strategy combination A.

Proof. For round $t_0 \geq M$, there is a positive probability that the following occur together:

(1) On round t_0, all of the N samples are taken from the β_Γ most recent rounds of play, that is, if

$$\zeta(t_0 - 1) = (A^1, \ldots, A^{t_0 - 1})$$

then there is a positive probability that

$$\eta_k^{t_0} = \eta_k \circ \zeta(t_0 - 1) = (A_{-k}^{t_0 - (\beta + 1)}, \ldots, A_{-k}^{t_0 - 1}) \text{ for } k \in N.$$

(2) Over the next β_Γ plays, there is a positive probability that each deliberator k draws the same sample $\eta_k^t = \eta_k^{t_0}$ of past plays as deliberator k drew in round t_0.

Suppose that (1) and (2) do occur together, and let A be the strategy profile played at round t_0. Since $A_{kj} \in A$ is a best response to $\eta_k^{t_0}$, there is a positive probability that the deliberators play A consecutively β_Γ times. $\qquad \square$

Corollary 3.5.3. Given the memory restrictions of Lemma 3.5.2, if A^* is an almost sure fixed state of RS-Dirichlet dynamics, then A^* is a Nash equilibrium.

Proof. Suppose that A^* is not a Nash equilibrium. Then for some $k \in N$, $A_k^* \in A^*$ is not k's best response to A_{-k}^*. By Lemma 3.5.2, for each run of β_Γ rounds of deliberation after round $t \geq M$ there is a positive probability p^* that the following occur together:

(A) The deliberators play A^* consecutively β_Γ times, and

(B) At round $t_1 = t + \beta_\Gamma + 1$, the deliberators each sample from the most recent β_Γ plays.

If (A) and (B) both occur, then $\mu_k^t(A_{-k}^*) = 1$ since k will have sampled only past plays in which the opponents played A_{-k}^*, so k will play some strategy $A_{ki} \neq A_k^*$, and so $A^t \neq A^*$.

Over the infinite sequence of plays, the probability that (A) and (B) never occur together at the rounds $t = M + m\beta_\Gamma + 1, m \geq 0$, is at most $(1 - p^*)^m \to 0$ as $m \to \infty$, so the probability that the deliberators will remain at A^* for all rounds of play is 0. $\qquad \square$

The converse of Corollary 3.5.3 is false. To see this, suppose that representatives of the Tories and the Whigs have played Chicken over time, that no one recalls the priors, that the history of past play is

$$\zeta(t - 1) = (A^1, \ldots, A^{t-3}, (A_1, A_2), (A_1, A_1))$$

and that $\beta_k^t \in \{1, 2\}, k = 1, 2$, for all rounds of play. If at round t the representatives each sample the $t - 2$nd play, then they play the Nash equilibrium (A_1, A_2) at round t, and the history of past play becomes

$$\zeta(t) = (A^1, \ldots, A^{t-3}, (A_1, A_2), (A_1, A_1), (A_1, A_2))$$

However, if at round $t + 1$ the deliberators each sample the $t - 1$st round of play, then they switch to the nonequilibrium strategy profile (A_2, A_2). Since there is a positive probability of this sampling scheme occurring, $A^t = (A_1, A_2)$ is not an almost sure fixed point of the RS-Dirichlet dynamics.

On the other hand, a *run* of enough consecutive plays of a strict Nash equilibrium A^* results in A^* being an almost sure fixed point of the dynamics. I prove this in detail, though the intuition underlying this fact is obvious: If RS-deliberators play a strict equilibrium A^* long enough, then no deliberator will be able to recall opponents having played anything other than A^*_{-k}, so every deliberator will want to stick with his end A^*_k of the equilibrium A^*.

Corollary 3.5.4. Given the memory restrictions of Lemma 3.5.2, if players play a strict Nash equilibrium A^* consecutively $2\beta_\Gamma$ times, then A^* is an almost sure fixed state of RS-Dirichlet dynamics.

Proof. Let $t_0 - 1$ be the last of $2\beta_\Gamma$ consecutive plays of A^*. Since the sampling is taken over the most recent $2\beta_\Gamma$ rounds, for every $k \in N$ we have $\mu_k^{t_0}(A^*_{-k}) = \kappa^t_{A_{-k}}/\kappa^t_k = 1$, to which $A^*_k \in A^*$ is k's unique best response, so $A^{t_0} = A^*$. By induction, $A^t = A^*$ for all rounds $t \geq t_0$.   □

For a fairly general class of games, RS-Dirichlet dynamics converges from any prior distribution with probability 1 to a strict Nash equilibrium. This result is quite similar to Theorem 1 in Young (1993), which we state for purposes of comparison. In order to state Young's result, we must first define the class of *weakly acyclic games*.

Definition 3.5.5. A *best reply graph* of a game Γ is a directed graph $G(\Gamma)$ with vertices $A \in S$ such that for each pair of vertices A, B, there is a directed edge $A \to B$ if $A \neq B$, there is exactly one $k \in N$ such that $B_{kj} \in B$ is a best reply to A_{-k}, and $A_{-k} = B_{-k}$. If A^* is a vertex of $G(\Gamma)$ from which there is no exiting edge, then A^* is a *sink* of $G(\Gamma)$. A game Γ is *acyclic* if $G(\Gamma)$ has no directed cycles. Γ is *weakly acyclic* if, from any initial vertex A of Γ, there exists a directed path to a sink A^*.   □

If Γ is weakly acyclic, then let $L(A)$ be the length of a shortest directed path in the best response graph of Γ from A to a sink A^*, and let $L_\Gamma = \max\{L(A)|A \in S\}$. Clearly A^* is a sink of a best reply graph $G(\Gamma)$ only if A^* is a strict Nash equilibrium. Hence a game $\Gamma = (N, S, u)$ is weakly acyclic if, and only if, for each strategy profile $A \in S$ there exists a finite sequence of strategy profiles starting at A of best replies by one player at a time that terminates in a strict pure strategy Nash equilibrium.

The class of weakly acyclic games includes a variety of different types of games in strategic form, including most games of pure coordination and all dominance solvable games. However, as Young (1993) notes, the game with payoff structure given by Figure 3.5.2 is not weakly acyclic, and both stochastic adaptive and RS-Dirichlet dynamics can fail to converge, even though this game has a strict Nash equilibrium.

Kay

		A_1	A_2	A_3	A_4
	A_1	$(2,1)$	$(0,0)$	$(1,2)$	$(-1,-1)$
Amie	A_2	$(1,2)$	$(2,1)$	$(0,0)$	$(-1,-1)$
	A_3	$(0,0)$	$(1,2)$	$(2,1)$	$(-1,-1)$
	A_4	$(-1,-1)$	$(-1,-1)$	$(-1,-1)$	$(3,3)$

Figure 3.5.2. Young's Counterexample

For either the stochastic adaptive or the RS-Dirichlet dynamics, if the deliberators can sample from only the 2 most recent rounds of play, and if the first two plays are (A_1, A_1) and (A_1, A_3), then the dynamics cycles without ever reaching an equilibrium. This counterexample shows that, like other inductive dynamical rules such as fictitious play, neither stochastic adaptive dynamics nor RS-Dirichlet dynamics converges in all cases.

I now state one of Young's (1993) main results, and prove the main convergence results of this section for RS-Dirichlet dynamics without external signals. The proof of Proposition 3.5.6 is similar to that of Theorem 1 in Young (1993).

Theorem (Theorem 1, Young 1993). Let Γ be a weakly acyclic game. If the players are stochastic adaptive deliberators such that at each round, each player has information from a sample of k past plays from the most recent m plays, then if $k(L_\Gamma + 2) \leq m$, the dynamics converges almost surely to a strict Nash equilibrium. □

Proposition 3.5.6. If Γ is weakly acyclic, and if RS-Dirichlet deliberators have the memory restrictions of Lemma 3.5.2, then RS-Dirichlet dynamics converges almost surely to a strict Nash equilibrium.

Proof. Following the construction in Lemma 3.5.2, for each round $t_0 = M + m\beta_\Gamma$, $m \geq 0$ of deliberation, there is a positive probability that all the deliberators sample according to the following scheme:

(1) At round t_0, each deliberator recalls the most recent β_Γ rounds of play, that is,

$$\eta_k^{t_0} = \eta_k \circ \zeta(t_0 - 1) = (A_{-k}^{t_0 - (\beta+1)}, \dots, A_{-k}^{t_0 - 1}).$$

(2) For each of the next $\beta_\Gamma - 1$ rounds of play, each deliberator k draws the same sample of past plays as deliberator k drew in round t_0, that is, for $t_0 \le t \le t_0 + \beta_\Gamma - 1$, $\eta_k^t = \eta_k^{t_0}$, and

(3) At round $t_1 = t_0 + \beta_\Gamma$, each deliberator recalls the most recent β_Γ rounds of play.

If (1) and (3) both occur, then over the β_Γ rounds $t_0, t_0 + 1, \dots, t_0 + \beta_\Gamma - 1$ rounds of deliberation the players play A^{t_0} consecutively β_Γ times, that is,

$$\zeta(t_0 + \beta_\Gamma - 1) = (A^1, \dots, A^{t_0 - 1}, \overbrace{A^{t_0}, \dots, A^{t_0}}^{\beta_\Gamma \text{ times}})$$

Hence, if (1), (2) and (3) all occur together, then at round $t_1 = t_0 + \beta_\Gamma$

$$\text{For } k \in N, \eta_k^{t_1} = \eta_k \circ \zeta(t_1 - 1) = (\overbrace{A_{-k}^{t_0}, \dots, A_{-k}^{t_0}}^{\beta_\Gamma \text{ times}}).$$

so $\mu_k^{t_1}(A_{-k}^{t_0}) = 1$. There are two cases to consider:

Case 1: If A^{t_0} is a strict Nash equilibrium, then on the t_1-st round of deliberation, the deliberators will all play A^{t_0} once again.

Case 2: If A^{t_0} is not a strict Nash equilibrium, then for exactly one $k \in N$ there is a strategy $A_{kj} \ne A_{ki} \in A^{t_0}$ such that A_{kj} is k's best response to $A_{-k}^{t_0}$. On round t_1, the deliberators will make a transition from A^{t_0} to $A^{t_1} = (A_{kj}, A_{-k}^{t_0})$.

Now, since the deliberators all recall only the most recent β_Γ rounds at round t_1, we may apply the argument from the previous paragraph and note that there is a positive probability that the deliberators play A^{t_1} consecutively β_Γ and that at round $t_2 = t_0 + 2\beta_\Gamma$, the deliberators recall only the most recent β_Γ rounds, so that they either play A^{t_1} once more or make a transition from A^{t_1} to $A^{t_2} = (A_{il}, A_{-i}^{t_1})$. Indeed, by repeating this argument L_Γ times, we note that there is a positive probability that

(A1) Over the $\beta_\Gamma L_\Gamma$ rounds from t_0 to $t_0 + \beta_\Gamma L_\Gamma$ the deliberators make each of the $n \le L_\Gamma$ transitions necessary to reach a strict equilibrium A^* from A^{t_0}.

Finally, there is a positive probability that over the next β_Γ rounds after round $t_0 + \beta_\Gamma L_\Gamma$, the deliberators will each remember the most recent $\beta_\Gamma + m$ rounds of deliberation, $1 \leq m \leq \beta_\Gamma$, that is,

$$\overbrace{\beta_\Gamma + m \text{ times}}$$

(A2) $\qquad \eta_k^t = \eta_k \circ \zeta(t-1) = (\overbrace{A_{-k}^*, \ldots, A_{-k}^*}), t = t_0 + \beta_\Gamma L_\Gamma + m$

In this case, for round $t \geq t_0 + M + \beta_\Gamma(L_\Gamma + 1)$, for any sample taken from the most recent $2\beta_\Gamma$ rounds of play,

$$\overbrace{\eta \text{ times}, \beta_\Gamma \leq \eta \leq 2\beta_\Gamma}$$

$$\eta_k^t = \eta_k \circ \zeta(t-1) = (\overbrace{A_{-k}^*, \ldots, A_{-k}^*})$$

that is, $\mu_k^t(A_{-k}^*) = 1$ for all $k \in N$, so the deliberators will have converged to the strict equilibrium A^*.

Let p^* be the probability that (A1) and (A2) occur together on any run of length $\beta_\Gamma(L_\Gamma + 1)$ from round $t_0 = M + m\beta + \Gamma$ to $t_0 + M + m\beta + \Gamma(L_\Gamma + 1)$, $m \geq 0$. By the arguments above, $p^* > 0$. Hence, the probability that deliberators never converge to a strict equilibrium on any of the runs of length $\beta_\Gamma(L_\Gamma+1)$ from round $t_0 = M + m\beta_\Gamma$ to $t_0 + M + m\beta_\Gamma(L_\Gamma+1)$, $m \geq 0$, is $(1-p^*)^m \to 0$ as $m \to \infty$. $\qquad\qquad \square$

The extension of RS-Dirichlet dynamics to *random sample conditional Dirichlet dynamics* (RSC-Dirichlet dynamics), that is, random sampling Dirichlet dynamics with external signals, is straightforward. Intuitively, RSC-Dirichlet deliberators are like conditional Dirichlet deliberators under the quasi-evolutionary interpretation, who observe "sunspots" at each round of deliberation but who can only use information from samples of the past plays when they update their probabilities over their opponents' strategies.

Definition 3.5.7. Let $\Gamma = (N, S, u)$, Ω, and the partitions $\mathcal{H}_k$ of Ω be given, and let an elementary event $\omega^t \in \Omega$ occur at each round of deliberation. The players are *RSC-Dirichlet deliberators* iff the sequence of probability distributions $(\mathfrak{P}^t)$,

$$\mathfrak{P}^t = (\mu_1^t(\cdot|\mathcal{H}_1), \ldots, \mu_n^t(\cdot|\mathcal{H}_n))$$

of the players' probabilities over their opponents' strategy combinations is defined recursively as follows:

(1) At the start of deliberation, Player k associates an *initial weight*

$$\gamma_{i A_{-k} \wedge H_{kj}} \geq 0$$

with each of $\tau_{A_{-k} \wedge H_{kj}}$ *initial states.* Player k's initial weight for the conjunction $A_{-k} \wedge H_{kj}$, $\gamma^0_{A_{-k} \wedge H_{kj}}$ is defined by

$$\gamma^0_{A_{-k} \wedge H_{kj}} = \sum_{i=1}^{\tau_{A_{-k} \wedge H_{kj}}} \gamma_i {}_{A_{-k} \wedge H_{kj}}.$$

Player k's conditional prior distribution $\mu^0_k(\cdot | \mathcal{H}_k)$ is defined by

$$\mu^0_k(A_{-k} | H_{kj}) = \frac{\gamma^0_{A_{-k} \wedge H_{kj}}}{\sum_{B_{-k} \in S_{-k}} \gamma^0_{B_{-k} \wedge H_{kj}}}, \quad H_{kj} \in \mathcal{H}_k$$

(2) For round t of deliberation and for each player k, let κ^t_k be a random variable with range $\{1, 2, \ldots, \beta^t_k\}$, let η^t_k be a random sample of size κ^t_k drawn without replacement from $\{M^t_k, M^t_k + 1, \ldots, t\}$, $1 \leq M^t_k \leq t$, and let τ^t_k be a random variable with range $\{1, 2, \ldots, N^t_k\}$, $1 \leq N^t_k \leq t$. For each $H_{kj} \in \mathcal{H}_k$, and each $A_{-k} \in S_{-k}$,

$$\kappa^t_{H_{kj}} = \sum_{i \in \eta^t_k} 1_{H_{kj}}(\omega^i)$$

and

$$\kappa^t_{A_{-k} \wedge H_{kj}} = \sum_{i \in \eta^t_k} 1_{A_{-k} \wedge H_{kj}}(\omega^i)$$

that is, $\kappa^t_{H_{kj}}$ and $\kappa^t_{A_{-k} \wedge H_{kj}}$ are the number of times that H_{kj} occurred and the number of times that A_{-k} and H_{kj} have both occurred, respectively, in the η^t_k sampled rounds of deliberation. At the $t + 1$st round of deliberation, player k updates his probability distribution $\mu^t_k(\cdot | \mathcal{H}_k)$ according to the rule

$$\mu^{t+1}_k(A_{-k} | H_{kj}) = \mu^t_k(A_{-k} | H_{kj})$$

if H_{kj} did not occur at the $t + 1$st round of deliberation, and, if H_{kj} occurred at the $t + 1$st round of deliberation, then

$$\mu^{t+1}_k(A_{-k} | H_{kj}) = \frac{\kappa^t_{A_{-k} \wedge H_{kj}} + \theta + \gamma^t_{A_{-k} \wedge H_{kj}}}{\kappa^t_{H_{kj}} + 1 + \sum \gamma^t_{B_{-k} \wedge H_{kj}}}$$

where

$$\gamma^t_{B_{-k} \wedge H_{kj}} = \sum_{i=t-\tau^t_k+1}^{\tau_{B_{-k} \wedge H_{kj}}} \gamma_i {}_{B_{-k} \wedge H_{kj}}$$

and where θ is defined as in conditional Dirichlet deliberation with full memory. □

The results proved for RS-Dirichlet deliberation with respect to strict Nash equilibria generalize straightforwardly to RSC-Dirichlet dynamics.

Lemma 3.5.8. If RSC-Dirichlet deliberators have a common information partition $\mathcal{H}$, and their sample sizes are bounded by β_Γ and $2\beta_\Gamma$ of the most recent rounds of past play on each H_k-subsequence of deliberation, that is, $\beta_\Gamma \leq \eta_k^t(H_k) \leq 2\beta_\Gamma$, and they cannot recall any of the states that determine the priors after some round K, then for each run of β_Γ rounds of deliberation after round $M = \max\{K, 2\beta_\Gamma\}$ there is a positive probability of β_Γ consecutive plays on any H_k-subsequence of deliberation of the same strategy combination A.

Proof. The proof is similar to the proof of Lemma 3.5.2. $\qquad\square$

Corollary 3.5.9. Suppose that in a game $\Gamma = (N, S, u)$ that the players are RSC-Dirichlet deliberators who condition a common information partition $\mathcal{H}$ and who have the same memory restrictions as in Lemma 3.5.8. If $f : \Omega \to S$ is an almost sure fixed state of RSC-Dirichlet dynamics, then f is an Aumann correlated equilibrium.

Proof. The proof is almost identical to the proof of Corollary 3.5.3. If f is not an Aumann correlated equilibrium, then for some $k \in N$ and some $\omega' \in \Omega$, $f_k(\omega') \in f(\omega')$ is not k's best response to f_{-k}. Let H_k' be the cell of $\mathcal{H}$ containing ω'. By Lemma 3.5.8, for each run of β_Γ rounds of the H_k-subsequence of deliberation after round $t \geq M$ there is a positive probability p^* that the following occur together:

(A) The deliberators play f consecutively β_Γ times, and

(B) At round $t_1 = t + \beta_\Gamma + 1$, $\omega^t = \omega'$ and the deliberators each sample from the most recent β_Γ plays.

If (A) and (B) both occur, then $\mu_k^t(f_{-k}(\omega')) = 1$, and k will play some strategy $g_k(\omega') \neq f_k(\omega')$, and so $f^t \neq f$.

Over the infinite sequence of plays, the probability that (A) and (B) never occur together at the rounds $t = M + m\beta_\Gamma + 1$, $m \geq 0$, is at most $(1 - p^*)^m \to 0$ as $m \to \infty$, so the probability that the deliberators will remain at f for all rounds of play is 0. $\qquad\square$

The following is the main convergence result of this section.

Proposition 3.5.10. Let Γ be a weakly acyclic game. If RSC-Dirichlet deliberators have a common partition $\mathcal{H}$, and if they have the same memory restrictions as in Lemma 3.5.8, then RSC-Dirichlet dynamics converges almost surely to a strict Aumann correlated equilibrium.

Proof. By the proof of Proposition 3.5.6, for each cell $H_k \in \mathcal{H}$, the H_k-subsequence of deliberation converges almost surely to a strict Nash equilibrium A_{H_k}. Hence the almost sure limit of RSC-Dirichlet dynamics is $f(\omega) : \Omega \rightarrow S$ defined by

$$f(\omega) = A_{H_k}, \ \omega \in H_k.$$

which, being a convex combination of strict Nash equilibria, is a strict Aumann correlated equilibrium.   □

§3.6   Deliberators with Variable States

In this section, I will consider a model of conditional Dirichlet deliberation which relaxes the assumption that each deliberator information regarding the "states of the world" is a cell of a *fixed* partition $\mathcal{H}_k$ of Ω for all rounds of deliberation. This model of *variable state conditional Dirichlet deliberation* allows for the possibility that at some rounds of deliberation, a deliberator might have a more coarse information partition of Ω than at other times. One can regard this intermittent "coarsening" of deliberators' partitions as a form of "noise" in the deliberators' information, which can lead to exogenous correlation in strategies.

As usual, to motivate this type of dynamics I use a version of the Battle of the Sexes example. In the Battle of the Sexes game defined by the payoff matrix in Figure 3.2.5, Kay and Amie receive information from an external event space Ω, such that

$$\Omega = \{\omega_1, \omega_2, \omega_3, \omega_4\}$$

where the ω_k's are equiprobable. For concreteness, one can interpret the points of Ω as the outcomes of two independent coin flips, such that $\omega_1 = HH, \omega_2 = HT$, $\omega_3 = TH, \omega_4 = TT$. If Amie and Kay are Dirichlet deliberators who are always able to observe the elementary event $\omega_k \in \Omega$, then their common information partition is $\mathcal{H} = \{\{\omega_1\}, \{\omega_2\}, \{\omega_3\}, \{\omega_4\}\}$. Starting with uniform conditional priors, conditional Dirichlet deliberation converges almost surely to the mixed Nash equilibrium defined by

$$\mu_1^*(A_1|\{\omega_j\}) = \frac{1}{3}, \qquad \mu_1^*(A_2|\{\omega_j\}) = \frac{2}{3}, \qquad 1 \leq j \leq 4.$$

$$\mu_2^*(A_1|\{\omega_j\}) = \frac{2}{3}, \qquad \mu_2^*(A_2|\{\omega_j\}) = \frac{1}{3}, \qquad 1 \leq j \leq 4.$$

However, suppose in this setting the deliberators have perfect memories, but at each round of deliberation there is a positive probability that Amie will fail to observe the outcome of the second coin toss, and there is likewise a positive probability that Kay will not gain information from the second coin toss. The probabilities that Kay and Amie will be deprived of their information from one of the coin tosses at a given round of deliberation are independent. One way to describe this situation more precisely is to say that at each round of deliberation, each deliberator observes a cell of the information partition $\mathcal{H}$, or a more "vague" set in the σ-algebra generated by the sets in $\mathcal{H}$, which is a union of cells in $\mathcal{H}$. Alternatively, one can say that each deliberator's information partition now depends upon the round of deliberation, and denote player k's information partition at round t by $\mathcal{H}_k^t$. If either deliberator fails to observe one of the coin tosses, then her information partition is a *coarsening* of the partition $\mathcal{H}$. For instance, if at some stage of t deliberation Amie observes only the first coin flip, then her information partition at this round is $\mathcal{H}_1^t = \{\{\omega_1, \omega_2\}, \{\omega_3, \omega_4\}\}$. At each round of deliberation, Amie and Kay each observe an event $H_k^t \in \mathcal{H}_k^t \subseteq \mathcal{F}$, where $\mathcal{F}$ is the σ-algebra generated by $\mathcal{H}$. They each update all of their conditional probabilities $\mu_k^t(\cdot|F_k)$, $F_k \in \mathcal{F}$, and each plays a strategy that maximizes her conditional expectation given $H_k^t \in \mathcal{H}_k^t$. One possible early sequence of this sort of *variable state conditional Dirichlet deliberation* (VSC-Dirichlet deliberation) is summarized in Table 3.6.1. At the 8th round of deliberation, Amie observes the results of both coin flips, and conditions on the cell $H_1^8 = \{\omega_1\}$ of her partition $\mathcal{H}_1^t = \mathcal{H}$. However, Kay observes only the outcome of the first coin flip, so she conditions on the cell $H_2^8 = \{\omega_1, \omega_2\}$ of her partition $\mathcal{H}_1^t = \{\{\omega_1, \omega_2\}, \{\omega_3, \omega_4\}\}$. At this round, Kay has observed the event $\{\omega_1, \omega_2\}$ four times in the past, since she has observed the elementary event $\{\omega_1\}$ three times and the elementary event $\{\omega_2\}$ once. Amie has played A_1 three times when Kay has observed H_2^8, so Kay's updated probabilities are

$$\mu_2^8(A_1|H_2^8) = \frac{n_{A_1 \wedge \{\omega_1, \omega_2\}} + \gamma_{A_1 \wedge \{\omega_1\}} + \gamma_{A_1 \wedge \{\omega_2\}}}{n_{\{\omega_1, \omega_2\}} + \gamma_{A_1 \wedge \{\omega_1\}} + \gamma_{A_1 \wedge \{\omega_2\}} + \gamma_{A_2 \wedge \{\omega_1\}} + \gamma_{A_2 \wedge \{\omega_2\}}}$$

$$= \frac{3+2}{4+4} = \frac{5}{8}$$

and

$$\mu_2^8(A_2|H_2^8) = \frac{n_{A_1 \wedge \{\omega_1, \omega_2\}} + \gamma_{A_2 \wedge \{\omega_1\}} + \gamma_{A_2 \wedge \{\omega_2\}}}{n_{\{\omega_1, \omega_2\}} + \gamma_{A_1 \wedge \{\omega_1\}} + \gamma_{A_1 \wedge \{\omega_2\}} + \gamma_{A_2 \wedge \{\omega_1\}} + \gamma_{A_2 \wedge \{\omega_2\}}}$$

$$= \frac{1+2}{4+4} = \frac{3}{8}.$$

Table 3.6.1

Battle of the Sexes

Played by VSC-Dirichlet Deliberators*

t	ω^t	H_1^t	H_2^t	s_1	s_2	$\mu_1^t(s_1\|H_1^t)$	$\mu_1^t(s_2\|H_1^t)$	$\mu_2^t(s_1\|H_1^t)$	$\mu_2^t(s_2\|H_1^t)$
1	ω_1	$\{\omega_1\}$	$\{\omega_1\}$	A_1	A_2	$\frac{1}{2}$	$\frac{1}{2}$	$\frac{1}{2}$	$\frac{1}{2}$
2	ω_4	$\{\omega_4\}$	$\{\omega_4\}$	A_1	A_2	$\frac{1}{2}$	$\frac{1}{2}$	$\frac{1}{2}$	$\frac{1}{2}$
3	ω_1	$\{\omega_1\}$	$\{\omega_1\}$	A_2	A_1	$\frac{0+1}{1+2}=\frac{1}{3}$	$\frac{1+1}{1+2}=\frac{2}{3}$	$\frac{1+1}{1+2}=\frac{2}{3}$	$\frac{0+1}{1+2}=\frac{1}{3}$
4	ω_4	$\{\omega_4\}$	$\{\omega_4\}$	A_2	A_1	$\frac{0+1}{1+2}=\frac{1}{3}$	$\frac{1+1}{1+2}=\frac{2}{3}$	$\frac{1+1}{1+2}=\frac{2}{3}$	$\frac{0+1}{1+2}=\frac{1}{3}$
5	ω_1	$\{\omega_1\}$	$\{\omega_1\}$	A_1	A_2	$\frac{1+1}{2+2}=\frac{1}{2}$	$\frac{1+1}{2+2}=\frac{1}{2}$	$\frac{1+1}{2+2}=\frac{1}{2}$	$\frac{1+1}{2+2}=\frac{1}{2}$
6	ω_4	$\{\omega_4\}$	$\{\omega_4\}$	A_1	A_2	$\frac{1+1}{2+2}=\frac{1}{2}$	$\frac{1+1}{2+2}=\frac{1}{2}$	$\frac{1+1}{2+2}=\frac{1}{2}$	$\frac{1+1}{2+2}=\frac{1}{2}$
7	ω_2	$\{\omega_2\}$	$\{\omega_2\}$	A_1	A_2	$\frac{1}{2}$	$\frac{1}{2}$	$\frac{1}{2}$	$\frac{1}{2}$
8	ω_1	$\{\omega_1\}$	$\{\omega_1,\omega_2\}$	A_2	A_1	$\frac{1+1}{3+2}=\frac{2}{5}$	$\frac{2+1}{3+2}=\frac{3}{5}$	$\frac{3+2}{4+4}=\frac{5}{8}$	$\frac{1+2}{4+4}=\frac{3}{8}$
9	ω_2	$\{\omega_1,\omega_2\}$	$\{\omega_2\}$	A_1	A_1	$\frac{2+2}{5+4}=\frac{4}{9}$	$\frac{3+2}{5+4}=\frac{5}{9}$	$\frac{1+1}{1+2}=\frac{2}{3}$	$\frac{0+1}{1+2}=\frac{1}{3}$
10	ω_2	$\{\omega_2\}$	$\{\omega_2\}$	A_2	A_1	$\frac{0+1}{1+2}=\frac{1}{3}$	$\frac{1+1}{1+2}=\frac{2}{3}$	$\frac{2+1}{2+2}=\frac{3}{4}$	$\frac{0+1}{2+2}=\frac{1}{4}$
11	ω_3	$\{\omega_3\}$	$\{\omega_3\}$	A_1	A_2	$\frac{1}{2}$	$\frac{1}{2}$	$\frac{1}{2}$	$\frac{1}{2}$
12	ω_1	$\{\omega_1\}$	$\{\omega_1\}$	A_1	A_1	$\frac{2+1}{4+2}=\frac{1}{2}$	$\frac{2+1}{4+2}=\frac{1}{2}$	$\frac{2+1}{3+2}=\frac{3}{5}$	$\frac{1+1}{3+2}=\frac{2}{5}$
13	ω_4	$\{\omega_3,\omega_4\}$	$\{\omega_4\}$	A_2	A_1	$\frac{1+2}{4+4}=\frac{3}{8}$	$\frac{3+2}{4+4}=\frac{5}{8}$	$\frac{2+1}{3+2}=\frac{3}{5}$	$\frac{1+1}{3+2}=\frac{2}{5}$
14	ω_3	$\{\omega_3\}$	$\{\omega_4,\omega_3\}$	A_2	A_2	$\frac{0+1}{1+2}=\frac{1}{3}$	$\frac{1+1}{1+2}=\frac{2}{3}$	$\frac{3+2}{5+4}=\frac{5}{9}$	$\frac{2+2}{5+4}=\frac{4}{9}$
15	ω_3	$\{\omega_3\}$	$\{\omega_3\}$	A_2	A_1	$\frac{0+1}{2+2}=\frac{1}{4}$	$\frac{2+1}{2+2}=\frac{3}{4}$	$\frac{1+1}{1+2}=\frac{2}{3}$	$\frac{0+1}{1+2}=\frac{1}{3}$
16	ω_2	$\{\omega_2\}$	$\{\omega_2\}$	A_1	A_1	$\frac{2+1}{2+2}=\frac{3}{4}$	$\frac{0+1}{2+2}=\frac{1}{4}$	$\frac{2+1}{3+2}=\frac{3}{5}$	$\frac{1+1}{3+2}=\frac{2}{5}$
17	ω_1	$\{\omega_1\}$	$\{\omega_1\}$	A_1	A_1	$\frac{3+1}{5+2}=\frac{4}{7}$	$\frac{2+1}{5+2}=\frac{3}{7}$	$\frac{3+1}{4+2}=\frac{2}{3}$	$\frac{1+1}{4+2}=\frac{1}{3}$
18	ω_4	$\{\omega_4\}$	$\{\omega_4\}$	A_2	A_2	$\frac{1+1}{3+2}=\frac{2}{5}$	$\frac{2+1}{3+5}=\frac{3}{8}$	$\frac{2+1}{4+2}=\frac{1}{2}$	$\frac{2+1}{4+2}=\frac{1}{2}$
19	ω_2	$\{\omega_2\}$	$\{\omega_2\}$	A_1	A_1	$\frac{3+1}{3+2}=\frac{4}{5}$	$\frac{0+1}{3+2}=\frac{1}{5}$	$\frac{3+1}{4+2}=\frac{2}{3}$	$\frac{1+1}{4+2}=\frac{1}{3}$
20	ω_3	$\{\omega_3\}$	$\{\omega_3\}$	A_2	A_2	$\frac{1+1}{3+2}=\frac{2}{5}$	$\frac{2+1}{3+2}=\frac{3}{5}$	$\frac{1+1}{2+2}=\frac{1}{2}$	$\frac{1+1}{2+2}=\frac{1}{2}$
21	ω_4	$\{\omega_4\}$	$\{\omega_4\}$	A_2	A_2	$\frac{1+1}{4+2}=\frac{1}{3}$	$\frac{3+1}{4+2}=\frac{2}{3}$	$\frac{2+1}{5+2}=\frac{3}{7}$	$\frac{3+1}{5+2}=\frac{4}{7}$
22	ω_3	$\{\omega_3\}$	$\{\omega_3\}$	A_2	A_2	$\frac{1+1}{4+2}=\frac{1}{3}$	$\frac{3+1}{4+2}=\frac{2}{3}$	$\frac{1+1}{3+2}=\frac{2}{5}$	$\frac{2+1}{3+2}=\frac{3}{5}$

*s_1 is the strategy that Amie plays at round t, s_2 is the strategy that Kay plays at round t, H_1^t is the event in $\mathcal{F}$ that Amie observes at round t, and H_2^t is the event in $\mathcal{F}$ that Kay observes at round t.

Since

$$E_2^8(u_2(A_1)|H_2^8) \;=\; 1 \cdot \frac{5}{8} + 0 \cdot \frac{3}{8} = \frac{5}{8}$$

$$> \;\; \frac{3\sqrt{2}}{8} = 0 \cdot \frac{5}{8} + \sqrt{2} \cdot \frac{3}{8} = E_2^8(u_2(A_2)|H_2^8).$$

Kay will play A_1 at round 8, so the deliberators miscoordinate once again at (A_2, A_1). However, then next time that ω_1 occurs, at round 12, Amie and Kay both observe both coin flips, so $\mathcal{H}_1^{12} = \mathcal{H}_2^{12} = \mathcal{H}$, and their updated probabilities are

$$\mu_1^{12}(A_1|H_1^{12}) \;=\; \mu_1^{12}(A_1|\{\omega_1\}) = \frac{2+1}{4+2} = \frac{1}{2}$$

$$\mu_1^{12}(A_2|H_1^{12}) \;=\; \mu_1^{12}(A_2|\{\omega_1\}) = \frac{2+1}{4+2} = \frac{1}{2}$$

$$\mu_2^{12}(A_1|H_2^{12}) \;=\; \mu_2^{12}(A_1|\{\omega_1\}) = \frac{2+1}{3+2} = \frac{3}{5}$$

$$\mu_2^{12}(A_2|H_2^{12}) \;=\; \mu_1^{12}(A_2|\{\omega_1\}) = \frac{1+1}{3+2} = \frac{2}{5}$$

Note that Kay has only observed the elementary event ω_1 three times in the past, while Amie has observed ω_1 four times in the past. Given their probabilities at round 12,

$$E_1^{12}(u_1(A_1)|H_1^{12}) \;=\; \sqrt{2} \cdot \frac{1}{2} + 0 \cdot \frac{1}{2} = \frac{\sqrt{2}}{2}$$

$$> \;\; \frac{1}{2} = 0 \cdot \frac{1}{2} + 1 \cdot \frac{1}{2} = E_1^{12}(u_1(A_2)|H_1^{12})$$

$$E_2^{12}(u_2(A_1)|H_2^{12}) \;=\; 1 \cdot \frac{3}{5} + 0 \cdot \frac{1}{3} = \frac{3}{5}$$

$$> \;\; \frac{2\sqrt{2}}{5} = 0 \cdot \frac{3}{5} + \sqrt{2} \cdot \frac{2}{5} = E_2^{12}(u_2(A_2)|H_2^{12})$$

and so Amie and Kay coordinate on (A_1, A_1). Since Kay and Amie can each recall all of the other's past plays in this kind of dynamics, the Absorption Theorem applies here, and so they will coordinate on (A_1, A_1) at all future rounds of deliberation at which they both observe $\{\omega_1\}$.

The three other subsequences of deliberation in this example also converge to strict Nash equilibria. At round 9 of deliberation, Kay observes the elementary event $\{\omega_1\}$ while Amie observes $\{\omega_1, \omega_2\}$. This results in their coordinating on

(A_1, A_1) on round 16 of deliberation, and so they coordinate at all future rounds at which they both observe $\{\omega_2\}$. At round 13, Amie observes $\omega_3\}$ while Kay observes $\{\omega_3, \omega_4\}$, and at round 14, Kay observes $\{\omega_3\}$ while Amie observes $\{\omega_3, \omega_4\}$. As the summary of deliberation in Table 3.6.1 shows, this results in their coordinating on (A_2, A_2) whenever they both observe either $\{\omega_3\}$ or $\{\omega_4\}$. Since the $\{\omega_1\}$- and $\{\omega_2\}$-subsequences of deliberation both converge to (A_1, A_1), and the $\{\omega_3\}$- and $\{\omega_4\}$-subsequences of deliberation both converge to (A_2, A_2), Kay and Amie will also learn to coordinate on (A_1, A_1) if either of them observe $\{\omega_1, \omega_2\}$, and they will learn to coordinate on (A_2, A_2) if either of them observe $\{\omega_3, \omega_4\}$. In this particular example, deliberation converges to the correlated equilibrium

$$f_1(\omega) = \begin{cases} (A_1, A_1) & \text{if } \omega \in \{\omega_1, \omega_2\} \\ (A_2, A_2) & \text{if } \omega \in \{\omega_3, \omega_4\} \end{cases}$$

Of course, this correlated equilibrium is only one possible outcome of such a sequence of Dirichlet deliberation in which the information partitions can vary. Given a different initial sequence of experimental outcomes, VSC-Dirichlet deliberation could converge to the correlated equilibrium

$$f_2(\omega) = \begin{cases} (A_2, A_2) & \text{if } \omega \in \{\omega_1, \omega_2\} \\ (A_1, A_1) & \text{if } \omega \in \{\omega_3, \omega_4\} \end{cases}$$

or to either of the pure strategy Nash equilibria (A_1, A_1) or (A_2, A_2). Moreover, the sporadic coarsenings of the partition $\mathcal{H}$ could be other than those described above. For instance, at certain rounds of deliberation Amie or Kay might miss observing the coin tosses altogether, in which case the partition conditioned upon becomes the trivial partition $\mathcal{H}_k^t = \Omega = \{\omega_1, \omega_2, \omega_3, \omega_4\}$. The leading idea behind VSC-Dirichlet deliberation is that the periodic coarsenings of the deliberators' information partitions can introduce an asymmetry in their knowledge of the past history of deliberation. As the example above shows, such an asymmetry can lead the various subsequences of deliberation into basins of attraction of strict equilibria, with the result that the entire system converges to correlated equilibrium.

Like the deliberational equilibria of conditional Dirichlet deliberation with fixed partitions, one may regard the limit points of VSC-deliberation as a kind of "sunspot equilibrium." The distinguishing feature of the fixed points of VSC-Dirichlet dynamics is that they can result from deliberators correlating their beliefs with external signals which yield variable *amounts* of information across time. As in conditional Dirichlet deliberation with fixed information partitions, the deliberators in VSC-Dirichlet deliberation are each using all of the information one has at any given time in computing expected utilities. However, at certain times the information the deliberator receives about the states of the world can be less detailed than at other times, which is formalized by the deliberators information partition being more coarse than at other times. As in previous models of conditional deliberation, if the deliberators find in the long run that the information they get from the sequence of external signals is statistically irrelevant to their plays, they will be no worse off for having conditioned on the coin flips.

I now turn to the formal definition and elementary properties of VSC-Dirichlet deliberation. The results of this section are quite similar to those of previous sections. The key point to keep in mind is that in VSC-Dirichlet dynamics, deliberators update several different conditional probabilities simultaneously, namely the probabilities conditional on the events $F_k^t \in \mathcal{F}_k$, $k \in N$, that the deliberators observe at round t, as well as the conditional probabilities for each event $F_{kj} \in \mathcal{F}_k$ such that $F_k^t \subseteq F_{jk}$. This is because, when k has observed F_k^t at round t, then if $F_k^t \subseteq F_{jk}$, then k knows that F_{kj} has occurred at round t as well. Note that the following definition is given in terms of an actual play interpretation of the dynamics.

Definition 3.6.1. Let $\Gamma = (N, S, \boldsymbol{u})$, Ω, and the partitions $\mathcal{H}_k$ of Ω be given, and let an elementary event $\omega \in \Omega$ occur at each round of deliberation. Let $\mathcal{F}_k$ denote the σ-algebra generated by the events in $\mathcal{H}_k$. The players $1, \ldots, n$ are *VSC-Dirichlet deliberators* iff they update their conditional probabilities recursively as follows:

(1) At the start of deliberation, each Player k assigns a value $\gamma_{\boldsymbol{A}_{-k} \wedge H_{kj}} \geq 0$ to each $\boldsymbol{A}_{-k} \in S_{-k}$ and each $H_{kj} \in \mathcal{H}_k$. For every $H_{kj} \in \mathcal{H}_k$, $\gamma_{\boldsymbol{B}_{-k} \wedge H_{kj}} > 0$ for at least one least one $\boldsymbol{B}_{-k} \in S_{-k}$. For each $F_{kj} \in \mathcal{F}_k$, define

$$\gamma_{\boldsymbol{A}_{-k} \wedge F_{kj}} = \sum_{H_{kj} \subseteq F_{kj}} \gamma_{\boldsymbol{A}_{-k} \wedge H_{kj}}$$

The prior conditional distribution $\mu_k^0(\cdot | \mathcal{F}_k)$ that each player has for the act combinations of his opponents in S_{-k} is defined by

$$\mu_k^0(\boldsymbol{A}_{-k} | F_{kj}) = \frac{\gamma_{\boldsymbol{A}_{-k} \wedge F_{kj}}}{\sum_{\boldsymbol{B}_{-k} \in S_{-k}} \gamma_{\boldsymbol{B}_{-k} \wedge F_{kj}}}, \quad F_{kj} \in \mathcal{F}_k$$

(2) At each round of deliberation $t \geq 1$, each deliberator k observes an event $F_k^t \in \mathcal{F}_k$, and plays a strategy $A_{kj} \in S_k$ which is a best response to her conditional distribution $\mu_k^t(\cdot | F_k^t)$, that is, k plays A_{kj} only if

$$E_k^t(u_k(A_{kj}) | F_k^t) \geq E_k^t(u_k(A_{kl}) | F_k^t) \text{ for all } A_{kl} \in S_k.$$

For each $F_{kj} \in \mathcal{F}_k$ such that $F_k^t \subseteq F_{kj}$, k knows that F_{kj} has occurred at round t as well. For each $F_{kj} \in \mathcal{F}_k$, $n_{F_{kj}}$ is the number of times that k knows that F_{kj} has occurred during the first t rounds of deliberation. For each $F_{kj} \in \mathcal{F}_k$ and each $\boldsymbol{A}_{-k} \in S_{-k}$, $n_{\boldsymbol{A}_{-k} \wedge F_{kj}}$ is the number of times that k knows that $\boldsymbol{A}_{-k}$ and F_{kj} have both occurred during the first t rounds of deliberation. At the $t + 1$st round of deliberation, player k updates her probability distribution $\mu_k^t(\cdot | \mathcal{F}_k)$ according to the rule:
If $F_{kj}^{t+1} \not\subseteq F_{kj}$, then

$$\mu_k^{t+1}(\boldsymbol{A}_{-k} | F_{kj}) = \mu_k^t(\boldsymbol{A}_{-k} | F_{kj})$$

and, if $F_{kj}^{t+1} \subseteq F_{kj}$, then

$$\mu_k^{t+1}(\boldsymbol{A}_{-k} | F_{kj}) = \frac{n_{\boldsymbol{A}_{-k} \wedge F_{kj}} + \theta + \gamma_{\boldsymbol{A}_{-k} \wedge F_{kj}}}{n_{F_{kj}} + 1 + \sum \gamma_{\boldsymbol{B}_{-k} \wedge F_{kj}}}$$

where

(a) $\theta = 1$ if k observes the opponents play $\boldsymbol{A}_{-k}$ at round $t + 1$, and

(b) $\theta = 0$ otherwise. $\square$

One can give an equivalent, but notationally more cumbersome, definition of VSC-Dirichlet dynamics by giving every deliberator a "base" partition $\mathcal{H}_k$, and specifying the dynamics in terms of time dependent partitions $\mathcal{H}_k^t$ such that at each round of deliberation t, either $\mathcal{H}_k^t = \mathcal{H}_k$ or $\mathcal{H}_k^t$ is a coarsening of $\mathcal{H}_k$. I have deliberately not specified the frequency with which a deliberator observes a particular event $F_k^t \in \mathcal{F}_k$. In words, Definition 3.6.1 says that the deliberators always play their best responses given *the most specific information each deliberator receives at each round of play*. Presumably, most of the time each deliberator will observe a cell of his information partition $\mathcal{H}_k$, but from time to time the deliberator will get information from a coarsening of $\mathcal{H}_k$ that is more vague than the information he would have received had he observed a cell of $\mathcal{H}_k$. However, the relative frequency of cells of $\mathcal{H}_k$ and of "vague" sets, which are unions of these cells in $\mathcal{F}_k$, in the sequence of deliberation may be distributed in a variety of ways. In particular, the "vague" sets might be uniformly distributed over time, or they might occur in "bursts," if the signaling device is occasionally interfered with.

The definitions of fixed points of VSC-Dirichlet dynamics are also quite similar to analogous definitions for other variations of the Dirichlet rule. An *almost sure fixed state* of VSC-Dirichlet dynamics is defined in the usual way, that is, $f : \Omega \to S$ is an almost sure state of deliberation if deliberators will with probability one follow the strategies determined by f for all rounds of play. The distributions of VSC-Dirichlet dynamics are a deliberational equilibrium if they are fixed for all the elements of each σ-algebra generated by each deliberator's information partition.

Definition 3.6.2. VSC-Dirichlet deliberators players are at *deliberational equilibrium* iff, for each $\omega \in \Omega$, and for each n-tuple of sets that deliberators observe with positive probability,

$$
\begin{aligned}
\mathfrak{P}^{t+1} &= (\mu_1^{t+1}(\cdot|\mathcal{F}_1), \ldots, \mu_n^{t+1}(\cdot|\mathcal{F}_n)) \\
&= (\mu_1^t(\cdot|\mathcal{F}_1), \ldots, \mu_n^t(\cdot|\mathcal{F}_n)) = \mathfrak{P}^t
\end{aligned}
$$

and, consequently, $\mathfrak{P}^u = \mathfrak{P}^t$ for all $u \geq t$, in which case the vector $\mathfrak{P}^t$ is called a *VSC-Dirichlet equilibrium*.

A function $f : \Omega \to S$ is an *almost sure fixed state* of VSC-Dirichlet deliberation if, should deliberators play f at some round t_0, then for all $t \geq t_0$, the event $\{f^t = f\}$ occurs with probability one. $\qquad\square$

For instance, in the Battle of the Sexes example given above, Amie's and Kay's sequence of plays converges to the almost sure fixed state (A_1, A_1) if $\omega \in \{\omega_1, \omega_2\}$, (A_2, A_2) if $\omega \in \{\omega_3, \omega_4\}$. Their conditional distributions for they events they observe in the sequence of deliberation converge to

$$
\begin{aligned}
\mu_1^*(A_1|\{\omega_1\}) &= \mu_1^*(A_1|\{\omega_2\}) = \mu_1^*(A_1|\{\omega_1, \omega_2\}) = 1 \\
\mu_2^*(A_1|\{\omega_1\}) &= \mu_2^*(A_1|\{\omega_2\}) = \mu_2^*(A_1|\{\omega_1, \omega_2\}) = 1 \\
\mu_1^*(A_2|\{\omega_3\}) &= \mu_1^*(A_2|\{\omega_4\}) = \mu_1^*(A_2|\{\omega_3, \omega_4\}) = 1 \\
\mu_2^*(A_2|\{\omega_3\}) &= \mu_2^*(A_2|\{\omega_4\}) = \mu_2^*(A_2|\{\omega_3, \omega_4\}) = 1
\end{aligned}
$$

On the other hand, the *unconditional* distributions eventually converge to

$$
\mu_1^*(A_1) = \mu_2^*(A_1) = \mu_1^*(A_2) = \mu_2^*(A_2) = \frac{1}{2}
$$

because the two coins are fair, so that in the long run, the frequencies of the events $\{\omega_1, \omega_2\}$ and $\{\omega_3, \omega_3\}$, and therefore the coordinated strategy combinations (A_1, A_1) and (A_2, A_2), both converge to $\frac{1}{2}$.

The following elementary result is analogous to Proposition 3.3.4.

Proposition 3.6.3. If $f : \Omega \to S$ is an almost sure fixed state of VSC-Dirichlet deliberation, then f is an Aumann correlated equilibrium with respect to every combination of partitions the deliberators update on with positive probability.

Proof. Suppose that f is not an Aumann correlated equilibrium with respect to all combinations of the deliberators' partitions that they update on with positive probability. Then for some collection of partitions $\mathcal{H}'_1, \ldots, \mathcal{H}'_n$ the deliberators might condition on, f is not an Aumann correlated equilibrium. That is, for some $k \in N$ and some $\omega' \in \Omega$,

$$E_k(u_k \circ (g_k, f_{-k}) | \mathcal{H}'_k)(\omega') > E_k(u_k \circ f | \mathcal{H}'_k)(\omega')$$

for some strategy $g_k(\omega') \neq f_k(\omega')$. Hence, if at round t_0 the elementary event is $\omega^{t_0} = \omega'$ and each deliberator observes her corresponding cell of the partition $\mathcal{H}'_k$, then k will deviate from f, so $f^{t_0} \neq f$. Since this occurs with positive probability, f is not an almost sure fixed state of VSC-Dirichlet deliberation. $\square$

As with RSC-Dirichlet dynamics, I believe that VSC-Dirichlet dynamics admits of plausible actual play and quasi-evolutionary interpretations, but not of a fictitious play interpretation. A fictitious play interpretation of this dynamics would imply that each deliberator not only knows the "basic" information partition of each of her opponents, as in the fictitious play interpretation of conditional Dirichlet deliberation, but also knows at each round of deliberation whether each opponent successfully observes all of the information he can from the signaling device. In other words, as with RSC-Dirichlet deliberation, a fictitious play interpretation of VSC-Dirichlet deliberation would make the deliberators out to be mind-readers, with the result that they would all know the same information at every round of deliberation, after all. In the example above, if at round 8 Kay fails to observe the second flip, but somehow reads Amie's mind and thereby learns the results of both coin flips, then Kay's information from the signaling device turns out to be the same as Amie's, when the whole motivation for introducing the VSC-model is to make it possible for the deliberators to occasionally receive unequal knowledge from the signaling device.

On the other hand, actual play and quasi-evolutionary interpretations of VSC-Dirichlet dynamics make intuitive sense, because these interpretations have less stringent requirements on the deliberators' common knowledge. Under either of these interpretations, all that a deliberator needs to know at any particular round in order to revise his current conditional probabilities is what his own signal is at that round and the strategy profile his opponents play at this round, not what the opponents' signals are. Allowing the partitions to be sporadically variable reflects the intuition that deliberators may sometimes fail to observe all of the information the signals would ordinarily provide them, perhaps because they are somewhat distracted from time to time or because some sort of "noise" interferes with the signal.

CHAPTER 4

The Emergence of Social Convention

This may properly enough be call'd a convention or agreement betwixt us, tho' without the interposition of a promise; since the actions of each of us have a reference to those of the other, and are perform'd upon the supposition, that something is to be perform'd on the other part. Two men, who pull the oars of a boat, do it by an agreement or convention, tho' they have never given promises to each other. . . . In like manner are languages gradually establish'd by human conventions without any promise. In like manner do gold and silver become the common measures of exchange, and are esteem'd sufficient payment for what is of a hundred times their value.

David Hume, *A Treatise of Human Nature*

§4.0   Introduction

As noted at the start of this book, the formal treatment of solution concepts for games and inductive deliberation given in Chapters 2 and 3 is motivated by the problem of explaining social coordination. In this final chapter, I will return to this problem, and consider how game theory and inductive deliberation can help give an account of a special kind of social coordination. In the classic passage quoted above, Hume observes that people are able to coordinate many of their activities without explicitly agreeing to coordinate, and he resolves this apparent paradox by explaining coordination in terms of reciprocal expectations. If a social coordination problem is "solved" in this way, that is, each agent acts so as to coordinate and expects others to do the same, the agents involved are said to follow a *convention*.

The notion of convention goes far in explaining how humans coordinate many of their activities without continually negotiating over *how* they will coordinate. At the same time this notion raises fundamental questions: (1) *Why do particular conventions persist over time?* and (2) *How does a particular convention arise in the first place?* Beginning with the seminal work of Schelling (1960) and Lewis (1969), a number of authors have addressed these questions by applying the noncooperative game theory developed by Von Neumann, Morgenstern, and Nash. There are two common threads in the game-theoretic literature on convention. First, a convention is usually defined as a certain type of equilibrium of a noncooperative game, which helps account for why conventions remain stable over time. Second, the emergence of particular conventions is often explained as the result of a *dynamical adjustment process*, in which the behavior of agents engaged in a repeated strategic situation converges to an equilibrium corresponding to a convention.

This chapter presents a new game-theoretic definition of convention, and applies inductive deliberation to give one account of the emergence of convention. Lewis (1969) gives a widely accepted definition of convention as a *coordination equilibrium* of a noncooperative game that satisfies common knowledge of a *mutual expectations criterion* (MEC) because it is *salient*, that is, the equilibrium is somehow conspicuous to all of the agents involved.[1] I propose an alternate definition of convention as an Aumann correlated equilibrium satisfying a *public intentions criterion* (PIC), and argue that this definition is more satisfactory than Lewis' definition.[2] A convention is defined as a function from a space of "states of the world," which formalizes salience, to strategy combinations of a noncooperative game that meet the PIC, so that the system is at equilibrium. I argue that many conventions correspond to correlated equilibria that are not Nash equilibria.

To account for the emergence of correlated equilibria corresponding to conventions, I apply the theory of inductive deliberation developed in Chapter 3. Choosing which correlated equilibrium of many to follow as a convention is an instance of the more general problem of equilibrium selection in game theory. As argued in Chapter 3, one way to address this problem is to have the players adjust their beliefs about each other recursively as inductive deliberators.[3] We have seen that players who are inductive Dirichlet deliberators can reach an equilibrium of a game from a state of initial indecision. This chapter applies Dirichlet deliberation and its variants specifically to the problem of explaining the emergence of convention. The approach taken here differs from other like-minded approaches in the literature in that players can receive external signals at each stage of deliberation, and they do not assume that strategy choices are stochastically independent.[4] We have seen that such deliberators can learn to play a

---

[1] Lewis attributes the intuitive notion of salience to Schelling (1960). See Lewis (1969), p. 35 and Schelling (1960), pp. 55–56.

[2] Shubik (1982) and Skyrms (1990) suggest that conventions can be defined as correlated equilibria, but neither gives an explicit definition. See Shubik (1982), p. 249, and Skyrms (1990), pp. 52–61.

[3] As noted in Chapter 3, Skyrms (1991a) and Vanderschraaf and Skyrms (1993) make similar arguments.

[4] For other dynamical explanations of the emergence of conventions, see Crawford and Haller

correlated equilibrium under the right conditions. In particular, *asymmetries* in the deliberators' knowledge of their situation can lead to their converging to a correlated equilibrium corresponding to a convention.

§4.1   Lewis' Characterization of Conventions

Lewis (1969) defines a convention as a state in which: (1) agents engaged in a game play a *coordination equilibrium*, and (2) their preferences to conform with this coordination equilibrium are *common knowledge*. A coordination equilibrium of a noncooperative game is a strategy combination such that *no* player can be better off if any player deviates unilaterally from this equilibrium.[5] For instance, in the 2-player game with payoff structure given in Figure 4.1.1, there are three coordination equilibria in pure strategies, namely (A_1, A_1), (A_2, A_2), and (A_3, A_3).

Kay

		A_1	A_2	A_3
	A_1	$(3,3)$	$(0,0)$	$(0,0)$
Amie	A_2	$(0,0)$	$(1,1)$	$(0,0)$
	A_3	$(0,0)$	$(0,0)$	$(2,2)$

Figure 4.1.1. Hume's Rowboat

Figure 4.1.1 repeats the 2-player Rowboat problem of Example 2 in Chapter 1. To review, Amie and Kay can each row in one of three ways, corresponding to the strategies A_1, A_2, and A_3. This is a *pure coordination game* (Schelling 1960, Lewis 1969),[6] that is, a game in which at each pure strategy combination the players all receive the same payoff. Amie and Kay each have three pure strategies and receive exactly the same payoff at each of the nine pure strategy combinations. This game models a situation in which there are at least three possible conventions, corresponding to the coordination equilibria (A_1, A_1), (A_2, A_2),

(1990), Young (1993), and Kandori, Mailath, and Rob (1993). Note that all of these papers model a convention as a Nash equilibrium, which I argue is too restrictive.

[5] Lewis (1969), p. 14.

[6] Schelling (1960), p. 84, and Lewis (1969), p. 14. Schelling calls pure coordination games of *pure collaboration*.

and (A_3, A_3). At any of these equilibria, the desires of the two players are perfectly coordinated, that is, each player has an incentive to play her end of the equilibrium, and she wants her opponent to play her end of the equilibrium as well. If the players select an equilibrium strategy profile, say (A_3, A_3), then the boat moves forward. Otherwise, the boat moves in circles. As with any Nash equilibrium, neither player will wish to deviate unilaterally from the equilibrium (A_3, A_3). In addition, neither player will want her *opponent* to deviate from the coordination equilibrium. If, for some reason, Kay were to deviate from her optimal strategy of playing A_3, then *both* players would suffer.

Note that a coordination equilibrium satisfies a much stronger condition than *strictness*. At a strict equilibrium, each player's strategy is her unique best response. For instance, in the Chicken game defined by the payoff matrices in Figure 4.1.2, the pure strategy equilibria (A_1, A_2) and (A_2, A_1) are both strict.

Kay

		A_1	A_2
Amie	A_1	$(6, 6)$	$(2, 7)$
	A_2	$(7, 2)$	$(0, 0)$

Figure 4.1.2. Chicken

If the players are at the equilibrium (A_2, A_1), then each player is strictly better off if she plays her end of the equilibrium than she would be were she to deviate. However, (A_2, A_1) is not a coordination equilibrium, since if Amie were to deviate from (A_2, A_1), she would actually improve Kay's fortunes (while harming herself). By a symmetric argument, (A_1, A_2) is not a coordination equilibrium, either. Chicken also shows that not every game has a coordination equilibrium.

Lewis' definition of convention requires not only that agents play their ends of a coordination equilibrium, but also that the agents have *common knowledge* that they all prefer to conform with the equilibrium given that every agent conforms with this equilibrium. Lewis formulated the notion of common knowledge for the express purpose of defining convention, though in the years since the publication of *Convention* game theorists have realized that various common knowledge assumptions underpin any solution concept for games.[7] Recall that a

---

[7]Lewis' definition of common knowledge appears on pp. 56–57 of *Convention*. For extended discussions of the role of common knowledge assumptions in game theory, see Brandenburger and Dekel (1988), Brandenburger (1992), and Chapter 2 above.

proposition A is common knowledge for a set of agents if

(1) Each Agent k knows that A,

(2) Each Agent i knows that each Agent k knows that A, each Agent j knows that each Agent i knows that each Agent k knows that A, and so on.

For Lewis, a coordination equilibrium is a convention only if the players have common knowledge of a *mutual expectations criterion*:

MEC Each agent has a decisive reason to conform to his part of the convention *given that she expects the other agents conform to their parts*.[8]

Lewis adds this common knowledge requirement to his definition of convention to rule out cases in which agents coordinate as the result of false beliefs regarding their opponents. Consider the Rowboat example of Figure 4.1.1, and suppose that on Friday Kay believes that Amie is not trying to coordinate her rowing style with Kay's rowing style, and likewise Amie does not believe that Kay is trying to co-ordinate with her. Rather, on Friday each believes that the other rows in the style corresponding to A_3 unconditionally, by habit. Nevertheless, Kay and Amie both want to coordinate with the other on Friday, so each will play A_3. In this case, the agents manage to coordinate, but Lewis does not count this sort of coordination as a convention, since each agent falsely believes that the other player does not care about coordinating. On the other hand, suppose that on Saturday, Kay now believes that Amie will choose A_3 because she believes that Amie wants to coor-dinate with her, and that Amie has similar beliefs regarding Kay. If these beliefs are common knowledge, then Kay and Amie both decide to play A_3 because of their expectations regarding what the other will do, and so they follow a conven-tion when they play the equilibrium (A_3, A_3). On Saturday, their coordination was the result of their common knowledge that they both wanted to coordinate, but on Friday, they coordinated as a result of false beliefs, and Lewis maintains that coordination predicated on false beliefs should not count as a convention.

For Lewis, then, a convention is a state at which agents play a coordination equilibrium as a result of their common knowledge that all conform with the equilibrium and that they do so in order to coordinate their activity.

A regularity R in the behavior of members of a population P when they are agents in a recurrent situation S is a convention if and only if it is true that, and it is common knowledge in P that, in any instance of S among the members of P,

---

[8]Lewis (1969), p. 25. The term "mutual expectations criterion" is mine, not Lewis'.

(1) everyone conforms to R;

(2) everyone expects everyone else to conform to R;

(3) everyone prefers to conform to R on condition that the others do, since S is a coordination equilibrium and uniform conformity to R is a coordination equilibrium in S.[9]

Lewis stipulates that the equilibrium of a convention must be a coordination equilibrium in order to capture the fundamental intuition that a person who follows a convention wants his intention to conform with this convention to be *public*. As noted above, Lewis argues that common knowledge of the MEC is a necessary condition of the definition of a convention. However, common knowledge of the MEC is not by itself sufficient to characterize convention, since common knowledge of the MEC can be satisfied at any strict Nash equilibrium. In Chicken, if Amie believes that Kay will play her end of the equilibrium (A_2, A_1), and Kay believes that Amie will play her end of the equilibrium, then both players will have an overriding reason to play their respective ends of the equilibrium. If these expectations are common knowledge, then the players have common knowledge of the MEC. However, this equilibrium is not a convention, since it is not a coordination equilibrium.[10] Chicken is a game of *partially conflicting interests*, since if a player chooses to play A_1, she would prefer that her opponent sacrifice her own interests by also playing A_1 rather than maximize her expected utility by playing A_2. The equilibrium of a convention is the equilibrium of a game of *mutual interests*, since every agent desires that all conform, thereby maximizing everyone's best interests. Consequently, conventions satisfy a *public intentions criterion*:

PIC At a convention, each agent will desire that his choice of strategy is common knowledge among all agents engaged in the game.

---

[9] Lewis (1969), p. 58.

[10] It will not suffice to amend the MEC so that each player will have decisive reason to conform to the convention *only if* she expects the others to conform. To see this, note that in the following game, if Kay expects Amie to play A_2 with probability 1, then Kay would still have a decisive reason to play her end of the coordination equilibrium (A_1, A_1) even though she does not expect Amie to play her end of this equilibrium.

		Kay		
		A_1	A_2	A_3
	A_1	$(3, 3)$	$(-1, -1)$	$(-1, -1)$
Amie	A_2	$(0, 0)$	$(-1, -1)$	$(-1, -1)$
	A_3	$(-1, -1)$	$(-1, -1)$	$(2, 2)$

The PIC, I think, reflects the nature of a convention better than the MEC. The PIC is perhaps best illustrated first by counterexample. Suppose that in Chicken, Amie elects to "play it safe" by choosing A_1. If Kay knows Amie's choice, then Kay will play the aggressive strategy A_2, and if their respective strategy choices are common knowledge, then Amie and Kay are at the equilibrium (A_1, A_2) and common knowledge of the MEC is satisfied. However, if Kay does not know Amie's choice, then Amie can serve her own best interests by appearing to be aggressive, in order to deceive Kay into playing it safe in hopes of gaining the higher payoff associated with the nonequilibrium point (A_1, A_1). So Chicken does not satisfy the PIC.[11] On the other hand, in the Rowboat game of Figure 4.1.1, if Kay intends to play A_3, then Kay will want Amie to know this, and Kay will want to know that Amie knows this, and so on, since this will give Amie a decisive reason to coordinate with Kay on A_3, with the result that *Kay's* best interests are served. Similarly, if Amie decides to play A_3, she will want her intention to be common knowledge, so at the convention corresponding to (A_3, A_3) the PIC is satisfied. Note that the PIC does not imply that agents will actually declare their intentions to each other before they act so as to conform with a convention. After all, convention is supposed to explain certain behaviors in terms of expectations rather than negotiation. Rather, the PIC implies that agents who conform with a convention would willingly disclose their intentions to one another if they were able to.

Lewis' game-theoretic account of convention captures several other important intuitions. Since Lewis does not require that all conventions correspond to pure coordination games, in Lewis' framework some conventions can benefit some individuals more than others. For instance, Battle of the Sexes with payoff structure given by Figure 4.1.3 is not a pure coordination game, but the two pure strategy equilibria (A_1, A_1) and (A_2, A_2) are coordination equilibria.

A coordinated pure strategy combination in Battle of the Sexes is an equilibrium corresponding to a convention, even though this convention is "unfair" to one of the players. Suppose this game describes Amie and Kay's Dining Out Problem of Example 4 in Chapter 1. If they both go to Amie's favorite restaurant, which corresponds to their both choosing A_1, and their choices are common

---

[11] Schelling (1960), p. 96, makes a similar argument with respect to zero-sum games. Shelling notes that in a zero-sum game, which he calls a game of *pure conflict*, the players can only achieve the (mixed) equilibrium by keeping each other in the dark as to their actual intended strategies. Typically in the literature, the justification for randomized strategies in zero-sum games is that randomizing one's own strategy keeps one's opponents uncertain as to which pure strategy one will actually play, for if a player's pure strategy becomes known to his opponents, then they will select strategies that strictly favor them and hurt the player. On the other hand, in a pure coordination game a player will want the others to know his pure strategy strategy choice, in order to ensure that they coordinate.

Kay

$$A_1 \qquad A_2$$

Amie	A_1	$(2,1)$	$(0,0)$
	A_2	$(0,0)$	$(1,2)$

Figure 4.1.3. Battle of the Sexes

knowledge, then Kay is less pleased than Amie, but at least they are to have their meal together, so Kay will accept the "unfair" convention. In general, no player will want to deviate from a coordination equilibrium corresponding to a convention, even if this equilibrium is not equally advantageous to everyone.

Furthermore, Lewis recognizes that while many conventions require everyone to do the same thing, some conventions can arise in which different agents perform different actions. Hence Lewis does not require that the players in a coordination problem coordinate by playing the same strategies, or even that the players have the same alternative pure strategies. Indeed, in the game with payoff structure given in Figure 4.1.4, Amie and Kay are at a pure strategy coordination equilibrium only when they play opposite strategies. This is the Telephone Tag game of Example 5 in Chapter 1, where A_1 is the strategy of receiving and A_2 the strategy of calling. Again, Kay and Amie can have a phone conversation only if one calls and the other receives, and each prefers to be the receiver, in order to avoid the charges of calling. There are at least two conventions of Telephone Tag, one characterized by Kay's and Amie's common knowledge that they will follow (A_1, A_2), and the other by their common knowledge that they will follow (A_2, A_1).

Kay

$$A_1 \qquad A_2$$

Amie	A_1	$(0,0)$	$(2,1)$
	A_2	$(1,2)$	$(0,0)$

Figure 4.1.4. Telephone Tag

Finally, Lewis explains the existence of certain *particular* conventions in terms of *salience*, a notion Lewis attributes to Schelling (1960).[12] A coordination equilibrium is salient to the players if it somehow stands out so that all

---

[12]Lewis (1969), p. 35.

expect each other to coordinate on this equilibrium. Lewis points out that salience need not necessarily arise from pre-game communication. In the rowboat example of Figure 4.1.1, the rowing convention corresponding to (A_1, A_1) might be salient because both Kay and Amie expect one another to try for the equilibrium that yields the greatest payoff. Salience may also result from precedent. The coordination equilibrium (A_3, A_3) in the rowboat game might be salient to the two players, despite the fact that it does not yield as high a payoff for each as (A_1, A_1) would have, because they have coordinated on (A_3, A_3) sometime in the past. Schelling (1960) reports on a variety of experimental results in which he presented subjects a variety of pure coordination problems without allowing them to communicate with one another before responding. These subjects were able to coordinate far more often than chance would predict, a phenomenon that Schelling attributes to certain solutions being particularly conspicuous to the subjects. In one of Schelling's most striking experiments, each of 36 subjects was asked where and when on a given day she would try to meet someone else in New York City trying to meet her without being allowed to communicate beforehand. An absolute majority of subjects said they would go to Grand Central Station, and nearly all of them coordinated on noon as the meeting time.[13] Schelling attributes this high rate of success partly to the subjects all being from Connecticut. As a result of their common background knowledge *their expectations were correlated on the same meeting place and time*, that is, this solution to the coordination problem was salient to the subjects even though they did not communicate before being confronted with the problem.

Salience can also result from the players correlating their strategies and their expectations with certain events external to the game. This *exogenous correlation* leads to conventions that do not correspond to Nash equilibria, a fact that Lewis does not discuss in detail in his work,[14] but that is consistent with his general point of view. To see this, consider the pure coordination game described by Figure 4.1.5.

In Example 1 of Chapter 1, this game was interpreted as an Encounter Problem, where Amie's and Kay's respective strategies are either to look on the first floor (A_1) or to look on the second floor (A_2). They find one another if and only if they search on the same floor. The players are at a coordination equilibrium corresponding to a convention if they play either of the pure strategy Nash

---

[13] Schelling (1960), pp. 55–56.

[14] Lewis wrote *Convention* before Aumann introduced the technical vocabulary of correlated equilibrium in his 1974 essay. On p. 129 of *Convention*, Lewis gives an example of a convention corresponding to a *Nash* equilibrium in *contingency strategies*. This example has a natural alternative description as an Aumann correlated equilibrium. However, this is the only such example I have found in Lewis' work.

Kay

		A_1	A_2
Amie	A_1	$(1,1)$	$(0,0)$
	A_2	$(0,0)$	$(1,1)$

Figure 4.1.5. The Encounter Problem

equilibria (A_1, A_1) or (A_2, A_2). They can also follow a "conditional convention": (A_1, A_1) if they spot their coworker Ron on the first floor, and (A_2, A_2) if they spot Ron on the second floor. This conditional strategy combination is not a Nash equilibrium, but it still satisfies the modified mutual expectations criterion and still results in both players receiving their best payoffs. This arrangement is admittedly more complicated than either of the unconditional pure strategy conventions, but it is hardly implausible. Such a conditional convention could easily arise if Amie and Kay have searched for one another in this office building often, and have become accustomed to *alternating* floors according to Ron's location, even if neither prefers meeting on one floor over meeting on the other floor. Of course, this particular convention corresponds to an Aumann correlated equilibrium, in which players tie their strategies to some event that is not part of the game. Here the external event is Ron's location in the building.

§4.2   Convention as Correlated Equilibrium

I now give a formal definition of *convention*, motivated by the discussion above. I first review elements of Aumann's analytical framework and fix notation. Recall that in Aumann's model, the players are engaged in a game $\Gamma = (N, S, u)$, and each player has a personal information partition $\mathcal{H}_k$ of a probability space Ω. The elementary events $\omega \in \Omega$ are the states of the world, and at each ω, every player k knows that the element $H_{kj} \in \mathcal{H}_k$ such that $\omega \in H_{kj}$ has occurred, but does not in general know which ω has occurred. H_{kj} represents k's private information regarding the states of the world. In general, while k does know the *partitions* of his opponents, k does not necessarily know the private information each of his opponents has regarding the states of the world. A function $f : \Omega \to S$ defines a system of exogenously correlated strategy n-tuples, that is, for each $\omega \in \Omega$, the players select a strategy combination

$f(\omega) = (f_1(\omega), \ldots, f_n(\omega)) \in S$ correlated with the state of the world ω. Informally, f is a correlated equilibrium if at each state of the world $\omega \in \Omega$, $f_k(\omega)$ is optimal for each player k, in the sense that $f_k(\omega)$ maximizes k's expected payoff given k's private information and k's expectations regarding his opponents. Recall from Definition 2.3.2 that $f : \Omega \to S$ is an *a posteriori correlated equilibrium* if, and only if, for each $k \in N$,

(a) f_k is an $\mathcal{H}_k$-measurable function, that is, for each $H_{kj} \in \mathcal{H}_k$, $f_k(\omega')$ is constant for each $\omega' \in H_{kj}$, and

(b) For each $\omega \in \Omega$,

$$(4.i) \qquad E_k(u_k \circ f | \mathcal{H}_k)(\omega) \geq E_k(u_k \circ (f_{-k}, g_k) | \mathcal{H}_k)(\omega)$$

for any $\mathcal{H}_k$-measurable function $g_k : \Omega \to S_k$, where for every player $k \in N$,

$(4.ii)$ $\qquad\qquad \mu_k(\cdot | H_{kj})$ is a probability measure on Ω, and

$(4.iii)$ $\qquad\qquad\qquad\qquad \mu_k(H_{kj} | H_{kj}) = 1$

for each $H_{kj} \in \mathcal{H}_k$. Again, these conditions follow immediately from the conventional definition of conditional probability if $\mu_k(H_{kj}) > 0$, but the requirement that every cell of every player's information partition satisfies $(4.ii)$ and $(4.iii)$ extends the standard definition of conditional probability to events of zero probability.

One can relax the assumption that each player's information structure is a *finite* partition by assigning each player information from a private σ-algebra of the state space Ω. This enables one to give a more general definition of correlated equilibrium, but, as Aumann (1987) notes, such a definition introduces some fairly cumbersome tools from measure theory into the picture, without adding to our understanding of the correlated equilibrium concept in any obvious way.[15] In this book, I have discussed only finite partitions. Clearly, this has kept the mathematical exposition simpler. Moreover, it may be the case that a rational agent can comprehend only a finite division of the "states of the world," so that finite partitions are entirely adequate. However, so far as I am aware, all of the discussion in this chapter applies equally well to the more general definition of correlated equilibrium in terms of σ-algebras.

In the following definition of convention, the agents refer to a common information partition of the states of the world. While each agent k has a private

---

[15] See Aumann (1987), p. 10.

information partition $\mathcal{H}_k$ of Ω, there is a partition of Ω, namely the intersection $\mathcal{H} = \bigcap_{k \in N} \mathcal{H}_k$, of the states of the world such that for each $\omega \in \Omega$, all of the agents will know which cell $H(\omega) \in \mathcal{H}$ occurs.[16] The agents' expected utilities in Definition 4.2.1 are conditional on their common partition $\mathcal{H}$, reflecting the intuition that conventions rely upon information that is public to all.

Definition 4.2.1. Given $\Gamma = (N, S, u)$, Ω, and the partition $\mathcal{H}$ of Ω of events that are common knowledge among the players, a function $f : \Omega \to S$ is a *convention* iff for each $\omega \in \Omega$, and for each $k \in N$, f_k is $\mathcal{H}$-measurable and

$$(4.iv) \qquad E_k(u_k \circ f | \mathcal{H})(\omega) > E_k(u_k \circ (f_{-j}, g_j) | \mathcal{H})(\omega)$$

for each $j \in N$ and for any $\mathcal{H}$-measurable function $g_j : \Omega \to S_j$.   □

In words, if any player j deviates unilaterally from the convention f, then every player $k \in N$, including j, is worse off. Hence Condition (4.iv) represents a slight departure from Lewis' notion of coordination equilibrium, since according to Lewis' definition any unilateral deviation from a coordination equilibrium makes the deviator worse off and no other player better off. One could give a more complex definition of convention that is more faithful to Lewis' technical requirements, but even on Lewis' own analysis I see no reason not to adopt the simpler notion of convention I give here. Note that if f is a convention, then f is clearly an Aumann correlated equilibrium. Moreover, this definition of convention satisfies the PIC. Since the agents in a convention refer to a common partition, at each $\omega \in \Omega$, a given player k's opponents all know exactly which strategy k will play, and k will want his opponents to know this. If any of k's opponents mistakenly believed that k would play a strategy $g_k(\omega) \neq f_k(\omega)$ at some $\omega \in \Omega$, then this opponent might be tempted to deviate from the convention, which would leave k strictly worse off. On the other hand, if k's opponent's all know that k will play $f_k(\omega)$ at every $\omega \in \Omega$, then they will all have a decisive reason to conform with $f(\omega)$, with the result that k is strictly better off.

Moreover, f is also a correlated equilibrium if the players condition their expected utilities in terms of their *private* information. If condition (4.iv) is satisfied, then if each agent were to compute her expected utilities conditional on her private information partition $\mathcal{H}_k$, which is a refinement of $\mathcal{H}$, then f_k is measurable with respect to $\mathcal{H}$ and condition (4.i) is satisfied. The details of this argument are carried out in the following:

---

[16] Since the intersection of any collection of partitions of Ω is again a partition, $\mathcal{H}$ is a partition of Ω which contains (by definition) cells common to every partition $\mathcal{H}_k$, $k \in N$.

Proposition 4.2.2. If $f : \Omega \rightarrow S$ is a convention, then f is an *a posteriori* equilibrium with respect to the players' private information partitions.

Proof. Let $\omega \in \Omega$ and $k \in N$ be given, and let H_{kj} be the cell of $\mathcal{H}_k$ containing ω. Let H be the cell of $\mathcal{H}$ such that $H_{kj} \subseteq H$. Since f is measurable with respect to $\mathcal{H}$, $f(\omega') = (f_1(\omega'), \dots, f_n(\omega'))$ is constant for all $\omega' \in H$. Hence $f_k(\omega')$ must be constant for all $\omega' \in H_{kj}$. We claim that

$$(1) \qquad u_k \circ f(\omega) \geq u_k \circ (g_k(\omega), f_{-k}(\omega))$$

for every function $g_k : \Omega \rightarrow S_k$ which is $\mathcal{H}_k$-measurable (and therefore constant over H_{kj}). For if (1) fails, then there is some $\mathcal{H}_k$-measurable function g_k such that $u_k \circ f(\omega) < u_k \circ (g_k(\omega), f_{-k}(\omega))$. Define $\tilde{g}_k$ over H by

$$\tilde{g}_k(\omega') = \begin{cases} g(\omega) & \text{for } \omega' \in H \\ f_k(\omega') & \text{for } \omega' \notin H \end{cases}$$

Then $\tilde{g}_k$ is $\mathcal{H}$-measurable, and

$$\begin{aligned} E_k(u_k \circ f | \mathcal{H})(\omega) &= u_k \circ f(\omega) \\ &< u_k \circ (\tilde{g}_k(\omega), f_{-k}(\omega)) \\ &= E_k(u_k \circ (\tilde{g}_k, f_{-k}) | \mathcal{H})(\omega) \end{aligned}$$

so condition (4.*iv*) fails, a contradiction. Hence, (1) must obtain. By (1) and the monotonicity of expectation,

$$E_k(u_k \circ f(\omega) | H_{kj}) \geq E_k(u_k \circ (g_k(\omega), f_{-k}(\omega)) | H_{kj})$$

for every $\mathcal{H}_k$-measurable function g_k. Since ω was chosen arbitrarily, we have shown that f_k is $\mathcal{H}_k$-measurable and that condition (4.*i*) is satisfied for every $\omega \in \Omega$, so f is an *a posteriori* equilibrium with respect to the partitions $\mathcal{H}_k$, $k \in N$. ☐

In other words, *while the correlated equilibrium corresponding to a convention relies upon public information regarding the states of the world, an individual agent's private information gives her no reason to deviate from the convention.*

Unlike Lewis' definition of convention, Definition 4.2.1 formally incorporates the notion of salience. Indeed, throughout his work Lewis leaves the notion of salience somewhat imprecise. This is perhaps not surprising, since salience can arise from so many different factors. On the other hand, salience is built into the correlated equilibrium definition of convention, since the correlated equilibrium that characterizes a specific convention is a function of "states of the world" on which the agents coordinate their actions. In other words, a convention f as defined in Definition 4.2.1 is salient to the players because they correlate, via f, their actions and expectations with various pieces of information at their disposal, which are formalized as elements of a partition of an event space Ω. For instance, in the office building example of Figure 4.1.5, if the players follow the convention corresponding to the pure strategy equilibrium (A_1, A_1), then the salience of this equilibrium is made precise by constructing a simple event space $\Omega = \{\omega\}$, and defining this convention as the correlated equilibrium $f(\omega) = (A_1, A_1)$. The single element probability space Ω is a simple formalization of all of the factors leading to the players' expectations that Amie and Kay will both choose A_1, such as precedents, external signals, or even the description of the game itself. The players follow the convention (A_1, A_1) rather than another convention like (A_2, A_2) because their expectations are correlated with ω. To take a slightly more complicated case, if Amie and Kay follow the convention of playing (A_1, A_1) or (A_2, A_2) depending on where Ron is, then one can construct the event space $\Omega = \{\omega_1, \omega_2\}$, where ω_1 denotes the event that Ron is on the first floor and ω_2 denotes the event that Ron is on the second floor. The convention

$$ f(\omega) = \begin{cases} (A_1, A_1) & \text{if } \omega = \omega_1 \\ (A_2, A_2) & \text{if } \omega = \omega_2 \end{cases} $$

is salient for the two players in virtue of how their beliefs regarding their own and their opponents' choices are correlated with the elements of Ω. Note that while one might argue that Ron's location in the building is not a true stochastic process, Kay and Amie will still have *subjective prior* probability distributions for the elements of Ω, reflecting their beliefs regarding Ron's location before they see him. Amie and Kay use these subjective priors to compute the expectations that characterize the convention f. In general, the event space Ω in the correlated equilibrium definition of convention makes explicit *what* the agents who follow a convention correlate their expectations on. But it raises the following question: How do the agents come to correlate on the elements of any particular Ω in any particular way? I will address this question below.

Extending Lewis' definition of conventions to include correlated equilibria also greatly expands the class of equilibria which characterize conventions. Suppose that a game Γ has the pure strategy coordination equilibria $A_1, \ldots, A_m$, $m \geq 2$, and that Ω is a lottery with m mutually exclusive outcomes $H_1, \ldots, H_m$, such that $\mu_k(H_j) = \lambda_j$ for each player j. Then if the players all condition on the partition $\mathcal{H} = \{H_1, \ldots, H_m\}$, and if $f : \Omega \to S$ is defined by $f(\omega) = A_j$ if $\omega \in H_j$, then (4.*iv*) is satisfied for every $\omega \in \Omega$, so f is a convention. Since there are infinitely many possible values for the λ_j's, any noncooperative game that has at least two pure strategy coordination equilibria has infinitely many correlated equilibria corresponding to conventions.

In particular, the definition of convention as correlated equilibrium accounts for certain conventions that are "fair" to both players, even though the corresponding game has no "fair" coordination equilibrium in pure strategies. Neither of the pure strategy Nash equilibria in Battle of the Sexes is fair, in the sense that the players receive equal payoffs. This game has a mixed Nash equilibrium at which Kay believes that Amie plays A_1 with probability $\frac{2}{3}$ and Amie believes that Kay plays A_2 with probability $\frac{2}{3}$, and at this equilibrium each player's expected payoff is $\frac{2}{3}$, so this equilibrium is "fair." However, at the mixed Nash equilibrium, both players are indifferent to the strategies they play, so this equilibrium fails the MEC and is consequently not a convention. Nevertheless, there are correlated equilibria of this game that are fair to both players, and that each player will prefer over the pure strategy equilibrium that is unfair to her. One such equilibrium is the coin-toss correlated equilibrium of Example 2.2.1, where Amie and Kay both play A_1 if a fair coin is tossed and lands heads-up ("H") and both play A_2 if the coin lands tails-up ("T"). Then the combinations (A_1, A_1) and (A_2, A_2) are each played with probability $\frac{1}{2}$, and the uncoordinated strategy combinations are played with probability zero. If we set $\Omega = \{H, T\}$, then we can denote this correlated strategy combination as a function $f : \Omega \rightarrow \{A_1, A_2\} \times \{A_1, A_2\}$, where $f(H) = (A_1, A_1)$ and $f(T) = (A_2, A_2)$. Neither player would unilaterally deviate from the strategy combination defined by f. As we saw in Example 2.2.1, if Amie computes her conditional expected payoffs, she will note that

$$E_1(u_1 \circ f | H) = 2 > 0 = E_1(u_1(A_2, A_1)) | H)$$

and

$$E_1(u_1 \circ f | T) = 1 > 0 = E_1(u_1(A_1, A_2) | T)$$

so she will not want to defect from the correlated strategy of playing A_1 if H and A_2 if T.[17] Similarly, Kay will want to adhere to her end of f. So we have repeated the argument given in Chapter 2 that f is a correlated equilibrium. Note, however, that f also satisfies (4.*iv*). For

$$E_1(u_1 \circ f | H) = 2 > 0 = E_1(u_1(A_1, A_2)) | H)$$

and

$$E_1(u_1 \circ f | T) = 1 > 0 = E_1(u_1(A_2, A_1) | T)$$

---

[17]I abuse notation by writing $E_1(u_1 \circ f | H)$ instead of $E_1(u_1 \circ f | \{H\})$, $E_1(u_1(A_1, A_2) | T)$ instead of $E_1(u_1(A_1, A_2) | \{T\})$, and so on.

so if Amie plays her end of the equilibrium f, she will not want Kay to deviate from f, and likewise, Kay will prefer that Amie plays the strategy determined by f given that Kay plays the strategy determined by f, as well. Hence, the correlated equilibrium f is a convention, and since the overall expected payoff at this equilibrium for each player is

$$E_k(u_k \circ f) = \frac{1}{2} \cdot E_k(u_k \circ f|H) + \frac{1}{2} \cdot E_k(u_k \circ f|T) = \frac{3}{2}$$

the payoff vector of f is equally advantageous to both players and also Pareto-dominates the payoff vector of the mixed equilibrium.

In the definition of convention, the players refer to a *common* information partition $\mathcal{H}$. This restriction is necessary to make the definition of convention conform with the spirit of Lewis' formulation. Consider the example, due to Aumann, summarized in Figure 4.2.1.[18]

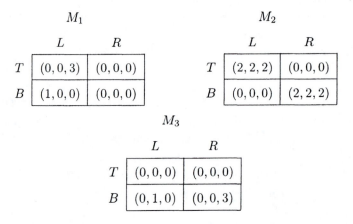

Figure 4.2.1. Aumann's 3-Player Example

Here Amie chooses the row, Kay chooses the column, and Ron chooses the matrix. The players are at a correlated equilibrium with payoff vector $(2, 2, 2)$ if Amie and Kay observe a coin flip and play (T, L) if the coin comes up H and (B, R) if the coin comes up T, and Ron (who doesn't know the outcome of the coin flip) plays M_2, and this correlated equilibrium is such that all players are made worse off if any player unilaterally deviates. In this example, $\mathcal{H}_{\text{Kay}} = \mathcal{H}_{\text{Amie}} = \{\{H\}, \{T\}\}$ and $\mathcal{H}_{\text{Ron}} = \{H, T\} = \Omega$, the trivial partition. As Aumann points out, this correlated equilibrium depends upon the players having

---

[18] Aumann (1974), p. 71.

different private information. If Ron had the same information partition as Amie and Kay, so that he would learn the outcome of the coin flip, he would break for either M_1 or M_3, which would drive Kay and Amie to play (B, L), to everyone's disadvantage. In other words, were Ron to discover Kay's and Amie's actual intended strategies, the correlated equilibrium would break down, so this correlated equilibrium fails the PIC.[19]

§4.3   Dynamical Explanations of Conventions

As Lewis fully realized, explaining the origin of conventions that agents in the world actually follow is a nontrivial problem, since social coordination problems generally have a number of distinct possible solutions. Lewis accounts for the emergence of conventions in terms of salience. Yet salience, as formalized in the definition of convention given above, simply shifts the key question up a level of abstraction. Where does salience come from? Lewis argues that a variety of factors, including pre-game communication, precedent, and environmental clues, can account for agents correlating their expectations on a particular coordination equilibrium. Agents can tie their actions to various "states of the world," thereby achieving correlated equilibrium.

At least in certain cases, Lewis' account of salience seems to push the "Why is *this* equilibrium salient?" question back still further. Quine (1936) argues that a conventionalist account of language cannot assume that all linguistic conventions are established by initial agreement, since persons require some minimal knowledge of a language if they are to explicitly agree on anything. Likewise, not all linguistic conventions can be established by proclamation, since people need some knowledge of a common language in order to understand any

---

[19]This correlated equilibrium still fails the PIC if the players condition on their common information partition, the trivial partition Ω. Suppose that Player 1 computes her expected utilities for her alternative strategies given Ω rather than $\mathcal{H}_1$, and that f is the correlated equilibrium described here. Then

$$E_1(u_1(f)|\Omega) = E_1(u_1(f)) = 2 \cdot \mu_1(L, M_2) + 0 \cdot \mu_1(B, M_2) = 2 \cdot \frac{1}{2} + 0 \cdot \frac{1}{2} = 1$$

and

$$E_1(u_1(B, f_{-1})|\Omega) = E_1(u_1(B, f_{-1})) = 0 \cdot \mu_1(L, M_2) + 2 \cdot \mu_1(B, M_2) = 0 \cdot \frac{1}{2} + 2 \cdot \frac{1}{2} = 1.$$

Similarly,

$$E_2(u_2(f)|\Omega) = E_2(u_2(B, f_{-2})|\Omega) = 1.$$

Hence, Player 1 and Player 2 are both *indifferent* to their choices if they condition on Ω instead of their private information.

proclamation. Crawford and Haller (1990) argue that, while pre-play communication can facilitate coordination in certain cases, explicitly introducing pre-play
communication into the game theoretic model of convention also involves the
players in the second-order coordination problem of associating meanings with
particular signals. If one accepts Quine's and Crawford and Haller's independent
arguments, then to avoid infinite regress, one must either reject a conventionalist
account of language, or admit that some conventions arise without communication. A similar regress problem confronts explanations of salience in terms of
precedent. How did the precedent come about in the first place?

Inductive deliberation can help one give a noncircular explanation of salience, and in turn give an account of the emergence of convention that does not
presuppose higher order coordination. Given the game-theoretic account of social convention presented here, the problem agents face when they wish to settle
upon one of many possible conventions is an equilibrium selection problem. The
theory of inductive deliberation is meant to provide an account of how players
engaged in a noncooperative game can learn to settle upon an equilibrium of the
game, even if their beliefs are not initially at equilibrium. Recall that in the theory
of inductive deliberation developed in Chapter 3, deliberators update their beliefs
regarding each other recursively according to the Dirichlet rule. In Chapter 3, we
saw that the original model of Dirichlet deliberation assumes, for mathematical
simplicity, that each player regards the strategies of the opponents as stochastically independent. The generalizations of Dirichlet deliberation developed in
Chapter 3 dispense with this independence assumption, and allow for the possibility of correlation in players' beliefs over opponents' strategies. Consequently,
the limits of these more general models of Dirichlet deliberation are correlated
equilibria that are not Nash equilibria. Such variations of the conditional Dirichlet model turn out to be well suited for giving an account of how deliberators
might achieve a correlated equilibrium convention.

We recall that conditional Dirichlet deliberation generalizes the basic model
of Dirichlet deliberation by dropping probabilistic independence and introducing
external signals that players observe at each round of deliberation. Each player k
has an information partition $\mathcal{H}_k$ of a finite probability space Ω, each element of
which occurs with positive probability.[20] At each stage of deliberation, a state of
the world $\omega^t \in \Omega$ occurs, and k learns that an event $H_{kj}(\omega^t) \in \mathcal{H}_k$ has occurred.

---

[20]This restriction is added to avoid mathematical trivialities. To justify it, one might argue that
in a deliberational context, a deliberator will want to condition only on events that can occur with
positive probability, since these are the only events that with positive probability can give the deliberator information during the sequence of deliberation. However, it is in principle possible to extend
the model of deliberation to include partition cells of measure zero, but this would complicate the
formalism without adding substantively to the deliberational model in any way I can see.

At the mth stage of deliberation, Player k's conditional probabilities are defined by the following:

$$
(4.v) \qquad \mu_k^m(\boldsymbol{A}_{-k}|H_{kj}) = \frac{n_{\boldsymbol{A}_{-k} \wedge H_{kj}} + \gamma_{\boldsymbol{A}_{-k} \wedge H_{kj}}}{n_{H_{kj}} + \sum \gamma_{\boldsymbol{B}_{-k} \wedge H_{kj}}}
$$

where $n_{\boldsymbol{A}_{-k} \wedge H_{kj}}$ is the number of times the opponents play $\boldsymbol{A}_{-k}$ given that H_{kj} has occurred, $n_{H_{kj}}$ is the number of times that H_{kj} has occurred, and the $\gamma_{\boldsymbol{B}_{-k} \wedge H_{kj}}$'s define k's conditional priors over the opponents' strategy combinations. We recall two natural ways to interpret inductive deliberation:

(1) *Actual Play Interpretation:* A fixed set of players play the game repeatedly, and update probabilities as functions of the frequencies of strategy combinations they observe. Each player chooses a strategy that maximizes expected utility at each round of deliberation, and updates his probabilities according to the inductive rule.

(2) *Representative Interpretation:* The n players correspond to n (possibly distinct) populations. At each stage of deliberation, one representative from each population is selected to play a round of the game. Each representative plays the strategy that maximizes expected utility given what the representatives in past plays have done, where probabilities for the current round are determined by the inductive rule, and then drops out.[21]

These interpretations of inductive deliberation presuppose that each deliberator knows the payoff structure of the game, or perhaps only his own payoffs, and the conditional frequencies of past plays. One need not assume that the deliberators are at equilibrium to start with, or that they attach any significance to the external signals at the start of deliberation. As argued before in Chapter 3, each player conditions her deliberations on the information from her private signals because these signals *might* be correlated with her opponents' strategies. If her private signals turns out to be uncorrelated with the opponents' strategies, then the deliberator's beliefs will evolve as if she had not conditioned her beliefs on them, that is, in this case, her secret information from the signaling device will

---

[21] As we have seen in Chapter 3, there is also the *fictitious play* interpretation of Dirichlet deliberation. Under the fictitious play interpretation, the players mentally simulate a sequence of successive plays by computing one another's expected utilities at each stage of deliberation, noting which strategy maximizes expected utility for each player, and updating probabilities according to the Dirichlet rule. However, the fictitious play interpretation of Dirichlet deliberation requires the stronger common knowledge assumptions that I do not wish to adopt for purposes of explaining the emergence of convention. Moreover, the extensions of Dirichlet dynamics introduced in §3.4–§3.6 do not admit of a plausible fictitious play interpretation.

turn out to be statistically irrelevant. However, if her opponents' plays turn out to be correlated with her private information regarding the states of the world, a deliberator can exploit this information by conditioning. We saw in Chapter 3 that deliberators who condition their beliefs in this manner can come to correlate their strategies with the states of the world and thereby learn to follow an Aumann correlated equilibrium. The process of deliberation itself generates this correlation. Since the external signals each player receives are not assumed to be *causally* connected with their actual play, the correlated equilibrium that can emerge from conditional deliberation can be regarded as a kind of "sunspot equilibrium" (Woodford 1990). Recall that conditional Dirichlet deliberators can converge to a correlated equilibrium even from uncorrelated priors. Hence, conditional Dirichlet deliberation and its generalizations can provide one account of the emergence of salience that does not presuppose any prior higher-order coordination on the states of the world.

In the remainder of this chapter, I will consider some of the relationships between correlated equilibrium conventions and conditional Dirichlet deliberation. Many of the results cited here turn out to be special cases of the results proved in Chapter 3. This chapter is meant to contribute toward a growing literature that explains convention in terms of dynamical adjustment processes. For instance, Crawford and Haller (1990), Young (1993) and Kandori, Mailath, and Rob (1993) present alternative dynamical approaches to explaining the emergence of convention, although these authors confine their work to conventions corresponding to pure strategy Nash equilibria. While game theorists are very far from a complete theory of convention, dynamics like the Dirichlet rule may go far in explaining the emergence of convention without communication or precedent.

In the special case in which conditional Dirichlet deliberators all have the same information partition $\mathcal{H}$, one can prove some fairly general convergence results for conditional Dirichlet dynamics. Such results are, of course, especially relevant to the emergence of conventions, since we define convention in terms of information from the *public* information that the various agents gain from their common partition of the states of the world. The key idea underlying these results is that when deliberators condition on a common partition $\mathcal{H}$, one can view the resulting dynamical process as a union of sequences of unconditional deliberation.

Definition 4.3.1. Given a set of conditional Dirichlet deliberators who condition on a common information partition $\mathcal{H}$ of the states of the world, the H_k-*subsequence of deliberation* $(\mathfrak{P}^{m_k})$ is the subsequence of updated conditional distributions $(\mathfrak{P}^m)$ of the deliberators such that $\omega^{m_k} \in H_k \in \mathcal{H}$.   □

If deliberators condition on a public information partition $\mathcal{H}$, then trivially the distribution of any H_k-subsequence with conditional priors $\mu_k^0(\cdot | H_k)$, $k \in N$, is the same as the distributions of a sequence of unconditional Dirichlet deliberation with priors $\mu_k^0(\cdot)$. This observation enables us to take advantage of the following result, first proved in Monderer and Shapley (1993):

Proposition 4.3.2 (Monderer and Shapley). If Γ is a game with identical payoff functions for each player $k \in N$, then unconditional Dirichlet deliberation converges to a Nash equilibrium. $\qquad\square$

Proposition 4.3.3. If Γ is a game with identical payoff functions for each player, and deliberators condition on a common information partition $\mathcal{H}$ of Γ, then conditional Dirichlet deliberation converges almost surely to a correlated equilibrium.

Proof. By Proposition 4.3.2, each H_k-subsequence of conditional Dirichlet deliberation converges to a Nash equilibrium of Γ if H_k occurs infinitely often in the sequence of deliberation. By the Borel-Cantelli lemma, this occurs with probability one. Hence, the limit of conditional Dirichlet deliberation is function $f : \Omega \rightarrow S$ such that f is constant on each $H_k \in \mathcal{H}$ and for each $\omega \in H_k \in \mathcal{H}$, $f(\omega)$ is a Nash equilibrium. Hence, f is a correlated equilibrium. $\qquad\square$

In a game with identical payoffs, when the limit of each H_k-subsequence of conditional Dirichlet deliberation is a strict Nash equilibrium, then conditional Dirichlet deliberation converges to a convention. However, it is possible for the limit to converge to a mixed equilibrium, which is not a convention since at a mixed equilibrium each player is indifferent to her pure strategy set.

On the other hand, a convention is always an *absorbing state* of conditional Dirichlet dynamics, in the sense that if conditional Dirichlet deliberators coordinate just once at each state of the of the world, then they will always coordinate at each state of the world, with the result that their beliefs will converge to the correlated equilibrium corresponding to a convention. This result relies upon Proposition 3.2.6, the Absorption Theorem of unconditional Dirichlet deliberation. Recall that the Absorption Theorem tells us that if unconditional Dirichlet deliberators play a strict Nash equilibrium A^* at any round of deliberation, they will play A^* at all future rounds of deliberation. The following result is similar to Proposition 3.3.5.

Proposition 4.3.4. A convention $f : \Omega \rightarrow S$ is an absorbing state of conditional Dirichlet dynamics in the case where deliberators condition on a common partition $\mathcal{H}$. That is, if conditional Dirichlet deliberators all condition on $\mathcal{H}$, and if for each $\omega \in \Omega$, there is a value t^ω such that the deliberators play $f(\omega)$ at round t^ω, then for all rounds $m \geq \max\{t^\omega | \omega \in \Omega\}$, the deliberators will always play the convention $f(\omega)$.

Proof. Let $\omega \in \Omega$, and let $H_k \in \mathcal{H}$ be such that $\omega \in H_k$. By hypothesis, there is a round t^ω at which the deliberators play $f(\omega)$. Since f is a convention, $f(\omega)$ is a strict Nash equilibrium, so by the Absorption Theorem the H_k-subsequence of deliberation remains on $f(\omega)$ for each round $m_k \geq t^\omega$ of deliberation such that $\omega^{m_k} \in H_k$. Since $\omega \in \Omega$ was chosen arbitrarily, and there are finitely many ω, for all $t \geq \max\{t^\omega | \omega \in \Omega\}$, the deliberators will play $f(\omega)$. $\square$

Conditional Dirichlet deliberators can converge to the equilibrium of a convention given the right priors, but in many intuitively plausible cases, deliberators may fail to converge to a convention. Often this failure is the result of perfect symmetry in the deliberators' beliefs and knowledge, which results in their converging to a mixed equilibrium rather than to a convention. In particular, deliberators might fail to converge to a convention if their priors are "uncorrelated," that is, if the priors satisfy probabilistic independence. For example, if Amie and Kay play the Battle of the Sexes game of Figure 4.3.1 as conditional Dirichlet deliberators with uniform conditional priors, then each subsequence of conditional Dirichlet deliberation converges to the mixed equilibrium defined by the distributions

$$\mu_1^*(\text{Kay plays } A_1) = \mu_2^*(\text{Amie plays} A_2) = \frac{1}{1 + \sqrt{2}},$$

at which each player is indifferent to her own alternative strategies. Hence, the PIC is not satisfied at this equilibrium, so the limit of this particular sequence of Dirichlet deliberation is not a convention.

Kay

		A_1	A_2
Amie	A_1	$(\sqrt{2}, 1)$	$(0, 0)$
	A_2	$(0, 0)$	$(1, \sqrt{2})$

Figure 4.3.1. Battle of the Sexes *II*

Nevertheless, inductive deliberators starting with uncorrelated priors can converge to a convention if they have *asymmetric knowledge* of the history of deliberation. One can introduce asymmetries in the players' knowledge in at least three ways:

(1) If each player recalls only a random number of the most recent m past plays, rather than the full sequence of past plays, then *random recall Dirichlet deliberation* (RRC-Dirichlet deliberation) introduces a knowledge asymmetry by making it possible for deliberators to have unequal memories of the past history of plays.

(2) If each player periodically fails to observe an element of his private information partition $\mathcal{H}_k$, then *variable state conditional Dirichlet deliberation* (VSC-Dirichlet deliberation) introduces a knowledge asymmetry by occasionally giving deliberators unequal knowledge of the states of the world that determine salience.

(3) If each deliberator is a representative of a population who can ask the members of his population for information on opponents' previous plays, then *random sampling conditional Dirichlet deliberation* (RSC-Dirichlet deliberation) introduces a knowledge asymmetry since representatives entering into a round of play can have knowledge of different samples of past plays.

In each of these extensions of the conditional Dirichlet model, we have seen examples in which correlation in the deliberators' beliefs emerges spontaneously despite the players having uncorrelated priors. This phenomenon implies that deliberators can converge to a convention even if their initial beliefs are uncorrelated. For instance, we saw that RRC-Dirichlet, RSC-Dirichlet and VSC-Dirichlet deliberators playing the Battle of the Sexes game of Figure 4.3.1 can all converge from uniform prior probabilities to the convention $f : \Omega \rightarrow S$, which is defined by

$$f(\omega) = \begin{cases} (A_1, A_1) & \text{if } \omega = H \\ (A_2, A_2) & \text{if } \omega = T \end{cases}$$

Indeed, for RRC-Dirichlet and RSC-Dirichlet deliberators, who have imperfect memories of past plays, convergence to some convention of Battle of the Sexes is *almost sure*. This is one instance of some general convergence results, with which I will close this chapter. First, we recall that in Dirichlet deliberation with full memory, if A^* is a strict Nash equilibrium then there is some number $\beta_{kA_k^*}$, player k's *transition frequency* for $A_k^* \in A^*$ such that, whatever k's priors are, if k's opponents play A^*_{-k} consecutively $\beta_{kA^*_k}$ times, then on the $\beta_{kA^*_k}$-th play k will play his end A^*_k of A^*. As in §3.4, we can set

$$\beta_{A^*} = \max\{\beta_{kA^*_k} | k \in N\}$$

and

$$\beta_\Gamma = \max\{\beta_{A^*} | A^* \text{ is a strict Nash equilibrium of } \Gamma\},$$

called the *absorption frequencies* of the equilibrium A^* and of the strict equilibria of Γ, respectively.

Proposition 4.3.5. Let Γ be a 2×2 game Γ with two Nash equilibrium conventions, let the players be RRC-Dirichlet deliberators with a common partition $\mathcal{H}$ of Ω such that each deliberator k recalls at least $\min\{t, \beta_\Gamma\}$ rounds, and at most $2\beta_\Gamma$ rounds, of the H_k-subsequence of deliberation at every round of deliberation. Then RSC-Dirichlet deliberation converges almost surely to a convention.

Proof. Let H_j be a cell of $\mathcal{H}$. Since the Nash equilibrium conventions are strict equilibria, the hypotheses of Lemma 3.4.4 are satisfied. Hence, by Lemma 3.4.5, the subsequence (f^{t_u}) of RRC-Dirichlet deliberation defined by t_u such that $\omega^{t_u} \in H_j$ converges almost surely to one of the strict Nash equilibria of Γ. Without loss of generality, let this equilibrium be $f(\omega_l) = (A_i, A_j)$ for $\omega_l \in H_j$. Then, $(f^t(\omega^{t_u})) \to f(\omega^{t_u}) = (A_i, A_j)$ almost surely if $\omega^t \in H_j$ as $t \to \infty$, and by hypothesis

(1) $$E_j(u_j \circ f | \mathcal{H})(\omega^t) > E_j(u_j \circ (g_j, f_{-j}) | \mathcal{H})(\omega^t)$$

Since $H_j \in \mathcal{H}$ was chosen arbitrarily, the entire system (f^t) converges almost surely to a correlated equilibrium f satisfying (1), which by definition is a convention.   □

   Proposition 4.3.5, which is in fact a simple refinement of Proposition 3.4.6, shows that RRC-Dirichlet deliberators with appropriately bounded memories converge almost surely to a convention in a variety of interesting 2×2 games, including the pure coordination Encounter Problem of §1.5 and the impure coordination problem Battle of the Sexes. The class of games for which RSC-deliberation converges is not limited to 2×2 games with two pure strategy equilibrium conventions. However, convergence theorems for more general pure and impure coordination games have not yet been discovered.

   On the other hand, we can show that RSC-Dirichlet deliberators with similar bounds on their memories converge almost surely for a wide class of coordination games. In this book, we have considered several examples of pure coordination games, such as the Encounter Problem and Hume's Rowboat. Schelling (1960) and Lewis (1969) defined the class of pure coordination games to be the games in which players' payoffs coincide exactly at each strategy profile. We have also considered games of *impure coordination* (Kavka 1986) such as Battle of the Sexes and Telephone Tag, in which the interests of the players coincide at every strategy combination, but where an outcome of the game can favor some players more than others. The class of impure coordination games can be defined precisely as a subclass of coordination games, both pure and impure.[22] Intuitively, a game of coordination is a game in which no player can gain at the expense of any other player. The following definition formalizes this intuition.

Definition 4.3.6. A game $\Gamma = (N, S, u)$ is a *coordination game* iff for each strategy profile $A \in S$, if there is a strategy profile $A' = (A'_k, A_{-k}) \neq A$ such that $u_k(A') > u_k(A)$, then for each $j \neq k$, $u_j(A') \geq u_j(A)$. A coordination game Γ is *pure* iff for each strategy profile $A \in S$,

$$u_1(A) = u_2(A) = \cdots = u_n(A),$$

and otherwise Γ is *(strictly) impure*. A coordination game Γ is *nontrivial* iff at least one strategy profile in S is a strict Nash equilibrium. ☐

In words, a nontrivial coordination game is a coordination game Γ having at least one Nash equilibrium convention.[23]

In order to derive the main convergence result for RSC-Dirichlet deliberation, a preliminary result is needed, which involves the notion of a *weakly acyclic* game (Young 1993) discussed in §3.5.

Lemma 4.3.7. If $\Gamma = (N, S, u)$ is a coordination game such that each pure strategy Nash equilibrium of Γ is strict, then Γ is weakly acyclic.

---

[22] I have not seen a general definition of coordination games that covers both the pure and the impure cases elsewhere in the literature.

[23] As the game given by the following figure shows, some trivial coordination games have no equilibria that are conventions. In this game, every strategy profile (pure or mixed) is an equilibrium, but no strategy profile is a convention, since each player is always indifferent to the opponent's choice of strategy. Note that this game has the unusual property of being both a pure coordination game and a zero-sum game.

Kay

		A_1	A_2
Amie	A_1	(0,0)	(0,0)
	A_2	(0,0)	(0,0)

Before proceeding to the proof of Lemma 4.3.7, we should note that the result can fail for coordination games that have Nash equilibria that are not strict. For instance, the best reply graph of the pure coordination game summarized by Figure 4.3.2 has a closed cycle

$$(A_1, A_1) \rightarrow (A_1, A_2) \rightarrow (A_2, A_2) \rightarrow (A_2, A_1) \rightarrow (A_1, A_1)$$

and consequently is not weakly acyclic.[24]

Kay

		A_1	A_2	A_3
	A_1	$(1,1)$	$(1,1)$	$(0,0)$
Amie	A_2	$(1,1)$	$(1,1)$	$(0,0)$
	A_3	$(0,0)$	$(0,0)$	$(1,1)$

Figure 4.3.2. A Non-Weakly Acyclic Game

On the other hand, Lemma 4.3.7 shows that a very wide class of coordination games are weakly acyclic. The lemma applies to the pure coordination games Encounter Problem and Hume's Rowboat, and to the impure coordination games Battle of the Sexes and Telephone Tag. The lemma also does not depend either on the number of players or the number of strategies at their disposal. For example, suppose 100 individuals each must privately choose a letter of the alphabet, and that each individual receives some positive payoff if, and only if, all select the same letter. The positive payoffs at each of the 26 Nash coordination equilibria could be the same for each player, but this is not essential. Lemma 4.3.7 shows that even this immensely complicated game, which has $26^{100} \approx 3.1429 \times 10^{141}$ pure strategy combinations, only 26 of which are equilibria, is weakly acyclic. One way to restate the lemma is as follows: For a coordination game Γ with any number of players and number of strategy profiles, if all of the pure strategy equilibria of Γ are conventions, then Γ is weakly acyclic.

Proof of Lemma 4.3.7. Recall from §3.5 that we must show that for each strategy profile $A \in S$, there is a finite sequence starting at A of unilateral best replies that ends at a strict Nash equilibrium. More precisely, we must show that there is a sequence

$$A^0, A^1, \ldots, A^n$$

---

[24] See Definition 3.5.5 for the definition of a best reply graph.

such that $A^0 = A$, A^n is a strict Nash equilibrium, and for $1 \leq i \leq n$, $A^i = (A_{kj}, A^{i-1}_{-k}) \neq A^{i-1}$ where $A_{kj} \in S_k$ is a best response for k to A^{i-1}_{-k}. We construct this sequence recursively as follows:

Step 0. Define $A^0 = A$.

Step i, for $1 \leq i$. There are two cases to consider. If A^{i-1} is an equilibrium, then by hypothesis A^{i-1} is strict and so the sequence (1) terminates at $A^n = A^{i-1}$. If A^{i-1} is not an equilibrium, choose $k_i \in N$ and $A_{k_ij} \in S_{k_i}$ such that $u_{k_i}(A_{k_ij}, A^{i-1}_{-k}) > u_{k_i}(A^{i-1})$ and set $A^i = (A_{k_ij}, A^{i-1}_{-k})$. Since Γ is a coordination game, $u_j(A^i) \geq u_j(A^{i-1})$ for all $j \neq k_i$. Proceed to Step $i + 1$.

Since there are only finitely many strategy profiles in S, either the sequence (A^i) terminates at a profile A^n which is a strict equilibrium, or the sequence cycles back to A^0, that is, for some $i > 0$, $A^i = A^0$. However, if the sequence (A^i) cycles, then by construction

$$u_{k_1}(A^0) = u_{k_1}(A^i) \geq u_{k_1}(A^{i-1}) \geq \cdots \geq u_{k_1}(A^1) > u_{k_1}(A^0),$$

a contradiction. Hence (A^i) must terminate at a strict Nash equilibrium. $\qquad\square$

We are now in a position to show that RSC-Dirichlet deliberators with certain restrictions on their recall of past play will achieve a convention of a coordination game of the sort defined in Lemma 4.3.5 with probability one.

Proposition 4.3.8. Let Γ be a coordination game such that each pure strategy Nash equilibrium is a convention. If the players are RSC-Dirichlet deliberators such that:

(i) Each player conditions on the cells of a common partition $\mathcal{H}$,

(ii) The players' sample sizes are bounded by β_Γ and $2\beta_\Gamma$ of the most recent rounds of past play on each H_k-subsequence of deliberation, that is, $\beta_\Gamma \leq \eta^t_k(H_k) \leq 2\beta_\Gamma$, and

(iii) No player recalls any of the states that determine the priors after some round K,

then RSC-Dirichlet dynamics converges almost surely to a convention of Γ.

Proof. By Lemma 4.3.7, Γ is weakly acyclic. This, together with (i)–(iii), implies that the hypotheses of Proposition 3.5.10 are satisfied. Hence, the deliberators will converge to a strict Aumann correlated equilibrium of Γ, which, by hypothesis, is a convention. $\qquad\square$

As noted in Chapter 3, the RSC-Dirichlet dynamics has the disadvantage of making sense only under some kind of population representative interpretation. Nevertheless, this disadvantage is perhaps not too great from the perspective of one trying to explaining social convention. In the real world, individuals regularly interact with different people, and may have no information to rely upon regarding what to expect from another than what people like themselves have experienced in past similar situations. Moreover, one might plausibly suppose that any individual about to interact with someone else will have knowledge of only a limited sample of past similar interactions. Indeed, it is the assumption of knowledge of the complete history of plays underlying conditional Dirichlet deliberation with full memory that seems problematic. The *limited* knowledge of the past that real individuals seem to have at their disposal resembles the weak knowledge assumptions of RSC-Dirichlet deliberation under its representative interpretation. RSC-Dirichlet deliberation gives a "quasi-evolutionary" account of how a convention can emerge gradually among the members of a population.

Interestingly, such an account of the emergence of convention is Humean in spirit. Hume, who argues that rules associated with property are *mere* conventions, writes

> Nor is the rule concerning the stability of possession the less deriv'd from human
> conventions, that it arises gradually, and acquires force by a slow progression,
> and by our repeated experience of the inconveniences of transgressing it. On
> the contrary, this experience assures us still more, that the sense of interest has
> become common to all our fellows, and gives us a confidence of the future
> regularity of their conduct.[25]

At the beginning of this chapter, I attributed to Hume the game-theoretic insight of characterizing a convention as an equilibrium that depends crucially upon the players' mutual expectations of reciprocal compliance. In this final passage, one might interpret Hume as having an intuitive grasp of how to explain equilibrium selection as the result of some trial and error process. Hume did not have the results of modern game theory available to him, and was therefore unable to verify how successful his explanation of convention might be. Hume's conclusions regarding social convention are being vindicated in our time. The convergence results given above form part of a growing body of results in game theory showing that under fairly general conditions, conventions will emerge as the result of a dynamical learning process.

---

[25] Hume (1740), p. 490.

References

Aristotle. (1980). *Nichomachean Ethics*. Translated by David Ross, revised by J. L. Ackrill and J. O. Urmson. Oxford and New York: Oxford University Press.

Aumann, Robert. 1974. Subjectivity and Correlation in Randomized Strategies. *Journal of Mathematical Economics* 1:67–96.

———. 1987. Correlated Equilibrium as an Expression of Bayesian Rationality. *Econometrica* 55:1–18.

Bernheim, B. Douglas. 1984. Rationalizable Strategic Behavior. *Econometrica* 52(4): 1007–1028.

Bicchieri, Cristina. 1993. *Rationality and Coordination*. Cambridge: Cambridge University Press.

Binmore, Ken. 1994. *Game Theory and the Social Contract.*, Volume 1, *Playing Fair*. Cambridge, Mass.: MIT Press.

Borel, Emile. 1921 (1953). La théorie du jeu et les équations, intégrales à noyau symmétrique gauche. *Comptes Renduc de l'Académie des Sciences* 173:1304–1308. Translated by L. J. Savage as 'The Theory of Play and Integral Equations with Skew Symmetric Kernels.' *Econometrica* 21:97–100.

———. 1924 (1953). Sur les jeux où interniennent l'hasard et l'habilite des joueurs. In *Théorie des probabilites*, edited by J. Hermann. Paris: Librarie Scientifique. Translated by J. L. Savage as 'On Games that Involve Chance and the Skill of Players,' *Econometrica* 21:101–115.

Brandenburger, Adam. 1992. Knowledge and Equilibrium in Games. *Journal of Economic Perspectives* 6:83–101.

Brandenburger, Adam and Eddie Dekel. 1987. Rationalizability and Correlated Equilibria. *Econometrica* 55:1391–1402.

———. 1988. The Role of Common Knowledge Assumptions in Game Theory. In *The Economics of Missing Markets, Information, and Games*, edited by Frank Hahn, 46–61. Oxford: Clarendon Press.

Brown, George W. 1951. Iterative Solutions of Games by Fictitious Play. In *Activity Analysis of Production and Allocation*, edited by T.C. Koopmans, 374–376. New York: Wiley.

Carnap, Rudolph. 1928 (1967). *Der logische Aufbau der Welt*. Translated by Rolf A. George as 'The Logical Structure of the World'. Berkeley: University of California Press.

Carnap, Rudolf. 1980. A Basic System of Inductive Logic, Part 2. In *Studies in Inductive Logic and Probability*, edited by Richard C. Jeffrey, 7–155. Berkeley: University of California Press.

Crawford, Vincent P. and Hans Haller. 1990. Learning to Cooperate: Optimal Play in Repeated Coordination Games. *Econometrica* 58:571–595.

De Finetti, Bruno. 1937 (1980). La Prevision: ses lois logiques, ses sources subjectives. *Annales de l'Institut Henri Poincare* 7:1–68. Translated by Henry Kynurg, Jr. and Howard E. Smokler as 'Foresight: Its Logical Laws, Its Sujective Sources.' In *Studies in Subjective Probability*. Huntington, New York: Robert E. Kriegler Publishing Company, pp. 53–118.

Frege, Gottlob. 1892 (1980). On Sense and Reference. In *Translations from the Philosophical Writings of Gottlob Frege*. Translated and edited by Peter Geach and Max Black. Oxford: Blackwell.

Fudenberg, Drew and David Kreps. 1988. A Theory of Learning, Experimentation and Equilibrium in Games. Department of Economics, Massachusets Institute of Technology, and Graduate School of Business, Stanford. Mimeographed.

———. 1991. *Learning and Equilibrium in Games*. Unpublished manuscript.

Fudenberg, Drew and Jean Tirole. 1992. *Game Theory*. Cambridge, Mass.: The MIT Press.

Gauthier, David. 1969. *The Logic of Leviathan*. Oxford: Oxford University Press.

Glymour, Clark. 1992. *Thinking Things Through: An Introduction to Philosophical Issues and Achievements*. Cambridge, Mass.: MIT Press.

Hampton, Jean. 1986. *Hobbes and the Social Contract Tradition*. Cambridge: Cambridge University Press.

Harsanyi, John. 1977. *Rational Behavior and Bargaining Equilibrium in Games and Social Situations*. Cambridge: Cambridge University Press.

Harsanyi, John and Reinhard Selten. 1988. *A General Theory of Equilibrium Selection in Games*. Cambridge, Mass.: The MIT Press.

Hobbes, Thomas. 1651 (1991). *Leviathan*. Edited by Richard Tuck. Cambridge: Cambridge Univerity Press.

———. 1655 (1962). *De Copore*. Reprinted in *Body, Man and Citizen*. New York: Collier.

Hume, David. 1740 (1978). *A Treatise of Human Nature*. Edited by L.A. Selby-Bigge. Oxford: Clarendon Press.

———. 1777 (1975). *An Enquiry Concerning the Principles of Morals*. Edited by L. A. Selby-Bigge. Revised Third Edition edited by P. H. Nidditch. Oxford, Clarendon Press.

Jeffrey, Richard C. 1983. *The Logic of Decision*. Second Edition. Chicago and London: University of Chicago Press.

Kandori, Michihiro, George J. Mailath, and Rafael Rob. 1993. Learning, Mutation, and Long Run Equilibria in Games. *Econometrica* 61(1):29–56.

Kavka, Gregory. 1986. *Hobbesian Moral and Political Theory*. Princeton: Princeton University Press.

———. 1989. Political Contractarianism. Unpublished manuscript.

Kolmogorov, Andrey N. 1933 (1950). *Grundbegriffe der Wahrsheinlichkeitrechnung*. Translated by Nathan Morrison as 'Foundations of the Theory of Probability.' New York: Chelsea Publishing Company.

Lewis, David. 1969. *Convention: A Philosophical Study*. Cambridge, Mass.: Harvard University Press.

Luce, R. Duncan and Howard Raiffa. 1957. *Games and Decisions: Introduction and · Critical Survey*. New York: Wiley.

Maynard Smith, J. 1982. *Evolution and the Theory of Games*. Cambridge: Cambridge University Press.

Miyasawa, Koichi. 1961. On the Convergence of the Learning Process in a Non-Zero-Sum Two Person Game. Economic Research Program, Princeton University. Research Memorandum No. 33.

Monderer, Dov and Aner Sela. 1993. Fictitious Play and No-Cycling Conditions. Working paper, The Technion, Haiffa 32000 Israel.

Monderer, Dov and Lloyd Shapley. 1993. Fictitious Play Property For Games With Identical Interests. Working paper, The Technion, Haiffa 32000 Israel, and the Departments of Economics and of Mathematics, University of California, Los Angeles.

Nash, John. 1950. Equilibrium points in n-person games. *Proceedings of the National Academy of Sciences of the United States* 36:48–49.

———. 1951. Non-Cooperative Games. *Annals of Mathematics* 54:286–295.

Pareto, Vilfredo. 1927 (1971). *Manual of Political Economy*. Translated by A. S. Schwier. New York: Agustis S. Kelley.

Pearce, David. 1984. Rationalizable Strategic Behavior and the Problem of Perfection. *Econometrica* 52(4):1029–1050.

Quine, Willard. 1936 (1985). Truth by Convention. In *Philosophical Essays for A. N. Whitehead*. Edited by O. H. Lee. New York: Longmans. Reprinted in *Philosophy of Mathematics: Selected Readings*. Second Edition. Edited by Paul Benacerraf and Hilary Putnam. Cambridge: Cambridge University Press, pp. 329–354.

Ramsey, Frank Plumpton. 1926 (1931). Truth and Probability. In *The Foundations of Mathematics*. Edited by Richard Braithwaite. London: Routledge and Kegan Paul, pp. 156–198.

Richards, Diana. 1993. Nonconvergence in Full-History Bayesian Decision Rules. Working paper, Department of Political Science, University of Minnesota.

Robinson, Julia. 1951. An Iterative Method of Solving a Game. *Annals of Mathematics* 54:296–301.

Rousseau, Jean-Jacques. 1755 (1987). Discourse on the Origin and Foundations of Inequality Among Men. In *Basic Political Writings*. Translated by Donald A. Cress. Indianapolis: Hackett Publishing Company, pp. 25–109.

Rubinstein, Ariel. 1991. Comments on the Interpretation of Game Theory. *Econometrica* 59:909–924.

Savage, Leonard J. 1954 (1972). *The Foundations of Statistics*. Second Revised Edition. New York: Dover Publications, Inc.

Schelling, Thomas. 1960. *The Strategy of Conflict*. Cambridge, Mass.: Harvard University Press.

Shapley, Lloyd. 1964. Some Topics in Two-Person Games. In *Advances in Game Theory*, edited by M. Dresher, L. S. Shapley, and A. W. Tucker, 1–28. Princeton: Princeton University Press.

Shin, Huyn Song. 1991. Two Notions of Ratifiability and Equilibrium in Games. In *Foundations of Decision Theory: Issues and Advances*. Edited by Michael Bacharach and Susan Hurley. Cambridge, Mass. and Oxford: Blackwell, pp. 242–262.

Shirer, William L. 1960. *The Rise and Fall of the Third Reich: A History of Nazi Germany*. New York: Simon and Schuster.

Shubik, Martin. 1982. *Game Theory in the Social Sciences*. Cambridge, Mass.: The MIT Press.

Skyrms, Brian. 1984. *Pragmatics and Empiricism*. New Haven and London: Yale University Press.

———. 1990. *The Dynamics of Rational Deliberation*. Cambridge, Mass.: Harvard University Press.

———. 1991a. Inductive Deliberation, Admissible Acts, and Perfect Equilibrium. In *Essays in the Foundations of Rational Decision*, edited by Michael Bacharach and Susan Hurley, 220–241. Blackwell: Oxford.

———. 1991b. Inductive Dynamic Deliberation and the Genesis of Correlation. Unpublished manuscript.

Smith, Adam. 1776 (1992). *An Inquiry Into the Nature and Causes of the Wealth of Nations*. Edited by R. H. Campbell, A. S. Skinner, and W. B. Todd. Indianapolis: Liberty Classics.

Vanderschraaf, Peter. 1992. Endogenous Correlated Equilibria in Noncooperative Games. Technical Report Series, Report No. MBS 92-94, Irvine Research Unit in Mathematical Behavioral Sciences.

———. 1994. Inductive Learning, Knowledge Asymmetries and Convention. Technical Report Series, Report No. MBS 94-08, Irvine Research Unit in Mathematical Behavioral Sciences.

————. 1995. A Study in Inductive Deliberation. Ph.D. diss., University of California at Irvine.

Vanderschraaf, Peter and Brian Skyrms. 1993. Deliberational Correlated Equilibria. Technical Report Series, Report No. MBS 93-07, Irvine Research Unit in Mathematical Behavioral Sciences.

Van Huyck, John, Raymond Battalio, and Richard Beil. 1990. Tacit Coordination Games, Strategic Uncertainty and Coordination Failure. *American Economic Revue* 80:234–248.

Von Neumann, John. 1928. Zur Theorie der Geselleschaftspiele. *Mathematische Annalen* 100:295–320.

Von Neumann, John and Oskar Morgenstern. 1944. *Theory of Games and Economic Behavior*. Princeton: Princeton University Press.

Woodford, Michael. 1990. Learning to Believe in Sunspots. *Econometrica* 55:277–307.

Young, H. Peyton. 1993. The Evolution of Conventions. *Econometrica* 61:57–84.

Zermelo, Ernst. 1913. Über eine Anwendung der Mengenlehre auf die theorie des Schachspiels. *Proceedings, Fifth International Congress of Mathematicians* 2:501–504.

Index

AUTHORS

Aristotle, 3
Aumann, 6, 34, 47, 49, 54, 57, 66–71,
    78, 80–82, 85, 91, 93, 131,
    132, 135, 136, 193–195, 200

Battalio, 44
Beil, 44
Bernheim, 34, 53, 55, 60–64, 77, 78, 86
Bicchieri, 41, 50
Binmore, 42
Borel, 14, 24
Brandenburger, 6, 47, 60, 61, 82–88, 188
Brown, 103

Carnap, 4, 15, 103
Crawford, 186, 202, 204

Dekel, 6, 47, 60, 61, 82–88, 188

Frege, 7, 8
Fudenberg, 4, 82, 130

Gauthier, 15, 29
Glymour, 15

Haller, 186, 202, 204
Hampton, 15, 29, 41
Harsanyi, 67
Hobbes, 15, 28, 29, 31, 32
Hume, 3, 7, 14, 15, 24, 33, 35, 185, 212

Jeffrey, 91, 96

Kandori, 187, 204
Kavka, 8, 15, 29, 41, 209

Kolmogorov, 21
Kreps, 4, 130

Lewis, 6, 8, 35, 36, 40, 55, 185–193,
    196–198, 200, 201, 209
Luce, 29, 41, 48, 68, 70

Mailath, 187, 204
Maynard Smith, 108
Miyasawa, 125, 162
Monderer, 125, 205
Morgenstern, 5, 14, 15, 21–24, 27, 31,
    33, 47, 49, 50, 185

Nash, 5, 33, 34, 47, 50, 80, 186

Pareto, 21
Pearce, 34, 53, 55, 60, 61, 63, 64, 86

Quine, 201, 202

Raiffa, 29, 41, 48, 68, 70
Ramsey, 21
Richards, 126
Rob, 187, 204
Robinson, 125
Rousseau, 9, 10, 42
Rubinstein, 49

Savage, 21, 22, 82
Schelling, 6, 22, 36, 37, 45, 185–187,
    191–193, 209
Shapley, 125, 205
Shin, 92, 96
Shirer, 12
Shubik, 68, 186

Skyrms, 4, 6, 21, 22, 47, 78, 101, 102,
    135, 137, 141, 148, 186
Smith, 11, 15, 43

Tirole, 82

van Huyck, 44
Vanderschraaf, 34, 49, 54, 57, 66, 68,
    74, 78, 186
Von Neumann, 5, 14, 15, 21–24, 27, 31,
    33, 47, 49, 50, 185

Woodford, 137, 204

Young, 149, 154, 155, 159, 161–163,
    167, 168, 170, 171, 187, 204,
    209

Zermelo, 14

SUBJECTS

Absorption Theorem, 129, 179, 205

Bayesian rationality, 22, 33, 55, 88

characterization
    arbiter, 91
    lottery, 91
common knowledge, 55, 79, 101, 187,
    189
convention, 3, 185, 194
    as correlated equilibrium, 194–195
    of language, 7–8
    Lewis' characterization, 187
cooperations games, 120
coordination
    impure, 8, 209
        Dining Out, 8–9, 40
        Telephone Tag, 9, 41
    pure, 6, 209

Conventions of Language, 7–8,
    40
    Encounter Problem, 6, 36–38
    Hume's Rowboat, 7, 38–39
correlated equilibrium, 5, 53, 54, 201
    a posteriori, 83, 85, 195
    Aumann, 54, 69, 80, 83, 134, 176,
        186
    endogenous, 54, 66, 74, 76, 79,
        93, 111
    objective, 71, 77
    subjective, 77

Dirichlet dynamics, 105, 124
    convergence, 125–129, 162
    interpretations
        actual play, 110, 203
        fictitious play, 103, 110, 124,
            142, 184
        representative, 108, 110, 162,
            203
    models
        conditional, 138–140
        correlation-dynamics, 113
        independence-dynamics, 113
        random recall conditional (RRC),
            149, 156, 207
        random sampling conditional
            (RSC), 163, 166–167, 173
        variable state conditional (VSC),
            176, 181–182, 207
Dirichlet rule, 102, 103
dominance solvable game, 59
dynamical system, 105
    adjustment process, 4, 186
    see also Dirichlet dynamics,
        inductive rule

equilibrium, 4, 32
   -in-beliefs, 47
   deliberational, 105, 140, 144
   see also Nash equilibrium,
      correlated equilibrium
expected utility, 4, 15, 20, 21, 61, 90
external event space, 67, 131
   signals, 155
   see also lottery characterization

fictitious play
   see Dirichlet dynamics

game theory, 4, 6, 14
   see also noncooperative games

incoherence, 102
independence
   causal, 63
   evidential, 63
   in deliberation, 121
inductive deliberational dynamics, 4, 113,
   186
   correlation in, 113
   deliberators, 4, 54, 102, 122–124
   geometric interpretation, 105
   independence in, 113, 122
   rational deliberation, 99
   see also Dirichlet dynamics
inductive rule, 102
   see also Dirichlet dynamics

joint expected utility maximization, 5
   see also equilibrium

maximin rule, 26
maximize-expected-utility principle
      (*MEU*-principle), 100, 107
   see also Bayesian rationality
Minimax Theorem, 27, 31

mixed strategies, 5, 25
   dynamic setting, 99
   static setting, 99
   subjectivist interpretation, 99
mutual expectations criterion (MEC), 186,
   189

Nash equilibrium, 4, 33, 101
   -in-beliefs, 47
noncooperative games, 4, 14, 185
   dynamic setting, 60
   static setting, 60

orbit, 105, 109

payoff function, 61
prior probability, 102
Prisoner's Dilemma, 29, 59
probabilistic independence, 4, 47, 53, 64,
   66, 77
property rights, 3, 14
public good provision, 45, 120
public intentions criterion (PIC), 186,
   190–191
pure conflict, 22
   see also zero-sum games
pure strategy set, 61

ratifiablility, 91
rational agents, 21
   see also Bayesian rationality
rationalizability, 53, 82
   correlated, 61
   Pearce, 64
rationalizable strategy profiles, 55, 83
replicators, 108

salience, 186, 197
security strategy, 26
signaling games, 40

social coordination, 4

states of the world, 81, 132–138, 186,
        194–197
    information partition, 132

stochastic adaptive dynamics, 149, 154,
        163

strategies
    mixed, 5, 25
    pure, 17, 61

subjective probability measure, 21

subjectivist interpretation, 6

sunspot equilibrium, 137–138, 180

threshold, 45, 120
    see also public good provision

utility
    cardinal (numerical), 19
    ordinal, 17

utility function, 61
    see also payoff function

weakly acyclic games, 162

zero-sum games, 5, 22
    see also pure conflict